11⁹⁵

MW00414486

The Mystery of Romuald and the Five Brothers

Stories from the Benedictines & Camaldolese

Thomas Matus

SOURCE   BOOKS

HERMITAGE   BOOKS

CALIFORNIA

Text and translations copyright © 1994 Thomas Matus o.s.b Cam.
Ilustrations by *Sylvester*

First Edition 1994

Properly attributed quotations and copies of up to 100 words of
continuous text may be used without prior permission. For copying
by any means of longer passages, please enquire of the publisher.

Library of Congress Cataloging-in-Publication Data

Matus, Thomas.
    The mystery of Romuald and the five brothers: stories from the
Benedictines and Camaldolese / Thomas Matus. – – 1st ed.
        p.   cm.
    Includes bibliographical references.
    ISBN 0-940147-33-5 : $12.00
1. Romuald, Saint ca. 951-1027.   2. Christian saints--Italy-
-Biography.   3. Camaldolese—Biography.   4. Benedictines–
-Biography.   5. Camaldolese—History.   6. Benedictines–
–History.   I. Title.
BX4700. R59M38   1994
271'. 14—dc20
    [B]   94-31045
                                                                 CIP

ISBN: 0-940147-33-5

A Publication of Source Books and Hermitage Books

> P.O. Box 794
> Trabuco Canyon
> CA 92678
> U.S.A.

Printed and Bound in the U.S.A. by KNI, Anaheim

CONTENTS

PART ONE: ROMUALD OF RAVENNA

PART TWO: THE LIFE OF THE FIVE BROTHERS BY BRUNO OF QUERFURT

CONTENTS

PART THREE: THE LIFE OF BLESSED ROMUALD BY PETER DAMIAN OF FONTE AVELLANA

MAPS, ETC.

PART ONE: ROMUALD OF RAVENNA

1. THE MYSTERY OF MASTER ROMUALD

This is the story of a monk named Romuald, who was born in Ravenna on the Adriatic coast of Italy some time around the year 952, and who died at the abbey of Val di Castro, in the province of Fabriano, on Monday evening, June 19, 1027. Five years later he was canonized a saint.

This is also the story of my conversations with don Anselmo Giabbani, superior of the Camaldolese monastery in Rome. These conversations cover a span of more than twenty years and constitute an initiation into the understanding of monastic life as a life of freedom. What you will find here are only a few fragments of these conversations, presented in logical rather than chronological order.

"'Mystery' is too heavy a word," said don Anselmo. "*È una parola troppo grossa.* Where did you get the idea of calling Saint Romuald a 'mystery'?"

"I took the expression from Jean Leclercq's book on Saint Peter Damian," I replied, "where he refers to Romuald as 'the mysterious master'."

"I disagree with Leclercq," Anselmo said. "The Holy Trinity and the Incarnation are mysteries; Saint Romuald is not a 'mystery'."

"Father Leclercq didn't mean it in that sense. He meant," I suggested, "that Saint Romuald was indefinable. His life and personality were too...singular, and we can't fit him into any of our theoretical pigeonholes."

Anselmo nodded. "If that is what Leclercq meant, I might agree with him. Indefinable, perhaps, but not unknowable. No, I believe Leclercq intended to say that Romuald was a shadowy figure about whom we can know practically nothing; if this is what he says, he is wrong. The fact that a man is little known does not mean he is unknowable; if the meaning of Romuald's life is ill understood, this is not to say it is unintelligible."

1

I was inclined to agree with don Anselmo, but I had to keep raising objections. "We don't have anything written by him and very little written about him by contemporaries. What Peter Damian says is all second hand."

"We don't have anything Saint Romuald may have written, true," Anselmo replied, "and Peter Damian's *Life of Romuald* is not biography, also true. But we do have certain intangible monuments to Romuald's presence, such as a sort of collective memory of him that lives on in the communities he founded or influenced a thousand years ago."

"You mean at Camaldoli and Fonte Avellana?"

"Yes."

"Some people find it hard to believe that there is any connection at all between Camaldoli today and Saint Romuald."

Don Anselmo looked directly at me. "Do you believe there is?"

"I do. But a lot of people would deny that Romuald's lineage survives at Camaldoli."

Anselmo paused a second, and then went on. "It is more than a question of mere survival. Tradition is more than the repetition of the past. A wisdom quest or a spiritual practice is something alive; it is enriched and changed by those who receive it, just as a family's gene pool is enriched and changed through succeeding generations. The very fact that the life we live at Camaldoli today differs from the life lived there by earlier generations is itself a sign that a certain tradition lives on at Camaldoli."

"How can that be?" I asked.

"The more you know about Saint Romuald, the more you will see how Camaldoli, precisely in its constant mutations, has inherited a good portion of his spirit. Of course, the monks of today's Camaldoli do not live as Saint Romuald lived; perhaps we do not live as he would wish us to, were he here to tell us. But I would not be afraid to meet him. I am sure he would recognize that at Camaldoli, in spite of the changes time has wrought, his spirit lives on." Anselmo paused again, then added, "Of course what I am saying cannot be used to justify everything we do or don't do. We need to ask ourselves many questions, in the light of our history."

"In other words, don Anselmo, Camaldoli is a mystery too."

Anselmo laughed. "There you go again!", he said.

2. CAMÁLDOLI

Camáldoli, like Rome, can be approached from many directions. During the Middle Ages, one of the most important roads to Rome from northeastern Italy passed by the doorstep of Camaldoli. Soon I will explain why this road was important, but for now let me describe my own approach to Camaldoli. I came not from the south, by way of Rome, but from the north, from France through the Swiss Alps and over the Simplon Pass into Italy.

Shortly after midnight on August 9, 1967, the train crossed the Italian border and stopped at the station of Domodossola.

"Are we in Italy yet?" I asked a young Italian-American whom I had met on the train.

"I think so," he answered.

I rolled down the window, leaned out, and saw a large sign that said, "Domodossola." In the seemingly deserted station, a voice called out in Italian and another answered. I thought it might be the station master calling the customs officer to come check the passports.

I smelled the warm air. "I'm going to like it here," I said to myself, out loud.

❧

The night I arrived in Italy marked a turning-point in my life, the intersection between a beginning and an end. It ended five intense and in many ways hard years as a novice

3

and simply professed monk at New Camaldoli Hermitage in Big Sur, California. It began a time of healing, a time to gather up the loose threads of my existence and weave them into some kind of pattern. Living in Italy and with Italian monks proved crucial to this task.

As the train turned south and followed the western shore of Lake Maggiore toward Milan, the excitement of seeing Europe for the first time became a feeling of belonging and homecoming.

I wondered whether I would feel at home at Camaldoli and whether I would find it to be as I expected. I knew, of course, that Camaldoli is not one but two monastic houses situated at different altitudes on a mountainside in the Tuscan Apennines. Near the summit is *il sacro Eremo*, the Holy Hermitage; below it is *il Cenobio*, the Cœnobium or Monastery. 'Cœnobium' means a monastic house where the monks all live together; it also used to mean that they slept in a single dormitory hall, but now each monk has a private room. Of course "hermitage" is generally understood to mean a cabin in the woods or on a cliff or in a tree where one person lives alone and never, or almost never, sees anyone. But at Camaldoli the Eremo, like the Cenobio, is a community where the monks pray and work and take meals together. It is different from the Cenobio in that each monk sleeps and spends part of his day in a separate bungalow called a 'cell.'

The Latin word *Erémus* (from the Greek, meaning 'desert, uninhabited region') is an implied paradox. Any stable human presence inevitably transforms desert or wilderness into an inhabited area, an extension of society. Even the most stripped and solitary hermit enters the desert bearing his baggage of culture and social relationships, simply because he is a human being. The hermit in the desert is not just one more item in the landscape, alongside the rocks and the cactus.

I knew all this, of course, and yet the Camaldoli I discovered when I arrived was not quite what I expected it to be. As a novice in Big Sur, I had imagined that at Camaldoli solitude and community would be assigned to distinct monastic institutions. For this reason I could not understand why Camaldolese hermitages had retained so much of Benedictine common life. I began to understand the Eremo and the Cenobio only when I came to see that solitude implies community and that solitude is not in itself a value but a condition for the realization of certain values, including community.

❦

After eighteen hours on trains I arrived in Florence. I was tired and sleepy and eager to get to Camaldoli.

I telephoned the Eremo. With my carefully memorized Italian phrases I told them that I, a *studente camaldolese americano*, was now at the *stazione ferroviaria di Firenze*, and would they please send someone to pick me up?

"*Si, si. Benarrivato*," said the prior at the other end of the line. "*Restate là. Manderemo a prendervi don Marino.*"

I recognized the name "Marino," although I had not met him personally. He was a recently ordained priest who knew a few words of English.

Fighting to keep my eyes open, I waited for don Marino in the parking lot outside the station. The sight of the Gothic church of Santa Maria Novella across the street reminded me that I was in Florence, and I was glad to be here, although at that precise moment my body would have preferred to be in a bed anywhere, asleep.

An hour later Marino arrived, and seeing a rather thin, sleepy-looking young American in a black suit, he walked up and asked, "Are you from Big Sur?"

Leaving Florence, we did not take the more direct route over the mountains but followed the highway going south toward Arezzo. Along the way I admired the beauty of the Tuscan countryside, which was ripening for *la vendemmia*, the grape harvest.

5

Skirting the city limits of Arezzo, we began to climb the foothills into the Apennines. Soon, through the thick foliage of the trees that lined the winding road I began to catch glimpses of an immense, rambling stone structure, buttressed by a line of very high arches—the Cenobio of Camaldoli.

When I saw that Marino was going to stop at the Cenobio, I asked him if Father General was there.

"Yes," he answered. "I'll take you to his room."

The Right Reverend Aliprando Catani was then abbot general of the Camaldolese, but before he took office in 1963 he was at the Big Sur hermitage as "visitator" from the motherhouse. A very warm, simple man, he reminded me of Pope John XXIII. I was looking forward to seeing him again.

"You must be very tired," said don Aliprando, when Marino showed me into his office. I assured him I was, hoping that he would immediately send me to a room where I could lie down and sleep for an hour or two, or perhaps until next morning.

"No, you are from a hermitage," he said; "you must go up to the Eremo. I'll drive you there myself—I just got my driver's license."

"Is it very far?" I asked.

"Not far. About six kilometers," he answered, and I mentally calculated four miles. "They were working on one of the bridges this morning, but the road should be open now."

After we were out of sight of the monastery, the road up the mountain made a sharp turn and took us into a narrow corridor of beech and fir. At the end of the corridor we emerged into a broad, open area bordered on the right by grazing land and on the left by the high walls of the Eremo.

The walls date back to the seventeenth century and so are ancient by American standards, but when they were built the Holy Hermitage of Camaldoli had already been there for more than six hundred years. The walls, along with the Baroque overlay which suffocates the simple Romanesque

6

lines of the church, were added by another order of hermits who briefly took possession of the Eremo.

If you had come to Camaldoli in 1025, the year Saint Romuald founded the hermitage, you would have seen a broad meadow, in the midst of which five cabins clustered around a church and a lodge for common meals and meetings. Three kilometers down the mountain, where the Cenobio is now, you would have found a guest house, where a monk and two or three lay brothers provided food and lodging for travelers.

Saint Romuald wrote no rule for the hermits; the Rule of Saint Benedict was to guide their common life. For the life of the cell, his personal example and advice gave them all the rules they needed.

We entered the enclosure of the Eremo and walked up the flagstone-paved incline toward the church and the cells—small stone cottages arranged on a north-south axis in four rows.

The impression was overwhelming. I had spent the last few months at New Camaldoli preparing for this trip, studying Italian and looking at photographs of our monasteries in Italy. Now it was as if one of those black-and-white photos had suddenly taken on color and depth, and I was walking into it as through the magical picture-frame in a C. S. Lewis fantasy.

But perhaps this was not the way I experienced it. It was not déjà-vu but somehow the opposite: I was seeing something absolutely new for the very first time. Maybe it was like setting foot in Eden on the eve of the first Sabbath.

"Are you hungry?" Father General's question brought me back to present reality. He took me to the refectory and entrusted me to the care of an elderly lay brother with a sweet smile; then he left, saying he would be coming up to the Eremo next week.

Inside the refectory, as my eyes adjusted to the dim light, I began to observe the surroundings. Wooden benches and tables lined the walls, which were paneled half-way up to the ceiling. Above the paneling hung a few smoke-darkened paintings of monks, and over the head table was an impressive terra-cotta crucifix. The tablecloth was spotless, and the smiling lay brother gave me a fresh linen napkin and a plastic envelope to keep it in; then he spread a good meal of pasta, fish, bread, and red wine before me.

After I had eaten, the brother took me to a cell, dedicated to Saint John the Evangelist, where I was to stay during the next two months.

A cell looks larger on the outside than it actually is. Most of the bulk of the building consists of the thick, stone walls and an inside corridor surrounding the monk's living quarters, which are of quite modest dimensions. A wood-burning stove heats the room. My cell had modern bathroom facilities but no hot water; I would have to go to the kitchen with a bucket to get hot water for bathing.

I had just enough time to unpack my bags and take a short nap before the bell rang for Vespers. The common prayer here, as at Big Sur, consisted largely of Psalms sung in Latin to the Gregorian modes used in most Benedictine monasteries. The following year Camaldoli would begin singing the Psalms in Italian instead of Latin.

Dante speaks of Camaldoli and its founder more than once in his Divine Comedy. In the *Purgatorio* he mentions the Archiano stream *"che sovra l'Ermo nasce in Appennino,* which is born above the hermitage in the Apennines." The waters of the Archiano fill a small artificial lake just beyond the walls of the hermitage, and then they rush down a steep, narrow valley that at a certain point makes a sharp turn. A footpath accompanies the stream in its rapid descent to the monastery. Because of the turn in the narrow valley, hermitage and monastery are out of sight of each other, although you can see both from a peak about three hundred meters above the valley floor.

August 15, the Assumption of Mary, is a great feast at Camaldoli, one of the dozen or so occasions during the year when the monks in both houses (Eremo and Cenobio) come together for the solemn Mass, dinner, and recreation. After Lauds, the morning office of prayer, the younger monks at the Eremo set out on foot for the monastery; the elders would follow in a car.

We took a couple of shortcuts through the woods, once crossing the stream, and soon we could see the monastery. From that angle it looked like a medieval castle, with the Archiano guarding its eastern flank like a moat, across which a bridge connected the provincial road with the one leading to the hermitage.

The original name of the Cenobio was Fontebono, "good spring" in archaic Italian. The spring still flows into a stone fountain in front of the monastery. I tasted the water; it was ice-cold and sweet.

The abbot general, don Aliprando, presided at Mass, and all the other priests concelebrated. While I had taken my final vows, I was not yet ordained, and so I joined in chanting with the young Italian monks, most of whom would be with me in Rome that fall, beginning or continuing their studies. The singing was robust, full of joy, partly in Latin and partly in Italian.

Dinner followed, and then we gathered for recreation in the cloister garden. The garden was full of late-blooming perennials with those vibrant colors that only the mountain sunlight and the long months under snow can produce. The sixteenth-century arches along the north and east sides of the cloister had recently been glassed in, turning the portico into a greenhouse; they told me that geraniums flourished there throughout the winter.

I noticed don Anselmo in the garden and went over to greet him. We had met the previous year in Big Sur when he and Father General came for the triennial visitation of the American daughter-house.

Don Anselmo was then a man of stocky peasant build, with a peasant's sinewy hands. He walked with back straight, head slightly bent, the palms of his hands sometimes facing forward: these are gestures of humility, but strangely they gave one an overall impression of pride. He was almost completely bald; his face was broad and deeply lined, clean-shaven then, although he once wore a majestic beard. His eyes were large and very disconcerting; they did not seem to belong to his face. Were they the ingenuous, trusting eyes of a child, or the weary eyes of a man who has seen too much of human folly and can no longer bear it? Perhaps they were the eyes, prematurely wise, of children in countries at war, who have known privation and responsibility for others too soon. And indeed, Anselmo was a boy of six when the first world war began, and a young priest of thirty when Hitler and Mussolini started their war.

Don Anselmo's twelve years as abbot general (he was don Aliprando's predecessor) were a time of struggle, if not war, within the Camaldolese Order. The conflict was for the most part one of ideas: the progressive ideas of a far-seeing, almost prophetic abbot (don Anselmo foresaw the effects of an Ecumenical Council in the Catholic Church even before John XXIII summoned the bishops to Rome) and the ideas of a few monks whose false sense of certitude about the life they were living made them incapable of reading either the history of our Order or the signs of the times. By 1967, a year after the Council ended, everyone realized that the *aggiornamento* don Anselmo had been talking about for the past fifteen years had now become the official program of renewal for the entire Church.

Among don Anselmo's accomplishments during his years as abbot general, the most important were the renewal of serious scholarly work in the Order and the founding of New Camaldoli. He traveled to the United States in 1957, and the following year he sent don Aliprando and another monk from Camaldoli to look for a place to build a monastery. The place they found was Lucia Ranch, south of Big Sur on the California coast, where I became a novice in 1962. For the kind of monastic life I have been living as a Camaldolese Benedictine, I owe more to don Anselmo than to anyone else on earth.

As I chatted with Anselmo in the cloister garden, I mentioned that I would like to see the rest of the monastery. He called over one of the student-monks and ordered him, a bit gruffly, to be my tour guide.

The part of the monastery where the monks live now was built in the late sixteenth and early seventeenth centuries. A massive, two-storey structure attached to the church, it includes (with a separate entrance) a gift shop called Antica Farmacia.

During the Middle Ages, the Farmacia was in fact a kind of pharmacy. The monastery was situated on a well-traveled road that led from Ravenna on the Adriatic Sea, over the mountain pass behind the hermitage, and thence to Rome. Travelers would pause at the monastery, where the monks—practicing hospitality according to the Benedictine Rule—received them as Christ Himself. The needs of the guests often went beyond mere food and lodging, and the guest-master knew how to set broken bones and apply poultices to saddle sores and offer comfort and care to those who had contracted some disease along the way, and finally bury them if the disease proved fatal. The monks gradually expanded the simple facilities of the monastery's early period, and soon every Camaldolese hermitage and monastery was required by rule to maintain a hospital, staffed by skilled personnel on the monastic community's payroll and by one or more monks as chaplains and administrators. Later there arose active religious congregations founded specifically for health care, and the monks closed their hospitals.

The "pharmacy" at Camaldoli still contains the recipe books and utensils once used in preparing herbal remedies. With the addition of grape alcohol, some of the monks' potions became after-dinner cordials. The monastery sells four of them, one of which is like the famous Chartreuse and tastes better. The gift shop, with its cordials and other merchandise, is part of the inevitable folklore that Italians expect in their monasteries. Although the folklore aspect

11

bothered me, I tried not to give it much importance. The monks here obviously do not, and the preparation of the wares is a good, quiet form of manual labor.

On the south side of the church, opposite the monastic enclosure, is the guest house, where Camaldoli continues to exercise its ministry of the open door. If the monks no longer have a hospital, that is partly because people today suffer from wounds and fractures of a different sort that require different remedies.

Camaldoli is known throughout Italy and beyond the Alps for its seminars and retreats. When it is full, the Hospitium or guest house accommodates nearly two hundred persons. My first reaction, when I heard this, was to question the unbalanced ratio between the monks (at that time about forty in number) and their guests. The tail, I thought, would wag the dog.

But soon I realized that the monks at Camaldoli were every bit as aware of this problem as I was. Anyway, they reassured me, the guest house remains closed from October to May, except for the great liturgical feasts, and the snow and ice make a man a contemplative even if he is not particularly inclined in that direction.

My guide led me through the church to the guest house. Another route, from the second floor of the monastery, passes through the library. Church and library, prayer and culture, are the two bridges between the monks and their guests. As at the Eremo, here also the successive attempts at remodeling the church have left unfortunate results: an overblown Rococo of the late eighteenth century with, however, a certain ingenuous charm. The monastic choir above the sacristy is simpler; this is where the community prays during the long winter months when the church is unbearably cold.

The granite steps leading down into the Hospitium were like a time machine that took us back to the century when Camaldoli was founded. At the foot of the steps was a Romanesque cloister; strong stone pillars and rhythmical

arches defined a small, paved area open to the sky, surrounded by broad walkways and a ramp leading to a lower
level and another exit—a perfect architectural statement of
groundedness and peace.

At the sight of the cloister I was once more overwhelmed
by a sense of recognition, along with a moment of mental
pain. The cloister was once the focus of a monastic community, I thought, but now it is the entrance to something
like a hotel, with religious lectures instead of night-club
entertainment. But the beauty of the place held my attention
for the moment, and I let it soothe me.

Camaldolese architecture is a parable of Camaldolese
history. The Cistercian monks, founded a century after
Camaldoli, have their own architectural style too; it is
regular and orderly and consciously unadorned, in accordance with their literal interpretation of the Rule of Saint
Benedict. Camaldolese architecture is also plain but rather
less sophisticated than that of the Cistercians, and it is
always purposely asymmetrical, slightly off-center and literally eccentric, in accordance with Saint Romuald's
free-style interpretation of the Rule. The eleventh-century
cloister at Camaldoli is not quite four-square; each angle is
a bit more or less than ninety degrees, and it all tilts to fit the
narrow spur of the mountain on which it rests.

The young monk who was showing me the monastery
interrupted my reverie and hurried me on. To the left of the
entrance to the cloister was a small chapel; some think it
might be what remains of the original church or perhaps
even of a shrine that already existed here at the time of Saint
Romuald. Now it is a kind of crypt, with a slightly pointed
barrel vault sustained by one large column, of course off-
center.

Near the chapel were the conference rooms, each dedicated to one of the cultural luminaries of the Camaldolese Order:
Saint Peter Damian , a doctor of the Church; Guido of Arezzo,
inventor of the "sol-fa" scale names and the musical staff;
and Gratian of Bologna, the codifier of Canon Law.

A hallway took us from Romanesque to Renaissance; we were now in the fifteenth-century cloister, an elegant colonnade slightly marred on one side by a chapel added to the church two centuries later. Up another flight of stairs was the "Landino Room," named not after a monk but after Cristoforo Landino, a Renaissance philosopher. With his friends from Florence (including Marsilio Ficino and Lorenzo de' Medici), Landino made frequent excursions to Camaldoli, seeking the quiet of the woods and the company of the learned men among the monks. On the wall outside the room hung a five-hundred-year-old oriental rug, three meters by four, in deep reds and purples, a gift of the Greek Cardinal Bessarion to Ambrogio Traversari, the abbot of Camaldoli at the time of the Council of Florence.

Leaving the guest house by way of the library, we followed a narrow passage behind the organ pipes to the second floor of the monastery. I thanked my guide and went looking for my companions from the hermitage.

Back at the hermitage that evening, I tried to sort out the day's impressions. Bewildered by total immersion in a new language and a different culture, I now had to deal with the perplexing question of how to make the reality of Camaldoli fit the notions of Camaldolese history I had pieced together at the hermitage in California. It was hard enough for me, as an American, to understand what it means to live in a house that has been lived in continually for almost a thousand years. American roots simply do not go that deep. Moreover, we Americans do not deal well with complexity and a lack of definition. We want to know where we stand. At New Camaldoli in Big Sur, we would have preferred to say that we are contemplative not active, that our ideal is solitude not community. But we could not and can not define ourselves so simply, because the reality of Camaldoli and its history do not permit us to indulge in the illusory clarity of this definition. The history of Camaldoli has its own sort of clarity, but it is the clarity of a light that has passed through a prism of many facets.

By the end of summer I felt at home at Camaldoli, although I was eager to leave for Rome. There I would start work on a degree in theology at the Anselmianum—Rome's Benedictine university—while staying at our monastery of San Gregorio al Celio.

San Gregorio—Saint Gregory's on the Celian Hill— takes its name from Pope Gregory the Great, considered to be the first Benedictine to occupy the See of Peter. Toward the end of the sixth century, while still a layman, Gregory founded the monastery on his family estate overlooking the Palatine Hill and dedicated it to Saint Andrew the Apostle. Elected to the papacy, Gregory sent a group of monks from the Celian Hill to Canterbury in England, where they built a monastery and preached the gospel to the pagan clans in Kent. The Camaldolese took possession of San Gregorio al Celio in the sixteenth century.

On the evening of my arrival in Rome, I stood at the window of my room at San Gregorio enjoying the view of the floodlit ruins on the Palatine across the way. I thought of Byron and Shelley and Keats (the latter two are buried in the English cemetery a few blocks down the street from the monastery) and lost some of my intolerance toward Romanticism in general and the Romantic idea of monastic life in particular. To have such a view from the window of your cell is not a good reason for joining a monastery and is not reason enough for remaining there. But I may find, when I get to heaven, that my perseverance as a monk was due in part to the beauty I saw from my window, because the Palatine ruins have taught me how to read history with compassion and humility.

3. CLASSE

"I'm going to like it here," I said as I leaned out the window of the train, at the border station of Domodossola in the Italian Alps.

I did like Italy very much. Living in Italy was good medicine for me, and from the Italian monks I learned many things. In the fall of 1968, having asked the advice of don Aliprando and don Anselmo, I decided to remain in Italy, in Rome or at the Cenobio in the Tuscan Apennines, indefinitely and perhaps for the rest of my life.

What motivated me to make this choice? A romantic image of myself as an expatriate writer? I think not. My inability to live as a hermit? Probably, but not exclusively. Rome offered ample opportunities to study, and I wanted to extend my training in theology beyond the usual program required for ordination. In fact, I wanted to write a thesis on Yoga and get a Ph.D. in history of religion. About the Yoga thesis my Italian superiors were not wildly enthusiastic— those in charge at New Camaldoli had made me drop all Yoga practice as a condition for my admission to monastic vows—but in Italy the policy was to encourage the monks who wished to study and teach or write. And so they allowed me to continue my research.

Were these really the reasons why I decided to stay on in Italy, at the Cenobio in the Apennines? My real motivations now seem more mysterious and ultimately less selfish. It may have been simply a matter of vocation—God so willed it. The more I see it this way, the happier I am with my decision.

Two years after my arrival in Rome, don Anselmo was appointed superior of San Gregorio. I began to confide in him, although I found his personality disconcerting, to say the least: a peculiar blend of peasant gruffness and Renaissance refinement, a juxtaposition of qualities that I observed in other Tuscans as well.

❦

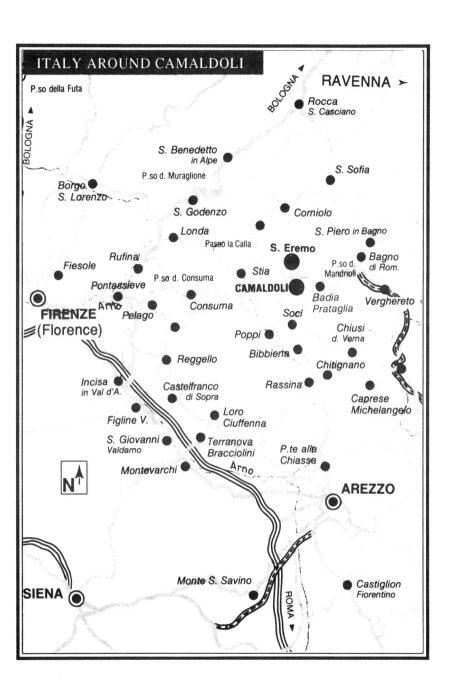

ITALY AROUND CAMALDOLI

P.so della Futa

BOLOGNA ▲

BOLOGNA ▲ RAVENNA ►

Rocca
S. Casciano

S. Benedetto
in Alpe

S. Sofia

P.so d. Muraglione

Borgo
S. Lorenzo

S. Godenzo

Corniolo

Londa

S. Piero in Bagno

Fiesole

Rufina

Paseo la Calla

S. Eremo

Pontassieve

P.so d. Consuma

Stia

P.so d.
Mandrioli

Bagno
di Rom.

Arno

Pelago

Consuma

CAMALDOLI

Badia
Prataglia

Verghereto

Soci

FIRENZE
(Florence)

Poppi

Chiusi
d. Verna

Reggello

Bibbiena

Chitignano

Incisa
in Val d'A.

Castelfranco
di Sopra

Rassina

Caprese
Michelangelo

Figline V.

Loro
Ciuffenna

S. Giovanni
Valdarno

Terranova
Bracciolini

P.te alla
Chiassa

Montevarchi

Arno

N ↑

AREZZO

SIENA

Monte S. Savino

ROMA ▼

Castiglion
Fiorentino

"Come in!" Don Anselmo's voice responded with its usual sharpness to my timid knocking on his door.

If I didn't know how to read don Anselmo's facial expressions, I would think he was annoyed to have me disturb him. But his brusque manner was the way he dealt with all those to whom he felt close, with whom he did not feel the need to use "manners" or any sort of diplomacy or mask.

"What am I supposed to do?" I began with a question that didn't make much sense.

"About what?" asked don Anselmo.

"About New Camaldoli, about myself, about my belonging to an Italian community and being both a member and a foreigner."

Anselmo almost smiled, and seeing I was in one of my negative moods, he assumed a tolerant attitude. "You know that the monks at Camaldoli respect you as a person and treat you like a brother. The fact of your being an American is secondary as far as they're concerned.

"Yes, I know that. They go out of their way to make me feel I belong." I paused. "I guess what keeps me unsettled is the thought of the community back in Big Sur. Why did I have to come to Italy to find the kind of monastic life that makes sense to me? Why couldn't I find it in California?"

"I think you must realize," said don Anselmo, now a little less tolerant, "that the difficulty Americans have in persevering at our hermitage in California may partly be due to causes outside New Camaldoli and even outside religious life itself. First, there is the extreme mobility of the American family; a child is likely to live in half a dozen different neighborhoods during his school years. Also, your individualism and your obsession with privacy are anything but helpful for a monastic vocation. Americans on a bus or a subway train may look like natural hermits—each one sufficient unto himself and absorbed in his newspaper or whatever—but self-sufficiency and self-centeredness are the hermit's worst enemies. If a candidate to any Benedictine community—our hermitage or any other monastery—does not lose this kind of individualism by the end of his novitiate, he will not persevere."

I was starting to feel a little uncomfortable. "I suppose you might say that the choice of Camaldoli in Tuscany as my permanent community was a very private choice. A sign I'm also a typical American individualist."

Anselmo had a "now-I've-got-you" look on his face. "I didn't say that; you did," he rejoined, and added, "I really think you waste too much energy examining yourself. You should stop asking unanswerable questions and get on with the work of simply being a monk. You should thank God that you are able to live out your vocation according to your conscience, whether here or in California or anywhere else. If you really are concerned about the future of New Camaldoli, you ought to examine the possibilities of helping them from where God has placed you. For one thing," Anselmo continued, gesturing to a book on his desk, "our American novices do not have access to the sources of Camaldolese history and spirituality, which are all in Latin and Italian. You might begin by translating *The Life of Blessed Romuald* by Saint Peter Damian. This has never been published in English."

"Father General also suggested this," I replied. "I've started a translation, but I don't know how much good it will do the monks in Big Sur. What I would prefer to translate is *The Life of the Five Brothers* by Saint Bruno-Boniface of Querfurt, since it gives a picture of Romuald as people saw him during his lifetime."

"Of course you must translate *The Five Brothers,* but don't forget Peter Damian," don Anselmo insisted. "Bruno-Boniface actually says very little about Romuald. His book is mostly about the disciples of Romuald who were martyred in Poland."

I started to argue with him. "And Peter Damian was writing more about himself than about Romuald. I mean, the Romuald he depicts in his book is actually a model for his own agenda of monastic reform. You can't read the book

19

without knowing Peter Damian's historical circumstances and his reform agenda. Most Americans have very little historical sense; they would read his *Life of Romuald* like any other piece of devotional literature, perhaps be edified, and then put it aside."

At that moment don Anselmo lifted his head and looked at me intently. It was not an accusatory look, but I began to feel a peculiar sensation of guilt. "I'm not going to tell you what to write or what to translate," Anselmo said, "but it is up to you to make Romuald and Camaldoli understandable to the Americans. You are an American, and you seem to have a sense of history. It is up to you."

His directness made me feel embarrassed, and I reluctantly accepted his compliment.

Anselmo continued. "If you don't want simply to translate these texts and publish them as such, you could do something else." He got up to open his window and then returned to his desk. "Perhaps you could take the contents of what Peter Damian and Bruno wrote and recast it into a narrative form that would mean something to an American monk or novice. But you could also relate the history of Saint Romuald to your own experience of the monastery. Think of yourself as a link in a chain that goes back to Saint Romuald in an uninterrupted succession of men who all faced the same problem: the problem of reinterpreting and reliving Romuald's experience of the monastic vocation in the context of their own day and age. This has been our concern at Camaldoli from the very start: continuity of values in the variability of times and circumstances and human attitudes."

I began to warm up to his idea, but I had one more question. "Of course Camaldoli is unique in Western Europe for its unbroken continuity over so many centuries. But that by itself does not mean very much. What is the real link between Camaldoli today and Romuald?"

"The primacy given to the experience of the indwelling Trinity," Anselmo answered without hesitation, "and the concept of a monastic education that begins with life in community and fosters the monk's growth toward greater and greater freedom—freedom, that is, to follow the inner guidance of the Holy Spirit. This is the whole meaning of the passage from the Cenobio to the Eremo: not the search for solitude, but the love of freedom. And the freedom to love."

श्री

With don Anselmo's encouragement, I started to translate *The Five Brothers* and Peter Damian's *Life of Romuald*. The work went slowly, and I found myself struggling to visualize Romuald's physical environment; nothing clear came to me from the texts. I had to go back to Ravenna.

I had been there once before, bringing with me art-book images of the grand mosaics that line the walls of the churches. I was now convinced that Romuald received more of his education as a Christian and a monk from those luminous images than he did from all the sermons he heard in the monastery. And since studying the mosaics of Ravenna was part of what led me to become a Catholic and join the monastery, the same may be true in my case as well.

By the middle of the tenth century, when Romuald was born, the ups and downs of political and military fortune had left Ravenna in a state of genteel decay. But the churches were solidly built of brick and mortar, and the mosaics shone with the same colors the mosaicist had seen, centuries before, as he cemented the tiny cubes of glass and marble to the walls of apse, vault, and nave. The unfading tesserae, set at uneven angles, still prismatically reflect the changing light and create a shimmering effect of subtle movement that brings figures and abstract patterns to life.

The mosaics were the Bible of the unlettered faithful. The twenty-six gospel scenes that line the nave of Sant'Apollinare Nuovo were their catechism, and the figures of Abel, Abraham, and Melchisedek in the apse of San Vitale taught them the unity of Old and New Testaments in one divine plan of salvation. Their senses were alive and

21

receptive to nature and art in a way that people today—
whose sight is cluttered with fine print and whose hearing is
dulled by the racket of machines—can only envy. And yet,
if you try, you can still share something of Romuald's
feelings and sensations when you visit Ravenna.

You enter the Baptistery of the Orthodox and look up at
the full and radiant faces of the Apostles, done in Roman
style as if they were portraits, concrete and real and present.
You see a sanity and wholesomeness in their faces, and they
look down at you with earnestness and intensity of expression, yet without passion, as if to say, "See, this is what you
must become." You come to Sant'Apollinare Nuovo to read
the mosaicist's gospel, and you see a youthful, beardless
Jesus healing and preaching and working signs and wonders; then—depicted with greater pathos by a later hand,
Jesus now has His beard—you see Him at table with the
Twelve and carrying His cross and appearing risen. And you
are surprised at the unbridged leap from the foot of Mount
Calvary to the empty tomb: there is no Passion scene—the
dead Jesus is not shown. But there is nothing peculiar about
this. Outside the pages of a few illuminated gospel manuscripts, no realistic representation of the crucified Savior
could be seen above any Christian altar until well after the
time of Saint Romuald. The cross was there, but bejew-
eled—it was the cross of Saint John's gospel; it was Pope
Leo's *gloria crucis*.

What does all this mean?

For one formed in the resurrectional light of Ravenna's
mosaics, the monk's life of asceticism and penance could
never degenerate into masochism, as at times it has done.
Not even the Abbé de Rancé and his reformed Trappists
could have lived their harsh and holy life under the glorious
cross that reigns over the altar of Sant'Apollinare in Classe,
where Romuald became a monk.

In the apse of the basilica at Romuald's monastery, you
can see, just as he did, not only the splendor of heaven but
also the nearness of heaven and the naturalness of heaven.

The warm, almost sensuous bodies in verdant and flower-studded pastures express a theology of the goodness of creation and of incarnate divinity; they affirm an eschatology of divine diaphany, of a universe become transparent to God. At the center of the apse is the *crux gemmata* flanked by Moses and Elijah, and you realize that this is a Transfiguration scene: the monastery—every monastery—is Mount Tabor. The Transfiguration of Jesus was the mystery that meant most to Romuald as a contemplative monk; to this mystery he dedicated the church at the Eremo of Camaldoli. Beneath the cross stands the holy bishop Apollinaris; he stands not as one who bears witness (with hands raised, palms facing forward) but in prayer (palms facing upward). The bishop-*orans*, buried beneath the altar, still leads the Church's liturgy.

If you look up at them with truly open eyes, these images will go straight down to the depths of your being and call forth everything you have to respond with.

❦

"How is your book coming?" don Anselmo asked me as we walked out of the refectory after dinner. His tone of voice was brusque as usual, but there was the hint of a smile on his face. It was obvious that he was genuinely interested.

I told him it was coming along slowly; that I had finished translating *The Life of the Five Brothers;* that I wasn't getting anywhere with Saint Peter Damian; and anyway Peter Damian wasn't writing history; there are gaps and inaccuracies in his stories about Romuald and his followers; he often seems to be grinding one of his axes; and maybe the best thing would be to extract and paraphrase, etcetera. Anselmo listened without saying anything.

When we got to his room, don Anselmo went to his desk and started looking among his papers. With his back turned to me, he said, in an offhand way, "As you write, try to remember the thoughts and feelings that accompanied your first years in the monastery."

23

"You mean I should be autobiographical?" I asked. "I don't think I'm ready to write my autobiography."

Anselmo turned to me and said, "All historical writing is in some way autobiographical. Every historian tends to project his own life's experience on the persons and events he is writing about. To a certain extent this is inevitable. So it is best to do so consciously."

He sat down at his desk, and I pulled up a chair opposite him. I was intrigued with what he was saying, but I still was not convinced. "My problem, don Anselmo," I objected, "is that I understand Bruno's or Peter Damian's Latin, but I am never sure I understand what they felt. It's getting to be an obsession: the remoteness of their eleventh-century Italy from our twentieth-century America. It's not simply a question of computers and space travel. Their minds functioned differently from ours."

"But they were men, and so are we," responded don Anselmo.

"Their minds functioned differently," I insisted. "They saw a different world, even when they were looking at the same things we see—the human face and body, the land, the sky. And even if we do understand what they wrote, I always have the feeling that the words have a different impact on us than they did on them."

Patiently, don Anselmo replied to my objection. "That may be so, but just like an American, you emphasize how different we are from men of the past. You seem to forget the identity of nature that unites us to them. Let me repeat what I said: when you write about Saint Romuald's vocation, try to remember what you felt and thought when you were learning to be a monk. Never forget: Romuald was a man and so are you."

"I don't know if that's enough. It hasn't been easy for me to be a monk."

Anselmo stiffened visibly and gave me a piercing look, but his voice remained calm. "Who do you think it has been easy for? That is not the question. You have had your inner struggles and doubts, and so had Saint Romuald. Do you think he never felt lonely? Do you think I never did? But that is not the point. The point is Romuald's faith-response to the crisis of his conversion and to the struggles he had to face in his life as a monk and a Christian. An authentic vocation is the work of the Holy Spirit. Try to remember what the Spirit did to you, and perhaps you will understand what He did to Saint Romuald."

❦

Romuald entered the monastery of Classe because of a murder. His father Sergio had a dispute with a kinsman over a piece of land and settled it with a duel. Romuald was present; filled with horror and remorse, he took upon himself the penalty for homicide, which was, according to Church law, forty days' penance in a monastery. Life was cheap then, in the Age of Iron.

While at Sant'Apollinare, Romuald was befriended by a simple fellow who had joined the monastery in his old age.

"Have you come to stay?" the old man asked.

"No!" Romuald responded abruptly. He found the brother's question deeply disturbing. After a few seconds he added, "I have come to do penance for a murder."

"Did you kill a man?"

"My father did."

"Why are you here, if you didn't kill anybody?"

"I was present and I saw him die. I have come to do penance for seeing it happen."

The old brother looked at Romuald for a moment. Then he said softly, "What will you do in return, if I make you see Saint Apollinaris with your own eyes?"

Romuald answered, "I'll become a monk!"

25

That night the sky was clear, and the light of a full moon filled the basilica of Classe with an alabaster radiance. Romuald stood next to the brother, their hands raised in imitation of the saint and their gaze fixed on his image in the apse.

The hours passed. At cockcrow Romuald began to see the hieratic figure, no longer on the flat plane of the mosaic but in three dimensions, rising in a cloud of incense from the altar and circling the church as if to honor its icons with the smoke of his thurible. Returning to the altar, the saint vanished.

In the days following their all-night vigil, the old man pressed Romuald to fulfill his promise, but the more vehemently he did so, the more Romuald resisted. Was the vision truly from God, Romuald asked himself, or only from his own imagination and the brother's suggestion? He consented to give his answer only if the vision would be repeated. So on the next full moon night, the two again kept watch in church, and once more Saint Apollinaris appeared and performed his incensing of the altars.

Still Romuald would not say yes. The brother, wearied at the young man's indecision, left him to his thoughts and prayers.

The robust and handsome son of one of Ravenna's most powerful citizens, already twenty and destined to a military career like his father's, whose future bride had already been chosen, was not the type of man whom people of the day expected to enter a monastery. A monk was ordinarily someone who had been raised in the monastery, either because he was the youngest son of a large family, for whom there could be no inheritance; or because he was the gifted child of poor parents, who would otherwise have no chance to develop his talents; or because he was an orphan. In the tenth century there was no real concept of vocational choice— not among the peasants, since their life was a struggle for survival, nor even among the wealthy and powerful, since family and political interests came first. After the year 1000, Europe would experience two centuries of warmer weather, abundant crops, and a population explosion, and hence more adults—*conversi*—would enter monasteries. But now it was not done.

To choose to belong to God—not to his father, not to his family, not to his social class—was a decision that would have no support except from within, from his conscience and his faith; we cannot imagine how difficult it was for Romuald to make this decision. He kept coming to the monastery, and he would often assist at the monks' Vigil office shortly after midnight, and when they retired for their second sleep, he remained in church to pray. The idea of choosing to be free for God made him dizzy, and yet it was more seductive than the most beautiful woman he had ever desired. One day he made his decision, and when the monks returned at sunup for the office of Prime, he stormed into the chapter hall. Falling to his knees in their midst, Romuald begged them through his tears to receive him into the community.

❦

"Don Anselmo," I asked, "tell me something of your own experience of becoming a monk."

He did not directly answer my question, but looking at me intently, he said, "There are exceptions, of course, but I believe that in most cases the idea of joining a monastery produces vertigo. You may even experience the dawning of the idea in your mind as a shock. But remember: a genuine monastic vocation involves being called repeatedly. The initial call does not hit you like lightning, do its job and vanish, never to bother you again. The lightning may or may not flash the first time, but the call comes again and again as long as you are on the monastic journey."

He continued to look at me, but now more gently. "At first, if you are a bit off-balance, monastic life will throw you off your feet. But in the end, if you let it, it will leave you standing, and you will realize that all the buffeting about was only a way of getting you to be normal and

27

natural, or in other words, simply to be yourself." He added, changing metaphors, "When it all starts, it feels like a thousand swords wounding you at once, Later, you discover that the wounds were there in the first place, and being a monk has healed them."

❦

The monks of Sant'Apollinare did not know what to do with Romuald's request to join the monastery. Romuald's father was a hard man, and who knows how he would react if they accepted his son into the community? They would take an old man (like Romuald's friend), but a lad of twenty, and a nobleman? It could not be done. The answer was no.

So Romuald went to the archbishop, Onesto degli Onesti, who before his election to the see of Ravenna had been abbot of Classe. On the archbishop's enthusiastic recommendation, the monks clothed Romuald in the monastic cowl.

But life in the monastery was not as he expected it to be. In accordance with what was prescribed for novices, one of the monks read him the Rule of Saint Benedict and translated its Latin into Romuald's Romance dialect. What Romuald heard the novice-master read and what he saw the monks do were two different things. For example, the Rule does not allow a second period of sleep after the pre-dawn Vigil service, but at Sant'Apollinare the monks went back to bed until sunup. And although they observed the liturgical customs and ceremonies of the great abbey of Cluny, they ignored much of what the great Cluniac abbots had said about silence and fasting and the reading of Scripture. When the novice-master slighted Romuald's objections and told him to accept things as they were, he was torn by doubts. Should he stay or should he leave? Should he voice his objections or remain silent? These thoughts beat upon his soul like waves of a winter storm on the seacoast beyond the abbey.

Perhaps another saint, endowed with other virtues, especially patience, would have persevered quietly in the monastery and gradually would have won his weaker brothers over to a more faithful following of their monastic vocation. As it happened, Romuald's personal mixture of strengths and weaknesses, of virtues and flaws, would not permit him to endure the imperfect life of his monastery, and he simply had to leave. But God turned his departure into a happy fault, a *felix culpa*, for the ultimately greater good of the Church and of the monastery of Classe.

༚

In his Life of Romuald, Saint Peter Damian speaks about a few of the monks plotting to kill Romuald. I asked don Anselmo, "Was murder really all that common in tenth-century monasteries?"

"This is not too strange to be true," he replied. "Life was cheap in those days, and people—even in monasteries—could talk quite casually about getting rid of someone they disliked. And there may have been family and political issues involved. In any case, the decadence of the monks at Classe—with a few individual exceptions—reflected the general decadence and moral squalor of Church and society in the early Middle Ages."

"Could Romuald have stayed in the monastery and still have remained faithful to himself and to God?"

Don Anselmo phrased his answer carefully. "Peter Damian tells us that, when Romuald heard about the plot to kill him, he decided to 'keep his mouth shut and pray to his Father in secret.' This may have saved his life, but it did not resolve the fundamental problem of living in a community of faithless, indifferent, and malicious men. If we look at Romuald's dilemma at Classe from a purely human point of view, the only solution we can see for such a crisis of conscience is rebellion or revolution—the person who listens to the voice of conscience must either reject the community or try to change it. But in a monastery, where it is a question of a Christian conscience animated by charity, the best protest is for the monk to isolate himself from the others, to become a hermit. This is the only way to avoid yielding to conformism, remain oneself and keep one's identity, without rejecting monastic life itself."

"History shows us many examples of monks who isolated themselves from others for false or pathological motives," I observed. "In other circumstances, there have been communities that imposed isolation by rule in order to safeguard an institution, to the detriment of the individual."

Anselmo agreed. "Underlying these examples there was always some form of theology or ideology which may have been theoretically orthodox but which in practice contradicted the truth of the human person and the truth revealed in the gospel. To be authentically human and Christian, the hermit's life must aim at deepening communion with God and neighbor, even when the choice of the hermitage is initially motivated by the need to free oneself from an impossible situation in the monastic community."

"Instead of becoming a hermit," I asked, "could Romuald have gone to another monastery?"

Anselmo smiled. "In the seventies of the tenth century, this would probably have meant jumping from the frying pan into the fire."

❦

After about three years at Classe, Romuald asked to leave the monastery. The abbot and his chapter readily agreed to let him go.

Romuald boarded a ship and sailed up the Adriatic coast to a place northeast of Venice now called Tor di Caligo. There he placed himself under the direction of a holy eccentric named Marino. Marino and Romuald lived in a rude fisherman's hut. They tilled a small field for food and caught fish in the lagoon.

Marino sang the entire Psalter every day. Rising early, Romuald with him, he would wander aimlessly, stopping now and then to sit under a tree and sing forty Psalms, then moving to another tree to sing thirty more, and so on.

They fasted three days a week, which meant they ate half a loaf of bread apiece and some dry fava beans, with water to drink. The other days they ate cooked food and drank a bit of wine.

Romuald did not go to Tor di Caligo for privacy; he and Marino were always together. Romuald chose the hermitage for the sake of poverty and asceticism, but at the same time he received an education of sorts. The two hermits each had a Psalter and would sit face to face and sing alternate verses of the Psalms. Romuald at first had a hard time reading the page. Every time he made a mistake, Marino would box him on the ear with a stick. Years later, Romuald used to laugh about Marino's teaching methods. He told his own novices about the day when he could take no more. "Please, Master," he said, "start hitting me on the other ear, since I am going deaf in this one." Marino, impressed with his disciple's meekness and humility, stopped using his stick.

So one year passed at Tor di Caligo, and then another, and Romuald began to feel that the years would march on into decades there, to the unending rhythm of daily Psalters, alternate fast days, and manual labor. But this was not to be; events in Venice were already reaching out toward Romuald, to draw him from the obscurity of Marino's hut into the light of history.

4. JOURNEY TO CUIXÁ

Rebellion was seething in the lagoon.

In the year 976, Venice had a petty tyrant for a doge: Peter Candiano IV, hungry for power and unscrupulous. Seeing that a marriage with Waldrada, the daughter of the marquis of Tuscany, would be to his political advantage,

Peter Candiano divorced his first wife and shut her up in a convent. Candiano's new bride brought him a rich dowry of lands, goods, and servants. To defend it all, he raised a private army of Tuscan mercenaries, much to the chagrin of the Venetians. Candiano's enemies, plotting to overthrow him, devised a plan which would involve the Orséolo family, eternal rivals of the Candiani.

The plan was extremely simple. The conspirators set fire to the west wall of the Orséolo palace. The flames leapt the narrow canal and began to devour the rafters of the basilica of Saint Mark, the cathedral church of Venice, and from there they reached out to embrace the palace of the doge.

Finding no way of escape, Candiano rushed out of the flaming palace, holding up his infant son as a human shield. The mob seized the child, butchered him before his father's eyes, and then killed the doge. Candiano's troops surrendered. There was no more bloodshed.

An Orséolo was immediately elected doge; his name was also Peter, a deeply religious man, then about fifty years of age. Peter Orséolo was acquainted with the hermit Marino and his young disciple from Ravenna. From time to time he would invite them to his palace, seeking their counsel in matters of conscience.

The circumstances of Peter Orséolo's election automatically implicated him in the rebellion, at least in the eyes of the Candiani. For this reason, Peter Orséolo's chief concern as doge was to cancel all visible effects and, as far as possible, all memory of the revolution. The two years of his rule were a time of feverish building activity, in which Saint Mark's Square began to assume the aspect it has today. The campanile was built, and Byzantine architects and were commissioned to create a new cathedral.

The Candiani had nurtured close ties with the Saxon emperors, as well as with the marquis of Tuscany. Peter Orséolo made it his policy to preserve these same alliances, but it was Orséolo's meekness and gentle character that calmed the wrath of the rival clan, and finally there was peace in Venice.

However, Emperor Otto II could not have ignored the political implications of the overthrow of his ally Candiano. He sent word to one of the most widely respected churchmen of his day, Abbot Garí of Cuixá, then on his way home from the Holy Land, instructing him to examine the situation and report back. Garí arrived in Venice during the summer of 978. Peter Orséolo welcomed the abbot and listened with great interest to the story of his pilgrimage.

In the course of their conversation, Orséolo surprised Abbot Garí with a riddle. "Can a shipwrecked man be saved, if he does not come to shore?"

"Certainly not," the abbot replied.

Peter continued. "Then tell me, what shore must I head for?"

Garí understood what he was hinting at. Peter Orséolo had long felt the attraction of monastic life, and now, in effect, he was asking to accompany Garí to his abbey in the Pyrenees and to become a monk there. Marino and Romuald, who were present on this occasion, encouraged him in this decision. Joining the monastery, they said, was the only way to disassociate himself from the plot that had put him into office.

Pleased that the whole political question had practically resolved itself, Abbot Garí accepted his unexpected postulant and agreed to leave with the doge for the abbey of Cuixá, just as soon as he returned from Rome.

❦

Garí left Venice and headed south by land over the Apennines, following the mountain road along which, fifty years later, Camaldoli would be built. In the meantime, the doge's plan remained a well-guarded secret, and Garí's return to Venice after visiting Rome aroused no suspicions. Nor did the doge's wife think it strange when he asked her to make preparations for a religious feast at one of his estates on the mainland. Peter promised to follow her the next day.

At sundown on August 31st 978, everything was ready. A ship loaded with church vestments and other precious gifts for the abbey lay at anchor in the lagoon. Shortly after midnight, Garí, the doge, and (the Cuixá chronicler states) "three noblemen of his duchy, John Morosini his cousin, John Gradenigo, and Romuald" embarked and sailed south to Chioggia. There they transferred their goods to wagons, mounted horses, and set off on the overland route by way of Verona and Lombardy.

When they realized that the doge had abandoned Venice, the members of the Great Council met to decide what was to be done. They sent messengers by every possible route westward and eventually found the abbot and his party. But Peter Orséolo, expecting that they would try to follow him, had shaved his beard and put on monk's garb, and with the hood pulled low over his eyes, he was unrecognizable.

Garí and his companions continued their journey, and in a few weeks they arrived at the foot of snow-covered Mount Canigou. As they approached the Abbey of Saint Michael, the bells were rung and the monks came out in festive procession to welcome their abbot with his cargo of relics, vestments, and other treasures. The former doge dismounted and walked the rest of the way barefoot to the monastery which was now his home, and where he would end his days, venerated as a saint by the monks.

Romuald had so far spent his life in the coastal plains and wetlands of northeastern Italy. Here he was to discover the beauty of Cuixá's green valley beneath the high and rugged Pyrenees. He would remain ten years at Cuixá, his longest stay as a monk in any one place.

Readers of Thomas Merton's *The Seven Storey Mountain* will recall that he speaks about the Abbey of Cuixá, or Saint-Michel-de-Cuxa, in the first chapter of the book.

> On the last day of January 1915, under the sign of the Water Bearer, in a year of a great war, and down in the shadow of some French mountains on the borders of Spain, I came into the world.

In a time before nation-states, Thomas Merton's birthplace was neither France nor Spain, and the mountains marked no border. The area was part of what would later be called Catalonia and was subject to the count of Barcelona. Merton continues, a few pages later.

> There were many ruined monasteries in those mountains... My mind goes back with great reverence to the thought of those clean, ancient stone cloisters, those low and mighty rounded arches hewn and set in place by monks who perhaps prayed me where I am now. Saint Martin and Saint Michael the Archangel, the great patron of monks, had churches in these mountains: Saint-Martin-du-Canigou; Saint-Michel-de-Cuxa. Is it any wonder I should have a friendly feeling about those places?

> One of them, stone by stone, followed me across the Atlantic a score of years later, and got itself set up within convenient reach of me when I most needed to see what a cloister looked like, and what kind of place a man might live in, to live according to his rational nature, and not like a stray dog. Saint-Michel-de-Cuxa is all fixed up in a special and considerably tidy little museum in an uptown park, in New York, overlooking the Hudson River, in such a way you don't recall what kind of city you are in. It is called The Cloisters. Synthetic as it is, it still preserves enough of its own reality to be a reproach to everything else around it, except the trees and the Palisades.

In the spring of the year following my visit to Ravenna, I journeyed to Cuixá, together with the novices of Camaldoli and their novice-master. At Cuixá a group of Catalan monks have reestablished a Benedictine community and are slowly restoring the abbey to something like its original splendor.

35

Traveling by car, we followed the Italian and French Rivieras to Marseilles and Perpignan and then turned southwest toward Prades.

As it was just after noon when we arrived in Prades, we looked for a place to stop in the shade and eat our lunch of prosciutto ham sandwiches and rosé wine from the Côte d'Azur. After lunch I asked directions of a couple of passersby, but neither knew the way to Rue du 4 Septembre, the street where Thomas Merton was born.

We turned back to the main avenue and drove slowly through town. Down a side street I saw what looked like the house Michael Mott described in his biography of Merton, but it was the wrong street. Finally a woman directed us there, and we found the house unchanged from the photograph in Mott's biography and indeed unchanged since Owen and Ruth Merton moved there from Paris, seventy-five years ago.

Having made our pilgrimage to Thomas Merton's birthplace, we left town and took the road south toward the mountains. In five minutes we were at the Abbey of Saint Michael.

Gentle hills embraced the abbey with its fields and orchards. Prades to the north and the village of Taurinya to the south remained out of sight from the monastery, which lifted its lofty bell tower up toward Mount Canigou. The summit of the grand massif was veiled by bright spring clouds.

We entered a driveway marked "Comunitat de Sant Miquel" and drove around to the back of the building. A slight, elderly man in lay clothes was there, speaking to a woman in the flower garden. In French I asked him if he were Father Josep the guest-master, with whom I had exchanged letters. He answered affirmatively in Italian, and welcomed us warmly.

Father Josep took us upstairs to our rooms and told us he would unlock the gate into the cloister. We could go in and look around on our own; he would come to show us the church in a few minutes. They had just harvested the cherries, he said, and he had to deliver the fruit to the farming cooperative to which the monks belong. Twenty minutes later he returned to give us our tour of the abbey.

"At Cuixá there have been four churches," Father Josep explained as he led us inside, "two dedicated to Saint Germain of Auxerre and two to the Archangel Michael. The first dates back to the ninth century, when Cuixá was still a dependent priory. The monks of its mother-house, the Abbey of Eixalada, took refuge here after a flood destroyed their monastery. In 938 they built a small chapel dedicated to Saint Michael in front of the church of Saint Germain. The latter was rebuilt in 956 but soon destroyed by fire. The fourth church was consecrated in honor of Saint Michael on September 30, 974, at the time of Oliba Cabreta, count of Barcelona, and Abbot Garí."

"Is this the church as we see it today?" I asked.

"Yes," he replied, "although you have to use some imagination to perceive the tenth-century form through the mutilations it has suffered due to changing architectural tastes and the ravages of time. Now the church has more the appearance of a cave than of a temple."

"Even so," I said, "it remains very impressive."

The guest-master agreed. "But imagine," he added, "how splendid it must once have looked: polychrome frescoes covered the walls; a great arch with the image of Christ in glory separated nave and sanctuary; and an elegant marble ciborium surmounted the high altar."

Noting the odd "keyhole" shape of the arches along the nave, I asked our guide if their form derives from Arab influence.

"No," he answered, "because they are really quite unlike the Moorish arches in some churches south of the Pyrenees. One theory relates them to the Christian monastic architecture of Cappadocia. Art historians now call them 'Visigothic arches.'"

Father Josep led us up to the high altar and lifted one corner of the altar cloth. "The white marble mensa was rediscovered in 1969," he told us. "It had been used to pave the balcony of a private dwelling in the town of Viná northeast of Prades. We are certain of its authenticity, since its dimensions correspond exactly with the measurements contained in an eleventh-century description of the church, and also because of the graffiti."

There were several inscriptions on the marble surface. The name "Oliba" was clearly legible; he was the son of Count Oliba (or "Olibano") Cabreta and Garí's successor as abbot of Cuixá.

Our tour of the abbey continued with a visit to the eleventh-century crypt, built to house what were believed to be relics of the manger of Bethlehem, where the Infant Jesus had lain. The vault was shaped like a torus, centered on a single, massive column.

To my question about the building materials, Father Josep replied, "You probably think the vault was made of poured concrete. In reality it is all stone masonry, constructed around a doughnut-shaped wooden form; the mortar, leaking through the stonework, retained the impression of the wood." He pointed above our heads. "You can even see a few slivers of the planks which adhered to the mortar."

From the crypt, our guide led us through a dark corridor up two flights of stairs to the cloister. "Here is the famous 'Cuxa Cloister,' one half of which was, as you know, taken to New York and set up in a park in Manhattan as part of a museum. Since 1950 we have been able to recover 27 of the original capitals and columns. Three more have just been found, and we hope to obtain them in order to complete the western side of the cloister. And we still dream of bringing the other 32 capitals back from New York."

He pointed out some of the details carved into the capitals. "Note that the imagery is all non-religious, or perhaps I should say, non-Christian. Some of the forms are clearly oriental: Assyrian, Indian, Chinese. Where they got the idea for these carvings we do not know. Most likely, they were copied from oriental manuscripts which Abbots Garí and Oliba gathered on their many journeys. Even before Marco

Polo, travelers from Europe sometimes succeeded in penetrating into the heart of Asia."

Taking us into a hall on the west side of the cloister, Father Josep showed us a papier-maché model of the abbey as it was at the end of the twelfth century and a drawing of the church as it must have looked when Romuald and Peter Orséolo arrived here in 978; it was already impressive then, even without the two towers and the great cloister.

"Cuixá is a monument to the past," the guest-master concluded, "but it is also a sign of the continual change a monastic community undergoes if it is alive to the reality of the present. The monastery buildings bear the marks of ten centuries, but we who live here, as heirs to Abbot Garí and his monks, are men of the twentieth century. We are still seeking God, as the monks did a thousand years ago, and we are trying to make the gospel come alive today. We live in a monument to the past, but we bear witness to a message that is always new: peace, reconciliation, and hope for the future of humanity."

After the tour, Father Josep took us to the gift shop and gave us postcards and color slides of the abbey.

Since it was still light, we walked around back of the church and went looking for the cell of Peter Orséolo. The guest-master had told us to cross the field and climb the hill to the east. We followed a path that led up the slope. Halfway to the top we came upon a stone aqueduct. Following the course of the water upstream, we reached a round concrete tank with a gushing fountain that fed the aqueduct. After taking photographs we decided to turn back and follow another path that ran along the slope of the hill only a few meters above the base. About 300 meters from the monastery we found the monument to Saint Peter Orséolo, erected last year for the one-thousandth anniversary of his death. Excavations at the site have brought to light a large boulder, into which had begun to be sculpted a human form; apparently it was to serve for Orséolo's burial but was abandoned when it started to crack. Around the boulder lie the foundations of what may have been his cell or perhaps a tiny chapel built at the time of his canonization in the early eleventh century.

It was nearing the hour of Vespers. We returned to the abbey, put on our cowls, and went to the monks' austere chapel. The altar there, Father Josep told us, contained the relics of Saint Peter Orséolo.

The following morning, after Lauds and breakfast, we set out for the other monastic monument in this part of the Pyrenees: the Abbey of Saint Martin, or Sant Martí del Canigò. We followed the road that skirted the monastery's orchards and wound up through the foothills in the direction of Font-Romeu, Andorra, and Spain. The last two kilometers on the road to Sant Martí were closed to motor vehicles. After a half-hour climb, we reached the monastery, perched dramatically on a towering spur of the mountain. The buildings are obviously a reconstruction, not a restoration in the strict sense. Original are the apse and half the nave, with the crypt beneath; the rest has been arbitrarily rebuilt according to a romantic view of medieval architecture. The community there is a charismatic-renewal group and includes both vowed religious and married couples with their children.

We were back at Cuixá by five, with plenty of time to visit the place which oral tradition identifies as the site of Saint Romuald's cell.

Father Josep suggested that, rather than climb the hill by the path in back of the abbey, we drive up beyond Taurinya and hike down through the old cherry orchard.

The trail to 'Saint Valentine's Tower,' as the local people call it now, left the paved road shortly before the turnoff to Sant Martí. We ate our fill of the ripe cherries on the trees, which had not been pruned in many years. Along the path we found a couple of small caves which clearly had been used, perhaps quite recently, by shepherds out at night in the hills with their flocks. Soon we came upon an almost cubical stone structure about ten meters high, with an apse and a Romanesque window, unglazed. The doorway had been bricked up, but a rough ladder under the window allowed us to look in. There was nothing inside but straw and bird droppings; the chapel obviously had been abandoned for decades.

The oldest among the local farmers remember "Saint Valentine's Tower" as a place of pilgrimage; some had even made their first Holy Communion there. Popular lore does not connect the chapel with Saint Romuald, but his presence at or near this place is well attested in monastery chronicles, and an archeologist has dated the foundations of the chapel to some time in the tenth century.

On the north side of the chapel the hill drops off, revealing a splendid panorama of the abbey and the valley all the way to Prades. To the east below the apse is level ground, which seems to have once been cultivated.

On the way back we stopped twice to photograph the chapel, which, at a point about 500 meters from the abbey, stood out sharply against the bright western sky.

The following morning we sang Lauds with the monks, joined them for breakfast, and prepared to leave. We thanked Father Josep for their hospitality. I left filled with thoughts of the church and Saint Romuald's cell and a strong desire to return. From what I had seen and felt there, it was clear to me why Romuald's ten years at Cuixá were the happiest years of his life.

❦

Upon arriving at Cuixá, Romuald built a cell on the hill overlooking the abbey. On Saturdays and Sundays he would attend services and take meals with the monastic community. After one year in the cloister as a novice, John Gradenigo joined him. The other two Venetians—Peter Orséolo and John Morosini—remained in the abbey enclosure a few years more. Eventually Orséolo built his cell behind the church, but Morosini decided to go back to Venice. He founded a monastery, San Giorgio Maggiore, just across the Grand Canal from the doge's palace and Saint Mark's Square.

After John Gradenigo joined Romuald in the hermitage, the two started to go out together every day to cut wood and work in the fields. At night Romuald would read about the early Egyptian monks; he tried to follow their example as best he could, especially in the practice of fasting. His daily rations, Monday through Friday, were a loaf of bread and a handful of garbanzo beans, and then on weekends and great feasts he went down to the abbey and ate cooked food and drank some wine.

Those first three years at Cuixá were not easy for Romuald. Above all, his mind boiled with thoughts. He, of course, ascribed their origin to the devil, but they also came from within him, from his store of memories, from his body. He thought of women. He thought of the property he was supposed to inherit and which his relatives were fighting over now. Half the time he thought he wasn't accomplishing anything with all his prayers and fasting and manual labor, and half the time he was afraid he might break under the strain.

But the thought that horrified him more than any other was the feeling that he was going to live to a very old age. His father was over fifty and still alive. He himself was healthy and getting healthier every week from the mountain air and the hard work and the garbanzo beans. At first I could not understand Romuald's problem, but then I realized that if I believed in heaven as deeply as he did, and if I were living in a century like his when life on earth was not easy at all, and if I were doing penance for my sins, I would most likely long for an early death and thank God if it came.

After three years, Garí called Romuald to his chambers and told him to stop working in the fields. He must now study and become a priest.

❦

Not having any first-hand accounts to go on, Saint Peter Damian drew on other lives of monastic saints in order to flesh out the story of Romuald's years at Cuixá. On Saint Athanasius' Life of Antony he patterned his account of

42

Romuald's fight with devils and sundry temptations, and from Saint Jerome's Life of Hilarion he borrowed the description of the hermit's manual labors and fasting. But the Bible gave him the model for the following episode: II Samuel 12,1-7, the prophet Nathan's parable to David, after the king had sinned with Bathsheba.

While at Cuixá, Romuald developed a close friendship with a local farmer. This kindly and generous man, richer in good will than in material possessions, provided Romuald with tools and made him furniture for the hermitage.

Now the poor farmer had a cow, which provided milk for his family and was his only livestock. A wealthy and greedy count, not wanting to slaughter any of his own herd, took the farmer's cow and sent it to the butcher. The poor man came to Romuald and told him the story, and Romuald immediately sent word to the count, asking him to give the cow back. But the count laughed at Romuald's request.

So the feast was made ready, and the cow was slaughtered and roasted. But God's justice prevailed, says Peter Damian, for when the count took his first bite, he choked on the food and died a horrible death without swallowing a single morsel.

There are two morals to this story. First, a sign of an authentic Christian hermit is the preferential option for the poor; if you are a genuine contemplative, you will see reality with the eyes of the have-nots. Second, all human justice is fallible; God's infallibly just judgment may be evident and take immediate effect, as in this instance, but most often it remains hidden to human eyes and inextricably interwoven with God's mercy. The hermit's role, like that of King David's court-prophet Nathan, is simply to point out where truth and justice lie, and let God take care of the rest.

After ten years at Cuixá, Romuald decided it was time to leave and go back to Italy. The year was 988.

Peter Orséolo had just died and been buried in the cloister with honors befitting a saint. Then John Gradenigo left

43

with Abbot Garí to accompany the count of Barcelona, Oliba Cabreta, to Saint Benedict's Abbey of Monte Cassino. Cabreta, having made his confession to Romuald, was going to end his days as a monk. Romuald was alone in the hermitage above Cuixá.

Meanwhile word had come that Romuald's father Sergio was in the Abbey of San Severo in Ravenna as a novice, but he was threatening to leave. Romuald decided it was his duty to make sure his father remained in the cloister.

On foot Romuald set out for Italy. Upon arriving in Ravenna he went straight to San Severo. Saint Peter Damian tells us that, after the beating his son gave him, old Sergio changed his mind about leaving and decided at last to take the cowl.

Here is the rest of the story from Peter Damian:

Sergio used to sit and say his prayers in front of an icon of the Savior. One day he had a vision of some sort. It seems the Holy Spirit appeared to him—in what form I do not know. Immediately he dashed out of the chapel and started running around the cloister asking everyone, "Where did he go? Which way did he leave? Did you see him come this way?"

"Who?" they asked.

"The Holy Spirit. I saw him! I saw him!"

They laughed. "You must be mad!" they said.

"No, no! I saw the Holy Spirit!"

A few days later he took to his bed and died. As the Lord said to Moses, "No man can see me and live."

5. RETURN TO CLASSE

After the death of his father, Romuald went back to Sant'Apollinare and asked the abbot to let him live as a hermit on the monastery's lands.

In a place called Peter's Bridge on the road through the marshes, Romuald built himself a hut. People who traveled that way would see his hut and come to visit him, and he welcomed them, heard their confession, and counseled them. But the damp climate began to undermine his health, and so he decided to move elsewhere. Peter Damian takes pains to convince us that Romuald was not in the least concerned about his health. But when he was ill he could not say his usual prayers and observe his customary fasts and vigils; so it made sense to seek out a more agreeable climate.

Romuald moved to Saint Martin in the Woods, a small stone chapel next to an abandoned cemetery. The chapel was more comfortable than a hut, and it was on higher ground.

One evening after sundown he was singing the office of Compline. The chapel was dark; he needed no light, since he knew the words and melodies by heart. In the pine trees the wind was howling. Romuald kept singing, the wind kept howling, and after a while the hair started to rise on the back of his neck. The wind howled louder; he sang louder. Then he thought: the cemetery! In his imagination the sound of the wind became the wails of ghosts and demons. He cried, "Jesus, dear Lord, why have you forsaken me?"

Suddenly the window next to where he was standing blew open and hit him on the forehead. He fainted and fell over backward. After a few minutes he regained consciousness, pulled himself to his feet, and, his head still bleeding, sang the rest of Compline. Romuald was left with a scar on his forehead. But he was never again afraid of ghosts. Or of the devil.

❦

After a year in the cemetery chapel, Romuald's health had not improved. He was getting stiff in the joints and having trouble breathing at night. It was time, he decided, to move again. South of Ravenna and inland on the slopes of the Apennines was an ancient Roman town called Bagno. Bagno means "bath," and like Bath in England it was a place with hot springs and steam and sulfur waters. Moreover it was in the mountains, and the air was ideal for the lungs.

Romuald moved to Bagno. He may also have taken the waters; the Rule of Saint Benedict neither forbids nor encourages bathing.

Bagno was then part of Tuscany under the reign of the Marquis Hugh. Hugh was the brother of Waldrada, widow of the murdered doge of Venice, Peter Candiano IV. These political connections had a certain importance at this moment in Romuald's life. Hugh felt indebted to Romuald, because Romuald had been instrumental in getting Peter Orséolo out of the country, so that Candiano's brother—and Hugh's firm ally—Vitale could be elected doge.

Hugh offered Romuald assistance, financial and otherwise, if he would stay and help reform the monasteries in his realm. So Romuald went to a locality above Bagno called Verghereto, and there, says Peter Damian, he built a monastery. Like the abbey of Cuixá, it was dedicated to the Archangel Michael. Peter Damian presents Saint Michael of Verghereto as Romuald's first foundation, although Romuald lived apart from the community. He advised the monks and served as a channel for the funds donated by Hugh, but he did not feel bound to the place, nor was he the monks' superior.

One day he received word from Ravenna that an abbey near the city had burned to the ground; so he sent the homeless monks some of the money he had on hand. When the monks of Saint Michael's heard about this they were furious. With sticks and clubs they came, and they drove Master Romuald out of town.

Bruised and depressed, Romuald headed south along the ridge of the Apennines. It was late in the year, and there was a sharp smell of winter in the air. He hoped to find a place to stay before it started to snow.

Never in his life had he experienced such feelings as filled his soul now. Romuald was a quiet man, but gentle and warm. He seldom laughed but often smiled, and his joy was contagious. When depression strikes a man like this, it is bitter and painful beyond words.

"Never again," he promised himself; "never again. I am a hermit. From now on the only thing that matters is the salvation of my soul. I am going to save my own soul and not bother any more about anyone else's."

He turned these thoughts over and over in his mind until, at a certain point, a deathly chill came upon him with a rush. What was happening? It was not the cold earth under his feet. What caused the dry taste of ash in his mouth? It was not his fast. At that moment a terror more intense than any physical fear flooded his brain, and he knew he had come very close to the edge. And that the thought he had been thinking would have led him straight to the heart of hell.

❦

Romuald ended his journey at the foot of Mount Catria in the Marches. Now Fonte Avellana, where, several decades later, Peter Damian would become a monk, was also at the foot of Mount Catria. The year was 993, and a small group of hermits had already begun to live a community life there under the Rule of Saint Benedict. It is strange that Peter Damian says nothing about a visit of Saint Romuald to Fonte Avellana; his silence may mean, quite simply, that Romuald never did visit the hermits.

Romuald was forty-one now, an age for looking back and taking stock of his life. His years at Cuixá had been the happiest years of his life. He felt that there, at last, he had found his place and fulfilled his vocation. But Romuald was the kind of man who never finds his place in this life, and his vocation was to be fulfilled, not in a quiet, semi-eremitical life in the shadow of a great abbey, but in constant wandering, in founding and reforming monastic communities, and in making a certain mark, especially through others, on the future of Europe and of the Church.

Romuald thought fondly of Cuixá and of Abbot Garí. He also thought of his two or three years with Marino near Venice, and of his three very painful years at Sant'Apollinare in Classe. And he dwelt on the memory of his vigils with the old brother and the visions of Saint Apollinaris and his decision to become a monk.

One night Romuald dreamt of Saint Apollinaris. The patron saint of Classe ordered Romuald back to the abbey where he had made his vows.

But there was more to the dream than just the order to return to Classe. Romuald now began to see his mission more clearly; perhaps he even saw that, five years hence, he would be elected abbot of his monastery. He knew, in any case, that his mission demanded preparation, both spiritual and intellectual. So Romuald embarked on a sort of second novitiate, dedicated to the reading of the Bible, the Rules of Saint Basil, the Conferences of Cassian, and other monastic texts that had nourished his inner life at Cuixá.

"How do you understand the relationship between monasticism and Christianity?" I asked don Anselmo.

"To see this relationship clearly," Anselmo replied, "you have to make a distinction between what belongs to Christian revelation and what belongs to the sociological phenomenon of monastic life. If you confuse the two and suppose that everything monastic is also Christian, you will exclude the possibility of change and reform in the monastery, when this becomes necessary. When you keep this distinction in mind, you find that monastic life can and must serve as an affirmation of the gospel. We become monks in order to live the Christian life and for no other reason."

"So monastic rules are to be judged in the light of the gospel?" I asked.

"Yes, and never the other way around."

"What are the chief characteristics of monastic life?"

"If you look at it as a sociological phenomenon," said don Anselmo, "you can see some special qualities that distinguish it from other ways of life. These qualities are usually expressed in negative terms: separation, silence, solitude, enclosure, and so forth. The emphasis here is on what is different from ordinary human behavior."

"But why use such negative terms?" I objected. "Wouldn't it be better to speak of the positive values of monastic life?"

"The point of emphasizing the negative characteristics of monastic life is to make it clear that, from a Christian standpoint, these have no value in and of themselves, but only in relation to some purpose they can serve. For instance, silence can be useful if you want to study, necessary if you want to sleep, indispensable if you want to meditate. The means of monasticism considered sociologically are ambiguous; they are justified and sanctified by the use that is made of them and by the end toward which they are directed."

"Then why do monastic writers use such expressions as 'holy' silence, 'holy' solitude, 'holy' rules...?"

"Let me make a distinction: sacred, yes; holy, no. Holiness is a quality of persons, not of things. God is holy, and God shares His holiness with us. Something is sacred not of itself but only if it serves the purpose of helping us to become like God."

"Could you define monasticism?"

"Monastic life is a kind of open space, a void which demands to be filled. Benedict and Romuald and other saints filled it with the gospel."

❦

In chapter nine of his *Life of Romuald*, Saint Peter Damian sums up Saint Romuald's new understanding of monastic practice, fruit of the five years of meditation and study that followed his return to Classe.

Fasting. Up to now, Romuald had been observing the Greek practice of fasting on bread, water, and beans without interruption, Monday through Friday. Now he adopted the

Roman Church's custom of breaking the fast on Thursday and keeping it again until Vespers on Saturday evening; this was thought to be somewhat easier. Romuald would not let his novices go all day without eating, even though he often did so himself. Perfect fasting, he said, means eating every day and feeling hungry every day. If you practice fasting with discretion, what seems hard at first will become easier. Romuald had no use for monks who started out doing heavy penance, and then weren't able to keep it up.

Vigils. About staying up at night to pray he was very cautious. What he didn't want anyone to do was to stay up and then fall asleep at dawn. Better to get a good night's sleep and stay awake in the morning.

Prayer. For Romuald, prayer was not "saying prayers" but praying with the heart. Better one Psalm with feeling, he said, than a hundred with a wandering mind. Constancy was the most important thing. Pray every day, whether you feel like it or not, and sooner or later God will grant you the prayer of the heart. And when your heart is fixed on God, there is no need to worry about stray thoughts. They may come and go, but they will not take your attention away from God.

❧

"What is the gospel, for Saint Benedict?" I asked.

"What it was for Saint Paul: the Word of God which proclaims the liberation of every human person from every sort of slavery," said don Anselmo. "The gospel fulfills its purpose when it makes us aware of our bondage and brings about that change of heart—conversion—which opens us to the word of life and to freedom."

"Can there be awareness of bondage without change of heart?"

"Of course. Every kind of political ideology in history has begun its propaganda with the words, 'You have nothing to lose but your chains.' Humanity has never been so aware of its chains as it is today. But people today are also beginning to realize that ideology can never change the human heart and can never make us free. If there is any wisdom in contemporary culture, it is found in the attitude of doubt and skepticism toward all forms of ideology."

"Mass media have caused the breakdown of ideological systems," I suggested; "people are better informed and hence ask more questions."

"People are better informed," countered don Anselmo, "but they do not know themselves better. The truth that makes us free does not come from the media but from the word of God speaking to our conscience."

I returned to our original subject. "How does Saint Benedict link monastic life with the gospel?"

"The link between them is in the attitude of listening. The first word in the Rule is, 'Listen!' Benedict immediately defines what he means: 'Incline the ears of your heart.' A monk listens with his heart, because only there can he hear the word of God. This attitude is the beginning of the monastic vocation. It focuses the monk's existence. The Rule expresses the same idea in negative terms, when it tells the monk 'to prefer nothing to the worship of God, to prefer nothing to Christ's love, to prefer nothing whatever to Christ,' Everything else the monk does is secondary."

"How did Saint Romuald relate his own monastic vocation to the gospel?"

Anselmo replied, "In the same way that Saint Benedict did. Romuald became a monk when he decided to give absolute primacy in his life to God's word and the love of Christ. But perhaps Romuald did add something new to the Benedictine experience: his insistence on the ambiguity of authority structures in monastic life and hence on the primacy of the voice of conscience. The gospel itself excludes any form of authority as power of domination over others, and the Rule of Saint Benedict forbids the abbot to teach anything over and above the commandment of Christ: love of God and love of neighbor."

"What about obedience?"

"Human obedience subjects the individual to laws and to the power of those who wield authority; it demands an attitude of passivity and submission. Monastic obedience is born in the heart and is the fruit of personal conviction; it is 'the obedience of faith' which is practiced through the works of love. The monk who obeys only his abbot is not obedient at all. The Rule commands the monks to obey each other and to 'honor all men.'"

"Was Saint Romuald obedient?"

"He was truly obedient, because he strove to listen to the word of God and to live accordingly in every circumstance of his existence, and also because he never sought to exercise authority over others. He was not interested in becoming an 'abbot of bodies,' and even in his exercise of spiritual direction he avoided imposing his will on others. If the monks would not listen to him, he simply went elsewhere. He did not care about his image, only about his conscience."

"What is conscience?"

"Conscience is the temple of the Holy Spirit, the Kingdom of God, the place of the covenant, the bridal chamber where the mystical marriage is consummated. Of course this refers to the conscience formed by God's word, the mature conscience. But because the word of God was made flesh in Christ, to form conscience means to form the Church, and when the Church or the monastery need reforming, you must reform the conscience of the members."

"Doesn't Romuald's emphasis on conscience lead to individualism?"

"Quite the contrary. A person of conscience is the opposite of the rugged individualist or the egotist. Not only God, but all other persons as well are reflected in your conscience and are a part of you. People of other faiths and cultures, followers of other philosophies, the poor, the ignorant, all those oppressed by the powerful and the wealthy, all those led astray by peddlers of lies—all of reality reverberates in your conscience, and you cannot remain indifferent. If you listen to your conscience, you will know that you can never enjoy peace without being aware of others, without vibrating in unison with the heart of Christ, who immersed Himself in this universe where you and I live, and who loved us to the shedding of His blood."

6. THE FIVE BROTHERS

Romuald was now approaching what would prove to be the most painful year of his life.

Early in 998 the eighteen-year-old Emperor Otto III appointed Gerbert of Aurillac, the greatest mind of the tenth century, as archbishop of Ravenna. Gerbert, a good friend of Abbot Garí, knew about Romuald and suggested that Otto make him abbot of Sant' Apollinare in Classe. In the fall of that year Romuald became the superior of the monastery he had left twenty years earlier.

Then in February of 999 the pope died. On April 2 Otto put Gerbert on Saint Peter's throne, with the name Sylvester II, and once again the bishopric of Ravenna was vacant. Political logic would have the new abbot of Classe step up and occupy it.

As a result there were constant comings and goings of emissaries between Rome and Ravenna, between cathedral and abbey, until Romuald could take no more. Although the monks at his abbey were an unruly lot, they nevertheless realized that the monastery needed reforming and were willing to have Romuald as abbot. But the pressures from without—from Romuald's own family, from other factions in the city, and now from papal and imperial politics—made it impossible for him to do what he believed necessary to reform the monastery. Romuald came to the conclusion that he was not saving anybody's soul and was damning his own; so he went and threw down the abbatial staff at the feet of Otto III and left for Monte Cassino to see his old friend John Gradenigo.

❦

How did John Gradenigo end up at Monte Cassino?

John had left Cuixá with Abbot Garí and Count Oliba Cabreta shortly after Peter Orséolo died. They were accompanying the count to the Abbey of Monte Cassino, where he was to put on the cowl.

At that time Garí was planning to continue on to Jerusalem, and John wanted to come along, even though Romuald had ordered him to remain at Monte Cassino with Count Oliba. But in the end he decided to go, and just as he was leaving the enclosure, a kick from one of the horses broke his leg. So there was nothing to do but put a splint on his leg and stay at the abbey.

Ten years passed. Now living in a hermit colony near the monastery with an ex-abbot of Cassino and a few other monks, John received a visit one day from a young monk of Benevento named Benedict, a lad of noble birth and great fervor. He had spent a year or two on his own as a hermit and had come to the conclusion that he needed more training in the spiritual life. So he asked John to accept him as a disciple.

Now John Gradenigo was about as self-effacing as a human being can be, and although he willingly gave counsel to young Benedict, he always insisted he was only quoting what Romuald used to say, just as Romuald had insisted that he taught nothing but what anyone could read in the Lives and Conferences of the Desert Elders. Benedict kept asking John about this famous Master Romuald. One day word arrived that Romuald was on his way to Monte Cassino. Benedict jumped on a horse and galloped off to meet him.

❦

In the fall of the year 1000, while at Monte Cassino, Romuald took ill and almost died. Benedict nursed him back to health and from that time never left his side.

In the meantime the young Emperor Otto was trying to set up court in Rome. He was obsessed with the idea of restoring the Roman Empire, a dream which the people of the city—patricians and plebes alike—did not share. Toward the end of November Romuald and Benedict came down to Rome and went to pay their respects to the emperor, who was staying on the Aventine Hill next to the monastery of Sant'Alessio, then a joint community of Greek and Latin monks. Two members of Otto's court, his chaplain Bruno of Querfurt and one of his chief officers, a man by the name of Tammo, had entered the abbey as novices, taking the religious names of Boniface and Thomas. Romuald befriended them and asked Otto and the abbot to let them come with him to a place near the city where he was going to build a hermitage.

At the hermitage, Romuald put Bruno-Boniface in Benedict's cell and had Benedict be his novice-master. The two became good friends; they were Romuald's favorite disciples.

Now Otto missed Bruno and Tammo and kept coming out to see them. Soon the hermitage was overrun with men from Otto's court, and Romuald decided that the hermits should move to a place north of Ravenna called Peréo. But they had hardly finished building their cells at Peréo, when Otto arrived with all his troops. Again the hermitage was turned into a military camp.

There had been riots in Rome, and Otto, to save his face, had retreated north to Ravenna. Now, as his dream of a new Roman Empire began to fade, he started dreaming of sending missionaries into Poland and Hungary, whose rulers had just accepted Christianity. Otto had known Bishop Adalbert of Prague, who, having renounced his bishopric, took the monastic cowl at Sant'Alessio and while preaching to the Prussians near Gdansk suffered martyrdom. Otto now believed he had a mission from God to complete Adalbert's work in the north, and he even conceived the idea of becoming a monk himself.

Otto decided to turn Peréo into a center for training missionary monks. Bruno of Querfurt was enthusiastic about the idea, and surprisingly Romuald went along with it. So Otto ordered that a monastery be built, with a Byzantine-style church in the round, and in October of 1001 he had it dedicated to Saint Adalbert the New Martyr.

The emperor's idea was to offer the monks a threefold option: community life for beginners, solitary life for those advanced in contemplation, and missionary work in Poland for the most fervent. The emperor's project was basically in harmony with Romuald's teaching, although it remained his idea, not Romuald's.

Personally, Romuald preferred the hermitage, which for him meant a small monastic community with little formality, the monks living either two by two or singly, doing some manual work but spending most of the day reading and chanting the Psalms. Romuald also encouraged the more usual, completely communal type of Benedictine monastery and founded a number of them, because he knew that most monks would need to spend their entire monastic life in community. For almost everyone, the hermitage would have to be a temporary experience, which might become permanent when a monk was too old to work or move about. But now, charmed perhaps by the emperor's boyish enthusiasm, Romuald accepted the idea of sending his monks off as missionaries and gave his approval to the project.

What were the concrete results of Otto's efforts? First of all, the news that Romuald, who had just resigned as abbot of Classe, was getting the emperor to build him another monastery, aroused the anger of many in Ravenna. Not that this bothered Romuald in the least. As long as he was doing what his conscience told him to do, he actually enjoyed seeing people outraged at him.

Secondly, the whole project came to nothing. The hermitage was occupied by Otto's court, and the new abbey at Peréo ended up with an abbot who was not the least bit interested in either hermitages or foreign missions.

But since Otto still wanted missionaries, Bruno got Benedict to volunteer, along with another monk named John (not to be confused with John Gradenigo, who stayed on at Monte Cassino and lived to a ripe old age). Otto took Benedict and John to Abbot Romuald, and everyone was surprised when, at the moment, Romuald said yes and gave the two brothers his blessing. But Otto and the others soon realized what Romuald really thought about the emperor's project, when they saw him pack up his Psalter and his summer cowl and sail off to Istria on the other side of the Adriatic Sea, leaving everyone with the impression that he might never come back.

❦

Otto sent Benedict and John on their way to Poland with packhorses and wagons and a letter addressed to Duke Boleslaw Chrobry, Poland's Christian ruler. Bruno said farewell to his best friend Benedict, promising to go see Pope Sylvester immediately; the brothers would need the pope's authorization to preach and do missionary work. Then Bruno would join them in Poland.

But as it happened, Bruno failed to keep his promise, and he never saw Benedict again.

After several weeks' journeying, Benedict and John arrived in Poland. Duke Boleslaw welcomed them with full honors as emissaries of pope and emperor, set them up on a large tract of wooded land, and provided for all their needs.

The brothers' first task was to learn the language. By identifying as much as possible with the people, they hoped to win the confidence of the pagan tribes and draw them to the gospel. Benedict and John also decided to set aside their monastic robes and dress like the local peasants. For the liturgy, the brothers most likely used the "Mass of Saint Peter" or Glagolithic Mass, which was a form of the Roman rite translated into Slavonic by Saints Cyril and Methodius.

In a short time three Polish novices joined them: Barnabas, already a priest, and two blood brothers, Isaac and Matthew. A local boy by the name of Christian offered them his services as cook and general handyman.

Months passed, and still there was no sign of Bruno. Benedict and John felt betrayed; they could not begin their mission until they had the document from Rome that Bruno had promised to bring them.

Then tragic news arrived: Otto was dead. He was just twenty-two years old.

౿

After Otto's death, Christendom turned on itself and began devouring its own innards. Arduin of Ivrea declared himself king of Italy and had Sylvester II, Otto's pope, driven out of Rome. As soon as Henry II, the son of Otto's great-uncle, was elected emperor, he declared war on Bohemia and Poland.

With their whole world turned inside-out, the brothers in Poland despaired of ever accomplishing what they went there for. Finally Benedict decided to leave and try to reach Bruno, who was now in Hungary. Benedict got as far as Prague and had to turn back.

Boleslaw did not want Benedict to travel; the risk of being caught in the cross-fire was even greater for him, an Italian, than for a Pole. So Boleslaw let Benedict send the Polish priest Barnabas, who would either find Bruno or would go see the pope himself.

In the meantime, a rumor had begun to circulate, to the effect that Boleslaw had given the brothers a large sum of money for the trip to Rome. A band of robbers started conspiring to break into the monastery, kill the monks, and take the duke's money.

On Wednesday evening, November 10, 1003, the vigil of Saint Martin, the monks sang Matins and celebrated Mass, and then they retired for the night. Before the first light of dawn, the robbers came armed into the dormitory where John, Benedict, Isaac, and Matthew lay sleeping. John was the first to become aware of the intruders. He leaned over and whispered something into Benedict's ear—perhaps it was his confession. He was the first to die, then Benedict. Isaac heard the commotion and started to yell, "God, help!

58

God, help!" But as the sword fell he muttered "God bless you," and died. Matthew ran for the door and was stabbed from behind. Outside, Christian came from his quarters with a stick to defend himself and was cut down in front of the chapel.

The robbers, not finding the money, set fire to the dormitory and the chapel and fled into the woods. A short distance away they stopped and looked back to see the flames. They saw nothing. And then they heard what sounded like music. Perhaps it was only the wind in the pines, but to them it seemed to be a hymn of victory. Terrified, they went back and looked into the monastery. The fire had sputtered out and all was silent. They ran off into the night.

7. VAL DI CASTRO

News of the death of the five brothers reached Bruno of Querfurt before Christmas and shocked him out of the paralysis of will that had kept him from fulfilling his promise to Benedict. Free now from indecision but burdened with bitter guilt at having betrayed those whom he loved most after Christ, he traveled north to see what he could salvage of the missionary project born at the hermitage of Peréo.

The emperor was dead and the pope was dead, and with them the policy of sending Latin missionaries only into territories not already evangelized by Greek missionaries sent by Constantinople. The new pope and the new emperor were intent on wresting at least Hungary and Bohemia away from the Greeks, since there was no hope of Latinizing Bulgaria or the Ukraine. Poland was another problem. Securely Latin, it was still trying to assert its independence of the major powers to the west and the east.

In the summer of 1004, after his consecration as archbishop, Bruno returned to Hungary and met with King Stephen at Gran. Both Stephen and Archduke Vladimir of Kiev were willing to accept a three-way treaty with the new emperor Henry II, but when Bruno brought the proposal back to Germany, Henry refused to sign, on the grounds that Vladimir and Stephen had favored the Greek missionaries and thus could not be trusted to remain loyal to the pope. The churches had already begun to excommunicate each other in the mission fields, a half-century before Humbert of Silva Candida laid the pope's bull of excommunication on the altar of Constantinople's Haghia Sophia.

Bruno left for Kiev to meet with Archduke Vladimir. From there he wrote Henry the following letter:

"Vladimir the great lord of the Russians kept me in his kingdom for an entire month, although I was anxious to move on. For him it was as if I wanted to commit suicide. 'Those people are savages,' he said. 'You will not win any of them to Christ, and they will torture and kill you.'

"He was terrified by what he saw was going to happen to me, but he could not bend my will. Vladimir gave me a military escort and himself accompanied me to the border of his realm. He dismounted and followed me and my companions on foot. We left through the gate in the enormous stockade Vladimir had built along the border, and we climbed the hill outside the gate. Carrying the cross before us, we sang the anthem, 'Peter, do you love me? Feed my sheep.'

"When we had finished singing, Lord Vladimir's messenger read us his parting words: 'I beg you for the love of God, do not throw away your life in the flower of youth. Your death would be my disgrace. But I know that on the morrow death will come to you, a cruel and useless death.'

"I sent him my reply: 'May God open to you the gates of paradise, just as you have opened for me the way to the pagans.'"

❧

Meanwhile, from 1001 to 1004, Romuald was in Istria, across the Adriatic from Venice in what is now Croatia, at a place called Porec, or Parenzo in Italian. He spent his first year there building a monastery, and then he retired to a cave. At Porec, writes Peter Damian, God bestowed on Romuald the fullness of the Holy Spirit.

Having read in the Lives of the Desert Elders how important was the gift of tears, Romuald used to worry about his inability to shed tears during prayer. However hard he tried, he could not wring a single drop of compunction from his heart.

Then one day, as he was singing the Psalms in his cell, his eyes lit upon the verse: "I will instruct you and teach you the way you should go; I will counsel you with my eye upon you." At that moment tears began to pour from his eyes; many mysteries of the Old and New Testaments were made clear to him; and he saw the meaning of his life and the direction he must follow.

And he cried out, "Jesus, dear Jesus, desire of my heart, joy of the saints, delight of the angels . . . !" As the Spirit descended upon him, his prayer went beyond words into utterances the human mind cannot comprehend. "We do not know how to pray as we ought," says Saint Paul, "but the Spirit himself intercedes for us with sighs too deep for words."

Romuald returned from Istria "impatient with sterility," says Peter Damian. What does he mean by this expression?

Remember what happened to Romuald after the monks threw him out of the monastery at Verghereto: how he began to wallow in self-pity and swore he would never bother about anyone's salvation but his own; and how his conscience revealed to him, in that very instant, that he was on the road to hell. Now, having lived half a century in an age of apocalypse, Romuald knew the obsession of the Apostle Paul, who cried, "Woe to me if I do not preach the gospel!"

So Romuald went looking for some good earth where he might plant the seed of God's word and bear fruit for his own and others' salvation. He found this earth in a lovely green valley ringed by hills and woods and watered by several springs: Val di Castro, near Fabriano.

At Val di Castro there was already a small chapel, served by a community of lay sisters. Romuald provided the sisters with another house and a plot of land, so that he and a few companions could establish a hermitage around their chapel. Romuald eventually built an abbey at Val di Castro and, close by, a monastery of nuns. (This was the first of two women's communities Romuald is said to have founded, but he must have founded several others besides these.)

Even as a simple hermitage, Val di Castro was a center of contemplative ministry, especially spiritual counseling and preaching. When Romuald preached, says Peter Damian, he was like a seraph clothed in fire, and his love for God set all his hearers aflame. Having now the gift of tears, he would sometimes be overcome with emotion in the middle of the sermon and have to run out of the church like a madman.

Without question Val di Castro was Romuald's favorite foundation; here he would choose to return when he was about to die. The monks were good men, but quite as imperfect as good men can be, and in their midst, says Peter Damian, Saint Romuald seemed "like a cedar of Lebanon in a briar-patch." On one occasion, after an argument with the man they had elected abbot—he was a satisfactory administrator, but not the contemplative that Romuald wanted him to be—Romuald left in disgust. But the monks of Val di Castro loved Master Romuald, and their love drew him back to them when his end was near.

❦

Countess Sibyl of Camerino was financing the construction of Val di Castro. Romuald had just been to see her and was on his way back to the monastery with the young novice who had accompanied him.

"Now there's a beautiful woman," Romuald mused. "The countess is so elegant and charming. A pity she has only one eye."

"No, father, you're mistaken," the novice, a bit surprised, replied. "She isn't missing an eye. In fact she has very beautiful eyes."

Romuald stopped and looked sternly at the lad. "Yes, I know she has beautiful eyes; but who told you to judge a woman by her looks?!"

The novice realized he had been caught and blushed. He promised he would be more careful in the future, and keep closer watch over his own wandering eyes.

❦

Once Romuald said, "Brothers, when you sit down to eat, wait a bit and let the others serve themselves first. Then when they've started eating you can go ahead and take something too. That way you'll still be observing the rule of sobriety without calling attention to yourself or being hypocritical."

❦

For all his austerity of life, Romuald always had a twinkle in his eye and a ready smile on his lips.

One day Brother Gregory had a terrific headache. Moaning with pain he went up to the window of Master Romuald's cell and said, "I can't stand this headache any longer."

Romuald leaned out the window and beckoned to a group of monks near by. "Let's cure Brother Gregory," he said. "Everyone stand around him, and when I say *three*, all of you blow as hard as you can on Gregory's forehead."

After this treatment, Gregory never had a headache again, says Peter Damian, and he even forgot what a headache feels like.

❦

Romuald interrupted his Sunday sermon. "Hurry!" he said. "There's a burglar breaking into Brother Gregory's cell!"

The monks rushed out of the chapter hall and found the thief trying to knock down the wall of the cell. They grabbed him and dragged him off to Romuald, who was waiting for them with a big smile on his face.

They asked him, "What do you want us to do to this guy?" Romuald answered, "I really don't know. Should we poke out his eyes? But then he won't be able to see. Or cut off his hand? But then he won't be able to work and may even die of hunger. And if we hack off his foot he won't be able to walk. Anyway, take him inside and give him something to eat. Then we can decide what to do with him."

When the burglar had eaten, Master Romuald, rejoicing in the Lord, gently corrected and admonished him with a few kind words and sent him on his way in peace.

❦

Then there was the time they brought a crazy man to Master Romuald. When the man had one of his fits, he would say and do the wildest things and couldn't remember any of it afterwards.

Romuald took the man's head in his hands and gave him a kiss.

Later the man said, "As soon as his lips touched me, I felt as if a strong wind were blowing all over my face and through my skull, and it put out the fire in my brain."

❦

During the recreation days preceding Lent one year, Master Romuald took a group of novices hiking with him in the mountains above their monastery. His idea was to find a place for a temporary hermitage, where they would stay and prepare themselves for Easter.

One morning they awoke in their camp to find themselves surrounded by white water. During the night a warm rain had melted the snow up the slopes and sent heavy runoff raging down the gorge on either side of them. There was no bridge, and now the water was too deep to wade through. So they could neither move on nor send word back to the monastery.

The only supplies they had with them were some chestnuts one of the novices had brought along in his sack. That morning, which happened to be the Sunday before Ash Wednesday, they started to peel the chestnuts, wondering if this might not be the last food they would take before Easter Sunday—if they survived so long.

Romuald, however, was his usual, cheerful self. He declared that, since today was Sunday, he was not going to eat anything unless somebody brought him fresh-baked bread for dinner. His disciples took these words as a prophecy and decided to wait. Around noon, in fact, three men appeared on the opposite shore with bread, wine, and other food in their packs. They saw the stranded monks, helped them cross the waters, and invited them to share their meal. The three men had come, they said, from a distant town on the other side of the mountain.

So they all thanked God for His gifts, and as the monks ate Sunday dinner, they realized that this, too, was a lesson from Master Romuald.

The core of Romuald's teaching was not rules and regulations of fasting and penance, but the ways of prayer. On the following page is the little rule of Master Romuald.

THE LITTLE RULE OF MASTER ROMUALD

SIT IN YOUR CELL AS IN PARADISE. PUT THE WHOLE WORLD BEHIND YOU AND FORGET IT. WATCH YOUR THOUGHTS LIKE A GOOD FISHERMAN WATCHING FOR FISH.

THE PATH YOU MUST FOLLOW IS IN THE PSALMS— NEVER LEAVE IT.

IF YOU HAVE JUST COME TO THE MONASTERY, AND IN SPITE OF YOUR GOOD WILL YOU CANNOT ACCOMPLISH WHAT YOU WANT, THEN TAKE EVERY OPPORTUNITY YOU CAN TO SING THE PSALMS IN YOUR HEART AND TO UNDERSTAND THEM WITH YOUR MIND. AND IF YOUR MIND WANDERS AS YOU READ, DO NOT GIVE UP; HURRY BACK AND APPLY YOUR MIND TO THE WORDS ONCE MORE.

REALIZE ABOVE ALL THAT YOU ARE IN GOD'S PRESENCE, AND STAND THERE WITH THE ATTITUDE OF ONE WHO STANDS BEFORE THE EMPEROR.

EMPTY YOURSELF COMPLETELY AND SIT WAITING, CONTENT WITH THE GRACE OF GOD, LIKE THE CHICK WHO TASTES NOTHING AND EATS NOTHING BUT WHAT HIS MOTHER BRINGS HIM.

In 1009 Bruno-Boniface of Querfurt was martyred by the Prussian tribes in what is now Lithuania,

When Romuald received word of Bruno's death, he decided that he, too, must go and shed his blood for Christ. He started to organize a mission to Hungary, and at the same time he built three new monasteries, in addition to the one at Val di Castro.

The following spring all was ready. Romuald sent two of his monks, Gregory and Ingelbert, to Rome to have them ordained bishops. On their return, they and twenty two others left with Romuald for Hungary.

Just as they reached the Hungarian border, Romuald became ill. When they turned back, he suddenly got well. So they tried again to cross over into Hungary, and this time Romuald's face swelled up and his stomach would not hold food. Then he said, "I understand it is not God's will for me to enter Hungary. But I know how you all feel about the mission. All of you are free to do what is in your heart. I am not ordering any of you to return with me. However, I feel sure that those of you who do continue on will not die as martyrs."

Fifteen of them entered Hungary; the two bishops went elsewhere; and seven returned to Italy with Romuald.

❧

In 1022 Emperor Henry II crossed the Alps on his third march into Italy. Henry was a man of many virtues, and for these he was canonized a century later. But he was also a man of blood, who to consolidate and extend his empire did not hesitate to ally himself with pagan tribes and wage war against his fellow Christians, especially the Poles in the north and the Greeks in southern Italy.

Romuald must have known this, because when Henry invited Romuald to his court, he was rebuffed with the excuse: "Abbot Romuald is on retreat and cannot break his silence."

The other monks begged Romuald to accept the emperor's invitation. Finally he agreed to do so and set out for Lucca in Tuscany, where Henry was holding court. Upon Romuald's arrival, the emperor went out to meet him and exclaimed, "Would to God that my soul were in your body!" But Romuald still would not talk.

Having made Henry wait one more day, Romuald broke his silence. He had much to say, especially about the emperor's violation of Church rights, his wars in Poland and Apulia, his social injustices. When he had finished, Romuald asked the emperor to give his monks the nearby abbey of Monte Amiata. The emperor agreed, deposed the existing abbot, and appointed the man Romuald had chosen. But the new abbot turned out to be just as bad as his predecessor, in Romuald's estimation. So when he received another invitation, this time from Tedaldo, the new bishop of Arezzo, Romuald left immediately.

Bishop Tedaldo wanted to establish a contemplative community near the northern confines of his diocese, with a church and a group of priests who would sing the Divine Office and celebrate the Mass there every day. And since the land set aside for the foundation was on the main road over the mountains from Ravenna and Bagno, the bishop also wanted the community to offer hospitality to travelers.

Romuald took to the idea immediately, because it seemed to embrace the full gamut of his own monastic experience and ideal: solitude (the hermit's cell), community (the daily celebration of the monastic liturgy), and mission (hospitality).

Five priests were ready to join the new community: Peter Dagnino, another Peter, Benedict, Gisso, and Teuzo. Romuald instructed them to build a cell for each monk, a church to be dedicated to the Transfiguration of Christ, and a guest-house half an hour's walk away. When all was ready, the bishop came and consecrated the church.

The year was 1025, and thus Camaldoli was born.

❧

"Romuald's full maturity as a man and as a monk is expressed in the foundation of Camaldoli," said don Anselmo. "Camaldoli gives institutional form both to the first commandment—to love God with all your heart, mind, and strength—and to the second—to love your neighbor as yourself. The meaning of the Eremo is the absolute primacy of God. Like Mary of Bethany at the feet of Jesus, the hermit-monk sits in his cell with no other concern than to listen to God's word. The meaning of Fontebono, the Hospitium, is the hermit's response to what God's word demands: attentiveness to the needs of others, readiness to welcome them and serve them."

"And the Cenobio?" I asked. "It was not part of Romuald's original foundation."

Anselmo replied, "The Cenobio was founded a few decades after Romuald's passing, not in contrast with what he had established—since he himself was a founder of monasteries of cenobites—but in order to complete his work. The Cenobio was necessary, first of all as a place of formation for novices, and also as a community for those charged with caring for guests and for the sick."

I started to ask another question, but Anselmo went on to say, "In any case, the Camaldolese hermitage and the traditional Benedictine monastery are expressions of the same monastic ideal and are structured according to the same model. Both have spaces for common activities: a chapel for liturgical prayer, a refectory for meals, a chapter hall for meetings."

"From the very start," I observed, "the singing of the Divine Office in common was an essential part of monastic practice at the Eremo."

"True," said don Anselmo, "but the originality of Camaldoli as an institution lies above all in the tension, freely accepted, between a pure contemplative life and the exercise of charity toward travelers and the needy. Romuald and the monks of Camaldoli took to heart the words of Scripture, 'How can you love God, whom you cannot see, if you do not love the brother whom you can see?'"

"At a certain point in history," I said, "this structure, with its inherent tension, was abandoned at Camaldoli."

"It was abandoned," said don Anselmo, "because, from about the thirteenth century on, Catholic theology was invaded by spiritualities grounded more in pagan philosophies than in the gospel, spiritualities which practically ignored the Incarnation and the union of God and human nature in Christ. Thus what God had united, man divided. Pre-Christian dualism was codified into a theology and a Canon Law which divided and opposed active religious and contemplative religious, apostolic orders and orders of hermits. This was the beginning of Camaldoli's decline."

Anselmo leaned back in his chair. After a few seconds he continued, calmly. "Saint Romuald was a man of unity. What he wanted at Camaldoli was harmony between contemplation and action, between solitude and communion, between prayer and service. He wanted the monks to learn how to love undividedly, and to let their love flow freely toward God, toward one another, toward the poor."

EPILOGUE

After my last conversation with don Anselmo, I returned to Camaldoli, continuing to revise my notes on the train. Halfway to Arezzo I looked out the window. The sky was filled with amorphous gray masses, but the ground was now dry. Last night in Rome I heard distant thunder outside my window, and it was still raining this morning when I boarded the train at Termini Station.

A few kilometers north of Chiusi the sun broke through the clouds and brightened the gentle Tuscan landscape. On a ridge paralleling the tracks a line of stone farmhouses and barns was silhouetted against the brightness.

Now the sky looked like the background of a Baroque fresco: massive, twisted shapes with patches of intense blue and dramatic shafts of sunlight on the horizon.

The train stopped briefly at Terontola. One half hour yet to Arezzo.

On my first night back at Camaldoli, I had the following dream:

I am at the Eremo with everyone. Great floods of water are coming up here, in waves like the rising tide of the sea.

No, it is not the sea, someone tells me. It is a canal bringing water to fill our cisterns.

The water spills over the machinery and down into the courtyard. They make it very clear to me that it is our own water. It flows from our own source.

❦

It cost Romuald an enormous effort to make the last journey of his life, from Camaldoli back to Val di Castro. His cough was getting worse. Arthritis and emphysema had bent his body, and he had to ride a mule all the way back rather than travel on foot, which was his custom.

At Val di Castro he had the monks build him a cell on the lower pasture, down by the stream. Somehow he found it easier to breath there, amidst the trees and the cascading water.

Throughout the spring of 1027 he tried to stay on his feet and keep the regular fast. But by June it was obvious the end was near. He took to his bed and became almost too weak to cough. Two brothers came down to his cell from the monastery every day and took care of him, but he would not let them spend the night.

It was the nineteenth of June. Romuald was calm, because he knew death would soon claim his body. The two brothers were with him all that day. At sundown, hearing the monastery bell, Romuald sent them away, telling them to come back at dawn to sing Lauds with him. They pretended to leave, but they went only a few paces from the cell and waited. Before long all was silent. They returned to the cell, forced the door, and lit a lamp. Romuald was lying face down on his bed, having given his life back to God.

❦

Several years had passed since I had last seen don Aliprando Catani. At the end of his term of office as abbot general, he had retired to his monastery of Fonte Avellana. In June 1984, during a chapter of the Order, we met again at Camaldoli.

After breakfast on the morning of the nineteenth, the feast of Saint Romuald, he told me the following story:

"I've always been devoted to Saint Romuald," he said, "because he helped me overcome my fear of death. As a child I was terrified of funerals, maybe because I had seen my dead grandfather turn over in his casket when rigor mortis set in. Well, one day in June 1927—this was during the nine-hundredth anniversary celebrations of our saint—my favorite uncle said, 'Let's take a drive to Fabriano and visit the body of Saint Romuald.' When he said 'body' I got goose-pimples, but a twelve-year-old boy can't turn down an outing with his favorite uncle."

Don Aliprando paused, smiling his Pope John smile, and then continued. "So we drove up to the church of San Biagio; it was illuminated inside and out with electric lights. At that time we didn't have electricity in our village, and so the sight was very impressive. We entered the church and went down the steps by the altar into the crypt, which was filled with lilies. The perfume was so strong it drugged my senses and made my head spin.

"There was the marble sepulcher, with its gold-plated fastenings—we couldn't see the body because the sepulcher was sealed. The lights, the flowers, the white-robed monks, the singing—all this took away my fear of death once for all. In my child's mind I grasped the meaning of the Resurrection for the first time, and I understood how Christ and His saints have overcome death, even though they died."

❦

The writing of this book has taken me on journeys to most of the places Saint Romuald lived. He has become for me somewhat less of a mystery, more human, more concrete; I hope I have been able to convey a sense of his humanity and concreteness in these pages. The mystery which remains I now see within me: the mystery of a monastic call.

I have also come full circle. I am writing these lines in Big Sur, at New Camaldoli Hermitage. I have been here a few months now, and will stay a few months longer; then I will return to Italy, where various duties and commitments keep me still.

Changes in myself and changes in this community have brought me closer to the beginnings of my monastic experience. The Big Sur hermitage is still associated in my mind with the pains and the joys of my first steps in the monastic life. But now I see both the joys and the pains in the perspective of a mystery greater even than the great saint that Romuald was.

Resurrection lies at the heart of human existence, written into the code of creation itself. To live truly as a human being means to hope that from and through death new life will come. Saints are those in whom this hope becomes fully conscious and whose lives anticipate the new creation. Martyrs are those who bear the clearest possible witness to this hope and to the new life it generates.

Master Romuald, the liturgy says, "was a martyr, yes, but a martyr of love." Martyrdom is not a deathwish but the very opposite, because it redeems the life not only of the martyr but also of those who cause the martyr's death: "Forgive them, for they know not what they do." The Life of the Five Brothers is a story of love and death: the love in the hearts of Romuald and his disciples for the Christ who rose from the dead, the love of friendship that bound them so strongly one with another, the love of the two disciples who joined Poland's first martyrs in overcoming, by the power of love alone, their own bodily death and the death in the hearts of their slayers. It is a story for all times.

PART TWO: THE LIFE OF THE FIVE BROTHERS
BY BRUNO OF QUERFURT

INTRODUCTION

Several things must be said, before a late-twentieth-century reader begins a hagiographic text from the High Middle Ages. First, and most obvious: that this literary genre has been totally absent from western literature since the Renaissance. Not that people no longer write about saints: see, for example, Robert Bolt's "A Man for All Seasons." But this fine play about the life and death of Saint Thomas More is not hagiography. By the same token, medieval hagiography is not biography, nor is it fiction; while it is not "historical" writing, as we understand the term, neither is it pure invention. Perhaps we should simply say, "It is liturgy." In fact, most early and medieval lives of saints were composed to be read in church, within the context of prayer and chanting and psalmody, as a celebration of "salvation history." And here is the second point, that all patristic and monastic writing about saints is conceived as a commentary on Holy Scripture; the Bible's account of historical and "collective" salvation is, in the lives of the saints, democratized. In other words, salvation history, relived in an exemplary way by the individual holy woman or man, is revealed as a reality which you and I—not yet saints but on the way there—can experience personally and directly. Hence the stories of the Bible and the lives of the saints constitute a hermeneutic circle, the one illuminating the other.

Bruno of Querfurt's Prologue begins with a cry for help. We assume that Bruno is simply giving vent to his tormented conscience, burdened with guilt for having betrayed his best friend. This, however, is not the case here; Bruno's torment was real, but even without these sentiments, he would have begun writing about the holy martyrs in the same way. The literary genre demands that he admit his personal inadequacy, as he assumes the task of recounting Christ's victory in His saints; all hagiographic texts begin with the author's act of humility and modesty. To a certain extent, Bruno's complaint about his own lack of literary talent is simple honesty; he writes a difficult, contorted, occasionally incorrect Latin, in which we seem to hear his thick German accent. On the other hand, Bruno's Life of Adalbert begins

77

*on exactly the same note; he is, in fact, following a prede-
termined form. He writes about real events of which he and his
contemporaries were eyewitnesses, but he always keeps an eye on
the great exemplars of early Christian hagiography: the* Life of
Antony *by Saint Athanasius, the* Life of Hilarion *by Saint
Jerome, and above all the second book of the* Dialogues *of
Saint Gregory the Great, which tells the story of Benedict,
the father of western monasticism.[1]*

PROLOGUE

Help me, God! I am a man of little talent, but I want to tell
a great story. Give me eloquence, understanding, and feeling. Let
me tell a tale of saints, men of pure hearts and good works, who
have received from Your hand the royal robe of martyrdom.[2]

Good Jesus, I know what I am. My sins have slain me and
left me to rot like a dead dog on a dunghill. I wallow in evil
like a sow in the mud.[3] Do not condemn me, dear Jesus, if I
dare to write about somebody else's virtues. And you, my
readers, my judges, forgive me for telling this story with no
style and without practicing what I preach. I simply must do
it, for I am driven by love.

I admit that I am a monstrous example of contradictory
behavior. But even if I cannot sing a good song, at least let
me bark like a dog! I will end up in hell if, like a guilty
bystander, I fail to tell what I have seen.[4] One thing is certain: as long as I keep dipping my pen into the inkpot of my
mind, I will have no time to think about sin or commit it. To
talk about good deeds is sometimes helpful, but writing
about them always is. Barlaam's talking ass told of God's
mercy and might,[5] and we humans, guided, as Scripture
says, by a little Child[6]—should we not show the way to
those who want to live rightly and be saved?[7]

With this hope I have begun. Now let me tell my story!
But first I need God's help, the touch of His hand, His word
that resounds from heaven. He is my help, who made earth

and sky, who fashioned both saint and sinner by His power. Give me Your blessing, Lord; show me Your goodness. You restore integrity to those who have lost their innocence; help me now to write well and to live well, and keep me safe for heaven, O Redeemer of the world. Rouse up Your might and save us![8] Come to my assistance! Make haste to help me![9] Friend of humanity, dear Jesus my God, my mercy, speak to me and say, "I shall finish the work I have begun in you, O sinner. Fear no more than you ought to. A few winters more, and when your time has come, I the Redeemer you long for will come to take you home."

Now as I take pen in hand and begin to write the life of these holy and fragrant martyrs, help me, Lord, in Your goodness.[10] All-powerful God, You are ever-present to save us—help me now to tell a good story and to live a good life. Let my enemies laugh no more. Let them behold my work brought to completion by Your great mercy and saving power. May the Apostle Peter and the holy martyrs intercede for me. Great Savior, as I set sail on a stormy sea, have pity on me, for your own name's sake. Put an end to my anguish and say to my soul, "I am your salvation!"[11]

---

[1]The following are the primary sources for the Latin text of Bruno's work, as well as of other information about Saint Romuald:

The Life of the Five Brothers: Monumenta Poloniæ Historica, Series nova, Tomus IV, Fasc. 3; recensuit, præfatione notisque instruxit Hedvigis Karwasinska. Warszawa: Panstwowe Wydawnictwo Naukowe, 1973.

The Life of Saint Romuald: Giovanni Tabacco, ed. *Vita beati Romualdi*. Roma: Istituto Storico Italiano per il Medioevo, 1957.

Thomas Matus, ed. *S. Pier Damiano, Vita di San Romualdo*. Camaldoli: Edizioni Camaldoli, 1988.

[2]"*...qui post album cor et opus bonum acceperunt pupureæ passionis aureum finem.*" Martyrdom, the saints' *passio* in imitation of Jesus Christ, is the paradigm of Christian holiness. The monk's singleness of intent and

ascetical effort has as its end a pure gift which God bestows on him gratuitously and not as a wage he has earned by his labor.

[3]In II Samuel 24,15, David compares himself to a "dead dog"—a man of little account who is not even worth killing—while II Peter 2,22 compares the sinner to the dog who eats its own vomit and to the sow who, having been washed clean, returns to the mud.

[4]The sin of the guilty bystander is the sin of omission: cf. James 4,17, alluded to again in the last chapter.

[5]The story of the talking ass is in the book of Numbers, chapter 22, verses 23 and following.

[6]The image is from the prophet Isaiah 11,6, where he dreams of the wolf lying down beside the lamb; the Child, for Bruno, is of course Jesus Himself.

[7]Literally, "show the way of salvation to those who are concerned to live rightly," but Bruno's *recte vivere*, "to live rightly" = "to live according to right reason," itself describes "salvation." The human person is saved, i.e., is restored to integrity, to spiritual sanity, by returning to human nature as rational, *rationabilis*, *logike*. Romuald, Bruno will tell us later, is "pater rationabilium eremitarum, the father of hermits who live according to right reason." In this case, being "reasonable" means, concretely, living according to the Rule of Saint Benedict: "*qui cum lege vivunt*." The great "law" that guides reasonable hermits is the law of discretion; like Benedict's Rule (*discretione præcipua*), Master Romuald is a man of "discretion" or, simply, "wisdom" (see below, *de discretione et perfectione Magistri Romualdi*).

[8]"He has raised up for us a mighty Savior" literally, "a horn of salvation": Luke 1,69, the *Benedictus* or Gospel canticle sung at Lauds, the morning office.

[9]From Psalm 70,2 (Psalm 69 in the Latin), the verse which opens every one of the Day Hours of the Divine Office.

[10]Cf. Psalm 51,2 (50 in the Latin), which used to be sung in monasteries every morning, and which now is sung on Fridays; the penitential Psalm *par excellence*.

[11]Psalm 35,4 (34 in the Latin).

1. BENEDICT'S VOCATION

The hero of Bruno's story is not Master Romuald, but Benedict of Benevento, Bruno's dearest friend and the co-founder of the little community which brought Romuald's eremitical style of Benedictine life to Poland. The intensity and purity of this friendship, centered not on the purely human affect but on a shared commitment to Christ and to Christ's way of love, colors the whole account and frequently leads the author to overstep the conventions of the hagiographic genre.

Yet the genre is always there, especially in Bruno's characterization of monastic life as "philosophy." We can grasp Bruno's meaning only if we remember that, throughout the classical and Hellenistic periods (with the sole exception of Aristotle), "philosophy" meant not so much a way of knowing (a "science of the whole") as a way of living; the philosopher's task, like the monk's, was neither to explain the world nor to change to world, but to know and change himself.

Young Benedict, Bruno tells us, begins his ascetical life by doing penance for a sin which he was not directly responsible for, that is, his parent's bribing of the bishop who ordained him (a transgression known technically as "simony"). Romuald, too, received his monastic call while doing penance for his father's duel with a relative. It is likely that both events are historical, but both also fit the conventional picture of the holy monk as a person of exquisitely sensitive conscience, so sensitive that others' sins weighed on him almost as heavily as his own.

Benedict (again like Romuald) embraces the Benedictine Rule and finds that, in the monastery he joins, the Rule is mostly honored in the breach. So he flees the cœnobium for the hermitage. But unlike Romuald, zealous young Benedict has a wise abbot who gently woos him back to the abbey and to a more discreet expression of his zeal.

The saint of whom I write came from Benevento, and his name was Benedict. The very sound of his name echos the benediction of his coming and going, the goodness of his living and dying.[1]   While yet a child, Benedict began to practice the true philosophy, the following of Christ.[2]   A bright lad, he learned his lessons well; devout and chaste, he avoided the pitfalls of youth.

Benedict's parents were eager to see him a priest; erring in their love for him, they paid the local bishop to ordain him, although their son had not yet reached the canonical age.[3]   When Benedict learned about the money, he did penance for his parents' sin by joining a community of canons regular. Even though his life there was exemplary, the Spirit soon moved him to give up everything for God, and he became a monk.

In reality, he was a monk already. He had taken chastity as his bride and kept his virginity with great zeal,[4] knowing that its reward is great in heaven. So when God called him, he entered the Monastery of the Holy Savior which over-looks the sea.[5]   There he found his Mother, the monastic Rule.[6]   He submitted to Her commands, even when they seemed harsh and painful, and soon he discovered what great sweetness flows from Her breasts, which feed God's servants. He was an exemplary monk, and in a few years he was ready to live as a hermit. The abbot would have let him have a private cell in the abbey, but Benedict could not endure the mediocrity and lukewarm observance of his brothers. The Holy Spirit's fire raged in his heart and drove him out into the wilderness.[7]

So he fled far from his place of birth and came to Mount Soracte, of which the pagan poet sang, "Do you see how deep the snow lies on Soracte's white peak?"[8]   (It was there that Saint Sylvester, fleeing persecution, took refuge. As he lay hiding, he devoted himself to Holy Scripture, until one day a messenger brought news which was beyond his wildest hopes: he was to baptize the emperor. And so he returned to Rome, entering the city with Emperor Constantine himself.)

Benedict spent about three years on the mountain. The hard life he led there made him vulnerable to every sort of temptation, as he himself admitted later.[9] Meanwhile, the abbot, although he praised Benedict's austerity, kept trying to woo him back to the monastery. When Benedict did return, the abbot built him a cell near the abbey, where he might enjoy that certain sweetness which God does not begrudge his lovers and where the hermit life would be easier for him and edifying for others.[10]

---

[1] A series of puns on Benedictus and Beneventum: *bene venisse, bene isse, bene vixisse.*

[2] "...the following of Christ" is a dynamic equivalent of *"Christo philosophari."* This expression, a key concept in medieval monastic vocabulary, once again links monastic practice to the evangelical and Pauline notion of "salvation": a person enters the monastery in order to live according to the gospel and so to be saved. On Christianity and Christian monasticism as "philosophy," see Henri de Lubac, *Exegèse medieval: Les quatre sens de l'Ecriture* (1957), p. 88; and Jean Danielou, *Etudes sur le vocabulaire monastique du moyen age* (Studia Anselmiana, vol. 48, 1961), chapter 2, "Philosophia," pp. 39-70.

[3] Simony, or the buying of ordination and ecclesiastical offices, was very common in those days; Saint Romuald, Bruno of Querfurt, Peter Damian, John Gualbert and others, especially in the monastic order, were vehement in their condemnation of it.

[4] "...great zeal," perhaps "excessive zeal," *nimio zelo*; Bruno seems to suggest, now and then, that Benedict's adolescent fervor was more than a little intemperate; later he would learn the wisdom of Master Romuald's *discretio.*

[5] We have no idea where this monastery was, although we might speculate that it overlooked the Bay of Naples. The title "Holy Savior" indicates that the monastery was dedicated to the mystery of Christ's Transfiguration, like Romuald's hermitage of Camaldoli.

[6] The "Mother Rule" is none other than that of Saint Benedict. The maternal metaphor is not found explicitly in the *Regula Benedicti*; however, the Rule does speak of the novice's experience of the hardness of

monastic initiation turning into an "inexpressible delight of love" (*Rule of Saint Benedict*, prologue 49).

[7]In this, Benedict's story as a monk parallels that of Master Romuald, who was constrained to leave his monastery for the hermitage, if he would remain faithful to his conscience (cf. Peter Damian, *Vita Romualdi*, chapters 3 and 4).

[8]Horace, *Carmina* 1,9,1, which Bruno cites incorrectly, evidently relying on his memory.

[9]Penance without discretion oversensitizes the monk; Benedict's excessive austerity—*nimio zelo*—although praiseworthy, is also a sign of spiritual immaturity. Bruno certainly had in mind, as he was writing this, the episode in the life of the first Saint Benedict (Gregory the Great, *Dialogues* 2,1), where a bird fluttering around his head provokes, in the young hermit of Subiaco, a violent response of sexual arousal and the equally violent reaction of stripping off his robes and throwing himself into a clump of stinging nettles.

[10]Literally, "easier and more worthy to be boasted of"—*levius et gloriosius*.

2. MASTER ROMUALD

Rare in the history of Christian literature are witnesses to the lives of "living saints"; Bruno of Querfurt's brief sketch of Romuald at the height of his career (he was in his early fifties) is one of them.

Bruno calls him "pater rationabilium eremitarum, *the father of hermits who live according to right reason." In this case, being "reasonable" means, concretely, living according to the Rule of Saint Benedict,* "qui cum lege vivunt." *The great "law" that guides reasonable hermits is the law of discretion; like Benedict's Rule (*discretione præcipua*), Master Romuald merits praise for his "discretion" or, simply, "wisdom."*

Romuald—like his disciple and friend John Gradenigo, whom we meet in this chapter—is totally free of presumption. "Presumption" is a typically monastic vice; it means I "take for granted" my own understanding of what monasticism is about. Monks are either damned by presumption or saved by discretion. They are damned if they take for granted their ability to achieve salvation by will-power and self-control; they are saved if they recognize that "all is grace" and work out their salvation "in fear and trembling," (cf. Philippians 2,12) avoiding that "bitter zeal which leads to hell" and practicing "the good zeal which monks ought to have" (cf. Rule of Saint Benedict, *chapter 72).*

Romuald and John were also free of the disease of spiritual subjectivism. Romuald's favorite medicine was "lectio divina," *the reading of Holy Scripture and such early monastic writings as the "Conferences of the Desert Elders ['Fathers']," by the fifth-century monk, Blessed John Cassian, who, after long sojourns with the hermits and cenobites in Egypt and elsewhere, settled on the island of Lerins, just off the French Riviera.*

Cassian's writings exerted a profound influence on Western monastic rules, such as that of Cassiodorus, the "Rule of the Master," as well as Saint Benedict's Rule, and formed the monastic thought of Saint Gregory the Great. The reformed monasticism of Cluny and other centers, such as Cuixá and Monte Cassino, took its inspiration from this family of texts—Cassian, Saint Basil in Latin translation, the Lives and Sayings of the Desert Elders—mentioned in the last chapter of the Benedictine Rule. Hence it is nothing but crass ignorance that leads some medieval historians to suggest that Romuald's return to these sources made him somehow "un-Benedictine." On the contrary, no one in the tenth or eleventh century was more Benedictine and even "Cluniac" than Romuald: he firmly believed that cenobitic formation was necessary for the vast majority of those who would become monks; he sent two of his disciples to study at Cluny; and he left no other written rule than that of Saint Benedict, to guide the common life in the hermitages and monasteries he founded.

*Master Romuald enters the scene here shortly after his resignation as abbot of Sant'Apollinare in Classe. His was not the first attempt to reform the Abbey of Classe; Saint Mayeul of Cluny had already tried to do so—with no lasting success—no more than a year before Romuald joined the community (about 972). As Saint Peter Damian tells us (*Life of Romuald ch. 22), *Romuald expected the monks to have all things in common and to regard one another as equals, with no special privileges for the learned or the high-born. Their inability or unwillingness to adhere to this fundamental principle of cenobitic life made it impossible for him to remain as their abbot.*

Never again would Romuald accept the office of Superior. He would always have his disciples elect one of their own number to govern the communities he founded; few of these abbots came anywhere near his standards.

Now at Monte Cassino there was a nobleman of mature years, John [Gradenigo] by name, a companion of [Peter Orséolo] the doge of Venice. When the doge decided to become a monk, John too, drawn to better things, renounced worldly power and riches. He showed such spiritual maturity as a novice, that immediately after monastic profession

86

he received permission to live as a hermit, subject to the authority of his spiritual father, [Abbot Garí of Cuixá]. The doge ended his days in God's service, clothed as a monk; and John, after the father abbot's death, continued to pursue the solitary life near the Abbey of Monte Cassino, where he earned great fame for his virtues.

Our young Benedict often came to visit Father John and even thought of sharing John's cell—a wise thought, for then he would not be wandering about following his own whims. Father John instructed Benedict in the way of salvation, but with humility, ascribing all his teachings to the wisdom and virtue of Master Romuald. "Romuald," he said, "is the greatest hermit of our day, yet he lives this beautiful life humbly and without presumption. He does not take for granted his own understanding of the life, but follows the Conferences of the Desert Elders; theirs was the doctrine he taught us."

Every time John spoke about Master Romuald (who was then in the prime of his life and famous throughout the land for his virtues), Benedict's heart burned within him. He wondered how it could be that a man like Father John, who was qualified to be a teacher in his own right, always presented himself as somebody else's disciple.

Shortly after he became emperor, Otto III—the last of that name but second to none for his piety—dragged Romuald out of the hermitage and made him take over as abbot of Classe. But because certain lay persons had too much influence on the abbey, Romuald was unable to do any good there. He began to realize that he was losing his peace of mind and purity of heart; so lest he damn himself without saving anyone else, he took the abbatial staff and threw it down at the emperor's feet. From then on he tried to stay as far away as possible from those who knew him too well, so that with solitude as his friend, he might at least save himself.

Romuald wasted no time. Leaving Classe like a fugitive, he went to Monte Cassino, the fountainhead of monks who follow the Holy Rule.[1] Romuald had a personal reason for going there: many years had passed since he last saw John

[Gradenigo]. He missed John and was eager to see him again. Romuald, the father of hermits who live according to right reason and follow the monastic Rule,[2] admired John's many virtues, especially his refusal to speak ill of people behind their back or to listen to those who do so.[3]

When news arrived that Romuald was coming, Benedict, like someone who has just inherited a great fortune, jumped on his horse and galloped off to meet him. From the moment they met, they were inseparable.

What Benedict loved most in Master Romuald was his refusal to compromise his ideal. The more harshly Romuald treated him, the more Benedict complimented himself on having found such a severe master. Benedict deemed nothing good or holy except what Romuald taught him to do. He zealously followed his teacher's orders, denying his self-will in everything. Romuald had nothing but praise for Benedict: "He is like a stone when he fasts or keeps vigil!" Romuald held him up to me and to all his disciples as an example of monastic life lived with purity and joy in God's presence.[4]

Autumn is a season when people generally fall ill, and in the autumn of that year, Romuald took to his bed and lay close to dying. Benedict strove to outdo everyone in nursing Romuald and serving his every need. As soon as he had regained his health, Romuald left for Rome, which itself was ailing. With him was Benedict, his faithful servant, a man of desires and a golden flower of obedience and humility. How could he let Romuald leave without him? He had joined his company in the quest for perfection, and this desire prompted him to endure every hardship and made him burn with the love of God to the very marrow of his bones.

---

[1] *...fons et origo regularium monachorum.*

[2] *...patrem rationabilium eremitarum qui cum lege vivunt;* the phrase is in the following sentence in the Latin text; we have placed it here purely for stylistic reasons, and because it echoes the phrase cited in the preceding note.

[3]This special virtue of John Gradenigo is praised by Peter Damian as well (cf. *Vita Romualdi*, chapter 15). Bruno ascribes the same quality to Benedict of Benevento; see below, chapter 19.

[4]The phrase "monastic life" translates "*innocentiam obedientiæ et castitatem morum*," which in turn echoes the monk's promises of *obedientia* and *conversatio morum* in the Rule of Saint Benedict, chapter 58. The Rule does not distinguish "evangelical counsels" (i.e., chastity, poverty, and obedience) from "precepts" (what is required of Christians, whether vowed to religious life or not), nor does it distinguish among the three "Benedictine vows," stability, obedience, and reformation of life, which are, in effect, three expressions that denote one and the same reality: "*conversatio*" or, simply, "monastic life."

3. OTTO'S VOW

Having accepted—however briefly—the abbacy offered him by the young emperor Otto III, Romuald's life is from now on interwoven with the events that will set the course of Europe in the second millennium and whose effects, especially in Central and Eastern Europe, we can still see today. One of these crucial events is the martyrdom of Saint Adalbert near Gdansk, in the year 997.

Adalbert, born in 956 with the name Wojciech, was a Bohemian nobleman and a disciple of Saint Adalbert of Magdeburg, whose name he took at confirmation. At the age of 26 he is elected bishop of Prague and, shortly after his consecration, meets Saint Mayeul, abbot of Cluny, who inspires him with the Cluniac ideals of humility, the worship of God, and fidelity to the Roman See.

Adalbert's monastic spirit and fierce independence of the local aristocracy win him more enemies than friends in Prague, and in 990 he flees to Rome with his half-brother Radim. While in Italy he comes under the influence of the Italo-Byzantine abbot Saint Nilos, who encourages him to enter the monastery of Saints Boniface and Alexis (Sant'Alessio) on the Aventine, a joint community of Latin and Greek monks. In 993 he is recalled to Prague, but driven out once more, he returns to his monastery on the Aventine, where the community elects him prior.

Three years later, the sixteen-year-old Emperor Otto, upon the death of John XV, has his cousin elected pope, with the name of Gregory V. While in Rome the young emperor meets Adalbert, and Otto's personal chaplain Bruno of Querfurt joins him at Sant'Alessio on the Aventine. The following year, after a last, futile attempt to establish himself at Prague, Adalbert meets death at the hand of the pagan Prussians in northern Poland. Poland's ruler, Boleslaw Chrobry, brings his body back to Gniezno and buries him with honors befitting a holy martyr.

Otto's pilgrimage to Adalbert's tomb in the year 1000 is decisive for future Polish history. The emperor recognizes Boleslaw's sovereignty and Poland's independence, both

political and ecclesiastical, from Germany, and his idea of
a new Roman Empire crystallizes and assumes the form of a
federation, ruled by the emperor (who would reside at
Rome) but not dominated by any one of the national groups
that it would unite.

The devout Emperor Otto was on his way back to Rome
from a pilgrimage to Saint Adalbert's tomb [in Poland].
When he reached the city, the people welcomed him with
great festivities, but their joy was feigned. Like a dire
presage of misfortune to come, a mighty rainstorm with
violent thunder and lightning accompanied his arrival. Abbot
Romuald—always a wanderer, now here, now there, gathering disciples in the power of the Holy Spirit[1]—took with him
Boniface and Thomas, two of Otto's closest friends, and
went off to serve God in solitude.[2]

Romuald's hermitage near Rome soon began to flourish
with the study of true philosophy, that of Christ. The Holy
Spirit fell like rain on the brothers' hearts, watering them
and bringing forth from their fear of God the leaves of virtue
and the fruits of holiness. But the devil was busy stirring up ill-
will, in order to deprive God's servants of their peace.

Even though the emperor had done nothing to merit their
contempt, the people of Rome rebelled against him, and he
was obliged to leave for Ravenna in order to save face. But
how could he go without first visiting the hermitage? For
some time now, Otto had been nourishing the thought of
leaving the world, and the love of God burned brighter in
him than in the heart of many a monk. At odd hours of day
and night, this rare soul would come to visit the hermits,
telling no one but God, since spiritual growth can take place
only in the secrecy of faith.

But it is hard to keep a king's comings and goings secret.
Otto tried to make sure that, except for his immediate
companions, whom he felt he could trust, no one knew what
he was doing. In spite of his precautions, however, people
kept following him—"where the carcass is, there will the

vultures gather."[3] The contemplative life suffered as a result of Otto's coming to see us and our being invited to visit him; and just as Rome had lost its empire and Otto had lately lost Rome, so the hermitage, having lost its peace and quiet, ceased to be a hermitage.

On one of his visits, Otto made a solemn promise: to renounce, for the sake of Christ's kingdom and its riches, the wealth and power which he possessed but neither loved nor enjoyed. Pressed on every side by misfortune—and it is often misfortune that turns people toward the way of salvation—he finally decided to give voice to the thoughts that had been on his mind for so long a time.

In the presence of God and His angels and before witnesses ("so that every case may stand on the word of two or three witnesses")[4] Otto vowed, "From this very hour I promise God and His saints that, when three years have passed and I have restored order in the empire, I shall renounce my throne and distribute the riches I inherited from my mother; then, naked, I shall give my all to Christ."[5]

Abbot Romuald was present, together with the two disciples [Boniface and Thomas]. Because of his age and his many years as a monk,[6] he answered in their name. "Hold fast to this desire, O king, and if the uncertain course of human existence does not grant you the time to fulfill it, know that in God's eyes you have already done so, for He knows what will be, and He judges men's outward deeds according to what is in their hearts."

---

[1]"...in the power of the Holy Spirit" translates "*in digito Dei*," literally "with God's finger," a common metaphor for the Holy Spirit in the Latin liturgy.

[2]In the text, Bruno-Boniface calls himself *Benignus*, a Latin synonym for "Bonifacius"; hagiographers were supposed never to name themselves in their stories. "Thomas" is, as Saint Peter Damian tells us, Tammo, a former officer in the imperial army. Both of them were now monks at the bi-ritual abbey on the Aventine. The Saint Boniface who was co-patron of this monastery was an early Roman martyr, whose name was assumed not

only by our own Bruno of Querfurt but also by the eighth-century English monk Wynfrith, who, having come to Rome and to the monastery on the Aventine, went forth from there to evangelize Germany (cf. C. H. Lawrence, *Medieval Monasticism: Forms of Religious Life in Western Europe in the Middle Ages* [London & N.Y.: Longman, 1984], pp. 57 ff). The spirit of Anglo-Germanic missionary monasticism, formed according to the Rule of Saint Benedict, would come to life again in the missions of Saint Romuald's disciples in eastern Europe.

[3]Matthew 24,28.

[4]Deuteronomy 19,15; Matthew 18,16.

[5]"...naked, I shall give my all to Christ" translates *"tota anima nudus sequar Christum."* The "virtue of nudity" is the total stripping of earthly possessions and of the desire for them. Similar expressions are found throughout early monastic literature (Jerome, Cassian et al.) and signify the initial "break" with the world which is a prerequisite for becoming a monk.

[6]"...many years as a monk" translates *"longa virtus,"* not "long virtue" but, like *conversatio* and *castitas morum*, simply "monastic life."

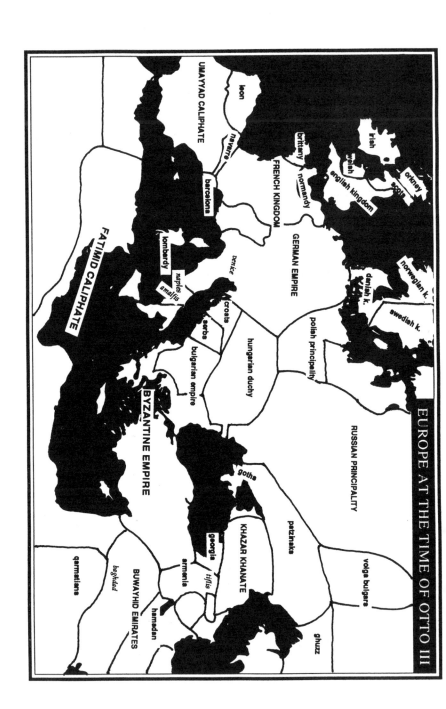

EUROPE AT THE TIME OF OTTO III

UMAYYAD CALIPHATE

leon

navarre

barcelona

FRENCH KINGDOM

brittany

normandy

FATIMID CALIPHATE

lombardy

naples

amalfis

venice

GERMAN EMPIRE

irish

welsh

english kingdom

scots

orkney

norwegian k.

danish k.

swedish k.

polish principality

RUSSIAN PRINCIPALITY

crcats

serbs

bulgarian empire

hungarian duchy

BYZANTINE EMPIRE

goths

petzineks

volga bulgars

qarmatians

baghdad

BUWAYHID EMIRATES

hamadan

armenia

georgia

tiflis

KHAZAR KHANATE

ghuzz

4. THE EMPEROR'S PROJECT

The scene now shifts from Rome to the wetlands north of Ravenna: the island of Peréo (cf. Peter Damian, Life of Romuald, *chapters 21 and 30). No longer surrounded by swamps, the place is now known as Sant'Alberto, a popular corruption of "Sant'Adalberto," the martyr Adalbert of Prague, patron saint of the monastery.*

At Peréo the hermits follow a rhythm of life quite similar to that of the early Palestinian lavras: they live two to a cell (Bruno's own cell-mate is Benedict of Benevento himself) and there they chant the weekday Offices; from first to second Vespers on Sundays and feasts all the hermits come to a common chapel for the Offices and the Mass, followed by the convivium, *the common meal*

The emperor, having fled Rome to save face, spends half his time in the company of Romuald's disciples, dreaming of becoming a hermit-missionary himself. His project of a monastic center for the formation of missionaries to Poland receives Romuald's consent, and Otto builds a cœnobium at Peréo. Inevitably, people back in Ravenna start asking why Romuald, who has just resigned as abbot of Classe, is letting the emperor build him another monastery, and just as inevitably, Romuald totally disregards what people say about him. This is perfectly in keeping with his vision of the monk as a person made free by uncompromising truthfulness to God and to oneself.

As a means of realizing his desire to become a monk, Otto conceived the following project: he would choose some of the more fervent brothers and send them to Poland[1]; there they would build a monastery in Christian territory but near an area where pagans dwell, secluded and surrounded by woods. This would offer a threefold advantage: the community life, which is what novices want; golden solitude, for those who are mature and who thirst for the living God; and the preaching of the gospel to the pagans, for those who long to be freed from this life in order to be with Christ.

95

Meanwhile, so that we might enjoy the first two advantages—since the third was not available here—as soon as we had established a hermitage Otto decided to build a cœnobium. He acted with the best intentions, for the salvation of the greater number, but on account of our sins his efforts produced the opposite effect: in the end he lost the hermitage without succeeding in founding the monastery.

When they saw the emperor doing this for Romuald, many persons cried scandal. They accused Father Romuald of greed, ignoring the pastoral motives that guided him. Above all else, Romuald desired that the emperor be saved through this good deed, but he also saw the monastery as a useful means for winning souls.

Romuald's personality, as a contemplative and a true servant of God, had one outstanding characteristic: whatever people would have liked to see him do, he tried at all costs to do exactly the opposite. Only when he could get them to insult, taunt, and slander him (provided he did nothing against his own conscience), would he consider himself worthy of esteem and capable of preserving his virtue.

Romuald was always totally consistent with himself. Here is an example: Romuald loved young Benedict for his total dedication to monastic living, and when it came time to appoint an abbot for us in the hermitage and for the emperor's new monastery, Benedict was Romuald's choice. In his humility, Romuald saw himself as abbot only of his disciples' souls, not of their bodies. Whenever the number of the brothers made it necessary to elect an abbot—whom they would have preferred to be Romuald himself—he had to choose one of them, since he would not accept it.

For the office of abbot at Peréo, Romuald—guided in his discernment of persons by the Holy Spirit—found no one better suited to the task than Benedict, to whom he applied the saying, "In his breast the thought of heaven made its stable abode, and in his way of life the virtues took possession of God's kingdom."[2] The brothers gladly agreed to Romuald's choice. But Benedict doubted his own ability to serve as abbot; so to be on the safe side of humility, he declared, "It is hard to accept the task of judging others, when one does not even know the state of one's own soul. The only people who should undertake the care of souls and the correction of others' lives are those whose seriousness, maturity, holiness, and moderation[3] make them fit to do so."

Now my friend Benedict had been appointed to guide me in the spiritual life, and we were living in the same cell.[4] So he turned to me, unworthy though I was, and had me ask the emperor to veto his election. Thus Benedict's willfulness thwarted Romuald's plans, with the result that another monk was consecrated abbot, one who resembled Benedict as much as mud resembles gold. Romuald was very angry, and when he found out whose fault it was, he called a chapter meeting and had Benedict and me strip to the waist and take the discipline,[5] even though Benedict had sinned only through an excess of humility, whereas I was the one who got the emperor to annul the election.

---

[1] The word translated here throughout as "Poland" is "*Sclavonia.*" The word, by itself, means "the lands of the Slavs," but Bruno of Querfurt uses it exclusively to refer to Poland or what was then called *Polanie.*

[2] Bruno seems to be quoting a text here, perhaps from the life of a saint, which has not come down to us.

[3] *Temperata discretio*, the great monastic virtue, which means first of all the humble recognition of one's own limitations.

[4] The practice of two monks sharing the same cell was common in the hermitages founded or influenced by Saint Romuald, including Fonte Avellana. This was not, however, the custom at Camaldoli, Romuald's last foundation; the bishop's charter makes a special point of the fact that each monk had his own cell, perhaps to balance the greater amount of time they spent together (at the daily liturgical offices, in the service of guests, etc.).

[5] See the penal legislation in the Rule of Saint Benedict, chapters 23, 24, 25, and 28. The "discipline" was a whip of cords—still used as a private penance at New Camaldoli when I was a novice—which did little more than irritate the skin. Its use in the Middle Ages did not necessarily instill or express sadomasochistic tendencies, as it would today

5. THIRST FOR MARTYRDOM

Speaking of his bondedness with Benedict, Bruno does not use the word "amicitia" *("friendship") but the expression* "privilegium amoris," *the "privilege of love" that united the group around Romuald. Biblical criteria (*"koinonia" *and* "agape": *Acts 1-4 and I John) guided their understanding and experience of this love; today's culture, guided by other criteria, tends to see all forms of love between persons of the same sex as tendentially, if not explicitly, homosexual. Homosexuality existed, of course, in the eleventh century as it does today, but not always as an expression (however inappropriate it might be deemed) of friendship; such relationships and practices also served as a form of dominance and were closely intertwined with authority structures. Romuald, in his aversion for the more alienating aspects of authority, sought to create egalitarian structures favorable to the climate in which wholesome friendship flourishes.*

Here we meet the other hero of the story: Brother John (not to be confused with John Gradenigo, who remained in his hermitage at Monte Cassino). Bruno's description mingles hagiographic commonplaces with genuine biography, blurring the image of this altogether lovable monk. John's "severity" is only that of the lifestyle he embraced; in real life, his disfigured countenance, softened by a habitual smile, shone with the radiance of a gentle, non-judgmental soul, totally free of "bitter zeal," that pseudo-ascetical harshness that leads some monks to hell (see the Rule of Saint Benedict, *chapter 72).*

During the long hours Benedict and I spent together—it was my privilege to enjoy his friendship and to hear him call me, "my brother"—I kept suggesting that he set out for Poland to preach the gospel, and I declared myself ready to do the same.

"The climate in this swamp is ruining our health," I said. "Can't you see that everyone here is getting sick, from the

abbot on down to the youngest novice? It is a miracle that no
one has died yet. How can we work with our hands, if our
legs aren't strong enough to carry us to church for holy
Communion on Sunday. How can we understand what we
read or put any feeling into our prayers if we are too weak
to get out of bed? You can't even fast, so long as the disease
has you in its grasp, and you can't practice any virtue except
one—patience—and you had better have plenty of it!

"Why should we stay in this swamp and die for nothing?
Wouldn't it be better to go someplace where we could live
as hermits and die for the gospel? Here, if we want to seek
God in the hermitage, we are not afraid to die. Would we be afraid,
then, if preaching the gospel meant that we would have to give
our lives for Christ? Don't say that it is pride for a sinner to
seek martyrdom. Many have received this grace in spite of
their past sins of impurity and idolatry. And anyway, we are not
looking for martyrdom in order to become saints, but only to have
our sins forgiven. For in fact, if Baptism washes away sins,
martyrdom totally extinguishes them."

Persuaded by my words, Benedict began to thirst for
martyrdom, and the idea of leaving for Poland gave him
another reason for not wanting to be abbot—although if he
had stayed and accepted the office, he could have done a
great deal of good for the monks, both in the cœnobium and
in the hermitage.

For the rest of the year, the brothers remained in the
hermitage, in spite of the fact that many of them came down
with malaria. In the meantime, Otto built them a chapel
dedicated to Christ's holy martyr Adalbert, to whom he was
greatly devoted. The chapel was built in the round and
adorned with marble columns.[1] The good emperor spent one
hundred pounds of silver on it.

Then Otto decided to return to Rome. His plan was to
take revenge on the city for the humiliation he had suffered
there. Would that he had never begun this journey, as it led
to his committing a grave sin against Saint Peter! Since
there were several bishops with him, he had them dedicate

the chapel [at Peréo]. As usual the people in the emperor's party overran the hermitage, thus becoming an occasion of sin for the two disciples [Boniface and Thomas] who spoke the emperor's native language [German] and were his best friends. Otto could not bear to see them troubled as they were by the crowds and their own relatives. So he obtained Romuald's reluctant permission for them to leave [Peréo] and retire to a more isolated hermitage, under the guidance of one of Romuald's senior disciples.

Of course all three of them, [Otto, Boniface, and Thomas,] acted with good intentions, and Romuald's disciple received the two young monks willingly, although with little enthusiasm. But their departure was objectively a sin, which could not go unpunished. For when they left [Peréo], they lost Master Romuald, and Romuald, having lost his disciples, set sail for Istria, his ancestral home, to beget new offspring in the Spirit.

The man of God Benedict was unaware of what was happening. I went to his cell, which was some distance away near the swamp. He was sick with malaria at the time and sat warming himself by the fire in front of his cell. Benedict was like the other half of my soul; he had to know that I had left Master Romuald. "The situation [at Peréo] was an occasion of sin for weak souls like mine," I explained. "but now I realize it was wrong for me to leave Master Romuald."

When he heard my story, Benedict said, "You have taken a great leap, my brother! We two ought to be one, and yet you did this without my knowledge. You lost your teacher, and you may never find anyone like him again. To me the thought of abandoning him is almost unthinkable, but if you are going to leave, I will too."

Then Benedict fell silent, and after a while he said softly, "Hand me my shoes, and let us be on our way." And he added, "Is nothing left of the desire and determination we once had in common? What has become of the king's noble plan, his secret intention to bear witness to Christ? What has become of the promise he made before the angels of God, to renounce all his wealth for the sake of eternal life?"

(And I thought: Even if a man decides to keep what he has, on the day he dies he gives up everything, whether he wants to or not.)

Benedict continued: "What of his desire to turn over the empire to a wise successor, so that stripping himself of royalty, he might set out as a monk for the holy city Jerusalem[2] and practice Christian philosophy in a hidden desert, far from the ways of men?"

I said in reply—I, the heedless disciple whom Benedict loved and whom he accepted, just as I was—"You know that the emperor wants you to leave for Poland before he does; he has not changed his plans about sending you there. Don't worry about me. I intend to follow in your steps as long as I live. It is only the king's wavering resolve that keeps me in this country; I have to wait until I see what direction his affairs are going to take."

This conversation took place as we were walking out of the woods toward the chapel. We found the emperor just risen from dinner; with his usual humility he went to see Master Romuald. In spite of our having offended our teacher by depriving him of his disciples, Romuald granted—contrary to our expectations—the king's request for two brothers as missionaries to the Poles: the good Brother John and the better (as he seemed to our human eyes) Benedict.

John was inferior to Benedict only in stature, but in the fervent love of God and in humility he stood head and shoulders above everyone else in the hermitage. He was a man of peace and moderation, and hardly anyone had ever seen him angry. As he had a natural aversion for vainglory, he hid his austere way of life behind a smiling face and tempered his youthful zeal with a wise mind and an inborn patience. Smallpox had blinded him in one eye, but his appearance was so radiant that he might have had three eyes instead of one!

From childhood he had chosen the better part,[3] and he regarded pleasure as an enemy. Shirking no task, he waged war on his lower nature. His observance in the monastery was beyond reproach. The unruly among the brethren he tamed, and disorderly behavior he rejected. He seasoned his every deed with the spice of humility and thus he won the abbot's confidence. Gentle and patient, he excelled in the fervent love of God and neighbor. Swiftly he grew to maturity, and when virtue had become easy for him, he endured whatever was hard and unpleasant out of love for Jesus Christ. (Remember what the Apostle Paul said: "For me to live is Christ and to die is gain."[4] And the Psalmist: "Great peace is theirs who love Jesus, and nothing can make them fall."[5] And again, "My heart and my flesh have found joy in the living God."[6])

---

[1]One sees round churches in Ravenna (San Vitale) and throughout the Byzantine world; this architectural form was quite typical of the Slavo-Byzantine churches in the areas where Saint Adalbert preached (cf. Francis Dvornik, *Byzantine Missions Among the Slavs* [New Brunswick, N.J.: Rutgers Univ. Press, 1970], p. 199).

[2]This "Jerusalem" is primarily metaphorical and means the "kingdom of God" as the goal of monastic practice. The secondary, i.e., geographical meaning is not excluded, however, since the model of itinerant eremitism was highly esteemed in the Christian East; remember, also, that Otto's religious formation was as much Greek Orthodox (he was the son of the Byzantine princess Theophano) as it was Latin Catholic.

[3]The "better part" is that of Mary of Bethany, who sat at the feet of Jesus and listened to His words (Luke 10,38-42).

[4]Philippians 1,21.

[5]Psalm 119 (Latin 118),165; the Latin Vulgate does not, of course, have the name "Jesus" in this verse, but the words "Your law."

[6]Psalm 84 (83),2.

6. FOND FAREWELLS

Benedict and John set out for Poland, their destiny overshadowed by prophecies.

No contemporary theologian could have expressed a more sober and intelligent attitude toward non-biblical prophecies and private revelations than what we find in this chapter. Bruno says Benedict had "learned to hope in the Lord alone"; from whom did he learn this preference for objective, public revelation over private visions, if not from Saint Romuald himself? Remember Romuald's doubting, almost skeptical attitude toward the apparitions of Saint Apollinaris which he witnessed as a young man. The apparitions did not convince him to join the monastery; the subtle stirring of God's love in his heart did. In a time when the "Fatima secrets" and the Medjugorje phenomena, not to mention the millennialism of Hal Lindsay and others, are stirring up anxiety, fanaticism, and even hysteria among simple believers, we need Saint Romuald's sober focus on God's true, total, and definitive revelation in the Incarnate Word. While others faced the year 1000 with trepidation or with wild expectations, Romuald and his disciples entered the new millennium with authentic Christian hope, convinced that indeed the Lord was coming, but that they had yet a great task to accomplish by the light of day, so as to prepare the way of His coming. We too, surrounded by symptoms of end-of-an-era psychosis, need to approach Christianity's third millennium with the same sober hope, committed to the building of God's kingdom in history.

A whole crowd of monks, both good and bad, joined King Otto on his trip down the river to Ravenna. The holy pair, Benedict and John, were ready for their trek across the Alps to Poland. The emperor, as a sign of his love for Christ, supervised all the preparations himself and made sure the necessary supplies were in order.

I cannot speak of our last evening together without tears in my eyes. Night was near, and in the waning light I began to traverse the heavens with Benedict. My sorrow was all the greater because of the great love that united us—and yet, miserable man that I am, I confess that I remember our last conversation together as a happy occasion.

I must not conceal what he said to me. Benedict, whose custom it was to address me lovingly as "my brother," this time kept calling me "lord bishop" with the same affection, thus prophesying what I was to become on account of my sins. He was not speaking lightly, and I have every reason to be afraid of what he prophesied. For just as virtue can turn into sin, so sin often gives birth to virtue;[1] hence, while I was yielding to the seduction of wanderlust, he was being guided to Poland by the spirit of holiness that had abandoned me (as in the Psalms, "Salvation is far from sinners.")[2]

Benedict had been the subject of two visions. The first was a dream that came one night to the bishop who ordained him: he dreamt he was pouring a great flood of oil over Benedict's worthy head. Later, someone else had a dream— I can't say who it was[3]—in which he saw Benedict take the chalice and drain all the consecrated Wine in one draught. (These are the gifts we pray for when we sing, "You have anointed my head with oil; Your chalice runs over, how glorious it is!"[4]

All of this would eventually come true, but Benedict was not interested in prophecies, nor did he seek salvation in the outward course of events. As a true man of God, he placed his trust in inspired Scripture rather than human speculations, for he had learned to hope in the Lord alone, who created all things out of nothing and ordered them to our salvation.

We continued to bid each other farewell, embracing and exchanging the holy kiss. As we walked and talked, in the manner of friends who are seeing each other for the last time, I kept telling him, "Dearest brother" (would that I had called him "my lord!"), "I beg you, for the sake of our common hope Jesus Christ, the Son of the Virgin, never forget that I shall always be with you, and you with me. Whenever you are at prayer or in choir, always remember to beseech the living God and to ask Him to fulfill in us, for the sake of His name, the desire He gave us both: that before we die a natural death, you and I may see the happy day when God in His mercy will allow us to shed our blood for the sake of the gospel[5] and, by the power of the Spirit, grant us the remission of our sins." (As it is written: "Whoever seeks to be saved, asks in the name of Jesus."[6])

I a sinner thus left a saint this pledge of my love: that wherever he went I would follow. I said this over and over again, so as to impress it upon his ears. For his part, blessed Benedict insisted that I learn Polish.[7] But the one thing he repeated most often, was that I must not come without the papal license to preach.

With these words my lord Benedict was taken from me, and never again would I see him in this place of toil.

Like two stars in the firmament, Benedict and John went forth to receive a noble end in the land of the Poles. Burning with love for Jesus, like wood in the fire, the man of God Benedict[8] was motivated by one desire only: to attain eternal life through a pure and undivided love for divine wisdom. John also, a man sent from God, though not as intense in his love for Christ, was of a stable and patient nature, not subject to changes of mood but always in command of his emotions. Less skilled in the spiritual life than Benedict, John was more gifted in practical matters. He would begin a work slowly but with a good spirit, and he would not stop working until he had finished. As for the observance of the vows, he practiced them like a true monk.[9]

They crossed the Alps and took a long detour that led them through many lands of unknown tongue before they reached Poland. After enduring great hardship they finally arrived at their destination, where they met the ruler of the Poles, Boleslaw. His name means "greater in renown," and he was the only prince of our day whose privilege it was to send such a rare soul as Saint Adalbert to preach and to have him fall as a martyr on Polish soil. As was his custom, Duke Boleslaw received the two servants of God with eagerness and deep gratitude, and he showed them every kindness. They soon found a peaceful place suitable for the contemplative life; Boleslaw built them a monastery, sparing no expense, and provided for their needs so that they would not have to work the soil.

---

[1]Bruno is alluding to Saint Gregory, *Moralia in Job,* book 11, chapter 49 (Migne, P.L. 75,982-983 no. 65).

[2]Psalm 119 (Latin 118),155.

[3]Bruno "can't say," because it is himself.

[4]Psalm 23; Bruno misquotes the Latin text (Psalm 22,5), which has "my" rather than "Your chalice"; and of course the text itself, being a translation of a translation (from the Greek, from the Hebrew), does not correspond to any current English translation.

[5]"...for the sake of the gospel" is *"per rationem"*; in this case, *ratio* is not "right reason" (as in "reasonable hermits") but "worthy cause."

[6]Bruno seems to be thinking of John 14,13-14 and 16,23, and perhaps also of Saint Augustine, *Tractatus in Johannem* ch. 73 (P.L. 35, 1824-26).

[7]"Polish" perhaps, but possibly also the Old Slavonic or "Church Slavonic" which was used in the Liturgy of Saint Peter, a Roman rite Mass translated by Saints Cyril and Methodius and then widely used in Bohemia and Poland with, scholars hold today, the approval of Saint Adalbert (cf. K. Lanckoronska, *Studies in the Roman-Slavonic Rite in Poland,* in Orientalia Christiana Analecta [Rome, 1961]).

[8]Bruno alludes to Gregory the Great's life of the first Saint Benedict (*Dialogues* book 2), who also receives the title *"vir Dei,* man of God."

[9]The "vows" are *"mores optimos,"* "monk" is *"famulus Dei."*

7. THE LAST ADVENTURES OF OTTO III

In its own right, this chapter is a remarkable document. Setting aside the hagiographic genre, Bruno gives us an eyewitness account of Otto's death, filled with fascinating details and with profound emotion. Bruno does not white-wash the ambiguity of this remarkable lad, ruler of half of Europe from the age of sixteen, heir to his grandfather's dream of a new Pax Romana and religious to the point of exaltation.

Otto's successor will be a man of different ideas and far different character. His distant relative Henry II, a political realist and German nationalist, will have no scruples about waging war on fellow Christians in Poland and Apulia. Otto's empire was to be a confederation of sovereign states united by fealty to an emperor in Rome and by a common religious faith; Henry's will be a military dictatorship under German hegemony. And yet, a century after his death, the Saxon warlord Henry II will be canonized a saint of the Catholic Church!

Speaking of Otto's desire to renounce his empire and become a monk, Bruno returns to the famous "triple advantage" (see above, chapter four): the cœnobium, the hermitage, and evangelization among the pagans. Here the idea is a bit less rigid, and we are told that these are different means to one and the same end, which is always (as we have seen) "salvation." There is nothing new in this idea, since it represents in a simplified form the enormous variety that characterized the first five centuries of the Benedictine way of life. Only later, with Robert of Molesme, the Cistercians, and the Carthusians, do we find the cœnobium separated from the hermitage (in fact, Saint Robert counseled the first Carthusians not to adopt the Rule of Saint Benedict, since they wished to follow a semi-eremitical life style) and the contemplative life separated from the proclamation of the gospel. The divisions within the monastic order were symptomatic of those which had

*already arisen within the Church; only today, after the
Second Vatican Council, are these divisions beginning to be
healed.*

That same year [1002], when winter arrived, Otto marshaled the imperial army, together with a special attack
force, and set out on his fateful march against Rome. That
the king should die without an heir was unthinkable; yet the
unthinkable happened, and Otto III met his end in the
miserable confines of a small castle—this great king, who
had done so much good. To err is human, and Otto was very
human; he forgot that it was the Lord who said, "Vengeance
is mine; I shall repay!"[1]

He failed to honor God, just as he failed to honor God's
holy apostle, the key bearer of heaven, Peter. "O Israel,
honor your Lord, the Holy One!"[2]

Otto loved Rome as he did no other city. On her people,
whom he favored above all others, he lavished riches and
honor. He had always dreamed of living in Rome and of restoring
the city to its pristine splendor. But "the plans of men are
vain";[3] Otto's boyhood dream was the cause of his sin.

He could not stand the sight of his native land, our
beloved Germany. He loved Italy and longed to make it his
home—Italy, overrun with warfare and destruction, plague
and death! He saw priests, bishops, and comrades fall at his
side. Many of his own household died, and the best among
his people were slain. The sword spilled the blood of his
nobles, and the death of those dear to him deeply wounded
his heart. Neither his crown nor his riches nor the army he
had mustered were of any help to him now. Neither spear nor
sword could deliver him from death, who alone has no
regard for kings.

King Otto was a good man, but he took a wrong turn when
he thought he could destroy the eternal walls of Rome. For
Rome's greatness lies in its having been chosen by God as
the resting place of His apostles, and not in its people, who
have always returned evil for good. Toward our native land,

dear Germany, Otto felt no affection. He preferred the adulterous beauty of Rome, who feeds on the death of her lovers. He clung to the illusion that he could restore the faded harlot to the beauty that was hers in the days of her pagan rulers, and nothing could make him give up this illusion.

Otto knew the history of Rome but did not learn its lesson (thus does the love of passing things blind the human mind). He knew the prophecy of our Holy Father Benedict, who could not lie, being filled with the same Holy Spirit who spoke through the saints of the Bible: "Rome," he said, "shall not fall prey to foreign armies but shall decay from within."[4] Having forgotten this just decree, Otto embarked on his folly, or rather, his two follies: first the dream of restoring Rome's ancient glory, and then the decision to lay siege to it.

To cut a long story short, the ungrateful Romans almost killed Otto and his German compatriots, because he wanted to make their city his home, contrary to the custom of his predecessors. The people of Rome took offense at his affection and would not requite his love. They forgot the huge sums of money he had lavished upon them. He might as well have thrown his gifts into the sea. Since it was not God's will for him to die in Rome, Otto was driven forth in disgrace from this wretched city, which he loved so dearly. The rage of the Romans exceeded all limits. Otto barely escaped with his life. Mortified, he fled north [to Paterno] and took refuge in Saint Peter's Castle[5].

Otto wanted revenge for the humiliation they had inflicted upon him. Alas for his sins! For in that moment death rose up in arms to punish him.

Since all is fair in war—at least, that is what people think, even though it is not true—Otto threatened, with oaths and curses, to take vengeance on Rome. He would not turn back, he said, until his foes were put to shame. Thus he was quick to anger, in the way of this world, and slow in keeping his promise to God, that he would renounce worldly ways and become a monk. The good emperor lost his honor by postponing the good he might have done and by fulfilling, if only in thought, the evil which his hurt pride drove him to do. "Man proposes, God disposes." "Woe to the one who wills the good but hastens not to do it, for soon he will lose it."[6]

His untimely death, however, was expiation enough for the sins of his youth. And he remained firm in his intention to become a monk, as he had promised in the presence of his elders.[7]

A whole army of monks crowded the room where he lay dying. Otto confessed all his sins; he purged his soul and made it whiter than snow.[8] "We firmly believe that repentance wipes out sin, even though the confession be made with the penitent's dying breath, provided he audibly bewails his sin."[9]

As he gazed on the relics of the saints and of the life-giving cross of Jesus, his tears fell in great drops on the ground, and we all wept with him. He received the Body and Blood of the Lord with reverence and joy, as he had done every day since he took to his bed. He received Communion as if his health of both body and soul depended on it.

He was conscious up to the very instant of his death, when, with a gentle sigh, he made us orphans and wounded the souls of those who loved him. Thus did Otto give up his spirit into the merciful hands of the Savior, in whom he had placed his hope. O bitter death! Untimely death, which in that moment plucked so many flowers from earth's garden, found none fairer than he, whose handsome face, worthy of the imperial dignity, was disfigured by the pox. Otto, of whose former beauty none could have their fill, whose fair aspect feasted the eyes of all who saw him, now became an object of loathing and horror.

So Rome remained unharmed, while Otto was wounded in payment of his crime. He was taken away before his time, lest his soul be disfigured by malice. Our guilty world was not worthy of such a king! If he had been allowed to live into his prime, he would have been an upright and beloved emperor. If I can trust my judgment, human eyes have beheld no better king than he.

But what God willed and allowed to happen was all for the best. It is only fitting that God's judgments, which are holy, should remain obscure to us, who are sinners.

Those who were there at the time remarked that Otto's last breath was so gentle that it seemed like someone sighing in his sleep. The holy Doctors of the Church teach us that when the faithful depart this life peacefully, they go straight to heavenly rest and the beatific vision. So let us not doubt; let us believe what they say. Even though he be called to account for his sins in purgatory, yet his works and his good intentions give us every reason to believe that Otto will soon be in heaven as a humble servant of the saints and a true son of the angels who never sinned.

Otto was more virtuous in the eyes of God than he was thought to be by men. Since he was young and accustomed to luxury and not yet married, his natural passions sometimes caused him to fall. But his ability to fast, to do penance, and to keep vigils, and his hidden practice of almsgiving, spiritual reading, and devout prayers, helped him to rise from sin and obtained for him God's mercy.

But it is to no avail if, as the Bible says, "One man builds up and another tears down"; "one prays, another curses."[10] Honesty compels us to admit that Otto's passions led him into sin. He was like a sick man, too weak to do what God commands him. However, Otto's weakness ultimately did him no harm, because he detested every sin he committed. "One sure way to a happy end in God is to recognize one's present unhappy state."[11] He longed to do better, and God's mercy strengthened his feeble will, enkindling in him an ardent desire for the three highest goods, any one of which is sufficient unto salvation: the monastic habit, the solitary life, and martyrdom.[12]

Otto's way to heaven was not by the practice of particular virtues nor by the gradual reforming of his life. As befits a man of courage, he resolved to renounce power and rank all at once. However, Otto mistook for virtue what in fact was vice in God's eyes, and we often reproved him for this. Otto's vice was his indifference to other people's weaknesses and needs, and his failure to administer law and justice for the sake of the poor throughout the empire.

Otto rarely acted like a king, whether at official functions or in his private life. On the contrary, he kept trying to practice virtues proper to monks. He was humble to a fault, his faith was unshakable, his generosity unbounded. No one in his right mind can deny that Otto did a great deal of good. His thoughts and affections were not for this world. Here he had no abiding city[13], but filled with love for God he sought the city that is to come. In the eyes of men he was an emperor, but in God's eyes he was already a monk. He had at his disposal all the carnal enticements that drag men to their ruin: gold and silver, an empire, and all the pleasures of power, but they were nothing to him. He was like one who had already renounced these things. Otto's death seemed to fulfill a prophecy of the Cumæan Sibyl.[14] The Sibyl was a pagan oracle who foretold many true things about Christ's birth, the redemption, and the last judgment. Speaking of kings and the destiny of Rome, she said of this Caesar, Otto: "A king to the purple born shall die at the gates of Rome in a land not his own." This is very close to the facts: the land rebelled against him, the city shut its gates, and the emperor was struck by death.

This was Otto: a father to monks, a mother to bishops, a son of kindness and mercy, a faultless servant of religion and the true faith, rich in good will while practicing the virtue of poverty, bestowing earthly goods on all without distinction, victorious over the carnal sins of youth, spurning his native land for the love of heaven. Golden Rome's beauty brought ruin upon him; but brief was God's wrath, and long was he mourned by those he left behind. Now his soul rests, assured of salvation and a better life in Christ Jesus.

[1]Romans 12,19, from Deuteronomy 32,25.

[2]A rather vague biblical reference, perhaps to Isa. 12 or Sir. 7,33.

[3]Cf. Psalm 94 (Latin 93), 11.

[4]Cf. Gregory the Great, Dialogues 2,15.

[5]This is not Rome's Castel Sant'Angelo across the Tiber, but a castle (which no longer exists) outside of Rome.

[6]Two more sayings, vaguely reminiscent of various Old Testament proverbs.

[7]"He remained firm in his intention to become a monk": see above, chapter three. The Latin has *"conversionis firmissima meditatio"*; both nouns are technical terms in monastic vocabulary, derived especially from the Rule of Saint Benedict.

[8]Cf. Psalm 51 (Latin 50),9.

[9]These words are most likely from some theological text which has not come down to us.

[10]Cf. Sirach 34, 23-24.

[11]We can not be sure whom Bruno is quoting here. H. G. Voigt, in his German translation of our text (Stuttgart, 1907) finds a similar expression in the writings of Romuald's great contemporary, Symeon the New Theologian, abbot of Saint Mamas in Constantinople. However, it seems rather unlikely, although by no means impossible, that Bruno could have had access to Symeon's writings.

[12]See above, chapter four.

[13]Cf. Hebrews 13,14.

[14]The ruins of the pre-Christian sanctuary of *Cumæ*, or *Kymai*, lie near Naples. Among the Cumæan oracles which are extant, these words quoted by Bruno cannot be found; they are most likely among the spurious oracles added by Christian hands to the Sibyl's "prophecies."

8. SALT IN THE WOUND

The mission in Poland, although blessed by Master Romuald, was in reality Otto's personal project, linked with his conception of empire. The young emperor's untimely death seemed to cancel the motives for which Benedict and John had left Italy.

Their one remaining patron, Poland's Duke Boleslaw Chrobry, now becomes the great survivor of Otto's "confederate" Roman Empire; for nearly twenty years after Otto's death, with typical Polish stubbornness and with remarkable success, he will continue to defend his people's sovereignty against Saxon domination. Still, our two brothers feel lost, since Bruno has apparently forgotten them. Without him, and without the papal authorization he is supposed to bring, Benedict and John have no reason to remain in Poland.

The news of the emperor's death wounded the holy brothers Benedict and John to the core. They had come from afar and endured much hardship for love of Otto's eternal salvation, and his death filled their hearts with infinite anguish.

One of Otto's finer qualities was his fondness for the company of good people—although, on account of his youth, he also enjoyed the companionship of vain and worldly men. He cultivated the friendship of anyone he knew to be virtuous, whether cleric or lay person, but he was especially fond of those who served God as monks[1]. Boleslaw Chrobry, on whose private land Benedict and John had their hermitage, bewailed Otto's death as no one else did, and with good reason, since one of the young emperor's unfulfilled desires was to honor Boleslaw above all his other vassals. If Boleslaw has remained faithful to their friendship, he must still cherish Otto's memory more than anyone else.

With the death of King Otto, Christendom turned on itself and began to devour its own innards. Wars raged and rumors of war as never before, with all the fury of a storm-whipped sea. All this was the wage of our sins! Meanwhile pagan tribes were at peace with one another. So they joined forces against Christians, while the Christian nations waged savage war among themselves.

But to rub salt in the wound[2], an even greater unhappiness befell me, in addition to the great unhappiness I had already endured. With peace no more and wars raging constantly, there was no way I could reach Rome and ask the pope to authorize our mission. The brothers kept wondering why I had not come with that authorization. Why the delay? they asked themselves. Wasn't I afraid of showing myself a liar? Had I no shame, having promised to come and then failing to do so?

They kept telling each other that they would never have dreamed of coming to Poland if I had not persuaded them and made the emperor organize the expedition. Italy had many lovely and lonely places suitable for the solitary life. It was not for the sake of solitude that they had gone to such trouble—as if they enjoyed the idea of living alone in a foreign country! No, they had come here to bear fruit for souls by preaching the gospel. A divine call had drawn them to this dreadful pagan land, and nothing else.

Benedict, with all his youthful energy, felt especially frustrated. He was eager to do good, and his zeal for perfection drove him to take the kingdom of heaven by storm. The armed struggle that was going on in the world was nothing compared to their inner struggle with anxiety and fear. For the world, vanity and pride were the cause of the conflict, but for them, it was God and the truth.

Their only fear was that they might die before they had fought the good fight in God's service. They were afraid they might never have to face the trials that are the way to heaven, and would thus end their life without glory and to no good purpose.

"Untimely death ends all good works," they said, "and Otto's death has killed the possibility of his ever becoming a monk[3]. This is a warning for us, the survivors. We must not sleep." And so with these words they strove to keep up their spirits. (I heard all this from one of their disciples, who is still alive.) Any day they expected me to arrive with the letter from Rome. After all, I was the one who had convinced them to leave for the missions.

If I could not come, it was all my fault. My sins held me prisoner. Not only were my sins more than I could count, but even my few and insignificant good deeds were contaminated with evil. As it is written, "He who helps a sinner shares in his sin."[4] And in the Psalms, "His ways are defiled at all times."[5]

In the hermitage in Italy I was not accomplishing anything, but I feared my own eagerness to leave. I remembered the gospel verse, "In whatever place you stay, hasten not to leave it."[6] The devil whose toy I was kept me far from my salvation, and yet I was going to preach the gospel to others! My desire to leave egged me on, but the miserable state of my soul kept me from going, fearful as I was of the consequences. I feared the devil was trying to deceive me with the hope of better things, so as to make me leave my cell in a state of sin, devoid of the virtues I was supposed to be acquiring there. "There are ways which men call right that in the end plunge into the depths of hell."[7] "Man toils to achieve his own ends, and brings perdition on himself."[8]

---

[1]"...as monks" is not in the Latin, but *"servus Dei"* means, precisely, "monk."

[2]Literally, "wound upon wound"; cf. Job 16,15 in the Latin.

[3]Again, "Becoming a monk" stands for *"conversionem."*

[4]Cf. Proverbs 16,5.

[5]Psalm 10,5 (Latin 9,26).

[6]Cf. Mark 6,10.

[7]Cf. Proverbs 16,25, cited according to the Rule of Saint Benedict 7,21.

[8]A distant allusion to Proverbs 16,26.

9. IN FEAR AND TREMBLING

The gossip of a traveling monk shocks Bruno's conscience out of its torpor. At last, and too late, he decides to leave for the missions.

In the meantime there was a monk traveling about, visiting various communities and taking counsel with the brethren. One day the Spirit led him to my cell. Among the matters about which he asked my advice was a terrible crime, and with a mournful voice he told me the story.

"I believe you know a monk in Rimini named Rothulf, a nobleman," he began. "Well, the people there all went after him and lynched him! Man of the world that he was, he had become an assistant to bishop Leo in the imperial court. Rothulf was eager to show his loyalty to the emperor, and he was also eager to make money. He acquired a lot of it through his dealings with the local aristocracy, and the mob came out to get him.

"He fled to the church of San Gaudenzio, claiming sanctuary. But they arrested him right in front of the altar and dragged him out of church. They weren't satisfied just to kill him. First they cut off his hands and feet, and then like dogs they tore him to shreds."

I could hardly believe this, and I was terrified. "Woe is me!" I said. "Just the other day I sat at table with him, and we shared the same dish. Death was the farthest thing from our minds. We were good friends, even though his involvement in politics broke every law in the books. I always thought that, because of our friendship, I might be able to win his soul for God."

I continued. "What can we do, brother? Truly, 'man's life on earth is warfare.'[1] Those who are alive with us today are taken away tomorrow. But not even a friend's death brings us back to the fear of God. We think our life here on earth

117

will never end, and we are madly in love with the bitter sweetness of passing things." Having told his tale the brother left, and my thoughts began to goad me. "Why wait any longer?" I asked myself. "Delay no more, be on your way! Better to be killed in a pagan land, preaching the good news of the Savior, than to stay in this swamp and one day die of malaria."

Then I remembered the brothers in Poland, and the thought gnawed at my conscience. But I answered myself with the same words Benedict used, whenever I came to him with some new idea: "I don't believe you!" he said. And he would mock me, quoting the prophet, "Wait and wait, a little more, a little more!"[2]

After a few days I finally made up my mind. The abbot encouraged me to go, and so with willing spirit but lagging feet I reached Rome at last. I had an audience with the pope and obtained his permission to preach the gospel.

Then I took the main route north, and after a toilsome journey over sea and land, I arrived in Regensburg, a city whose ancient name is Ratisbon, which means "good root." I ought to have continued on to Poland, where Benedict and John were anxiously waiting for me. But as a war was on, and the roads were filled with enemy troops, I turned my steed in the opposite direction. Of my unfulfilled promise and my dishonesty toward the brothers, not a shadow of memory remained in my heart.

I dismissed the idea of going to preach to the Prussians, even though the martyrdom of Saint Adalbert at their hands gave a better reason for going there than anywhere else. And so I boarded a ship and sailed east down the Danube toward the land of the Black Huns. I started to preach the gospel there, in the midst of unfavorable circumstances which I was too weak to deal with.

I kept saying to myself, "I shall give 'no sleep to my eyes, nor rest to my weary head'[3] until I find Christ." The search for Him must absorb all our energies, day and night— especially at night, when fear robs us of our peace. As long as we have the inner strength to seek God, we must, with His help, devote all our thoughts and our best efforts to this quest.

I have no way of knowing whether my Maker will take me soon. At that time, two years ago, I was "far from salvation."[4] But the moment was close when God's servants, according to His merciful will, would bravely suffer and merit their reward. I, a dog, was not worthy to be with saints, nor was I worthy to have pearls cast before me, a swine. It was my fault and no one else's. I was unwilling to make the journey to Poland.

There they waited, day and night. They were waiting for me, and I was not fit to be numbered with the saints, nor to join the company of the elect. I was a miserable Sarabaite,[5] following my own will, and all I cared about was keeping up appearances. So "I abandoned my honor to strangers, and my life to the cruel."[6] My law is what I like to do, and my pleasure is to let my lusts lead me in the ways of the world and make me a slave of many lords. I ought to be seeking my salvation, but I follow my fickle heart, lest God save me. "To the crooked You show yourself crooked."[7] "His delight is with corruption, that he might forget mercy."[8]

To forget mercy is the logical consequence of a corrupt life.

---

[1]Job 7,1; most of Bruno's quotations from Job are not taken directly from the biblical text, but from the *Moralia* of Gregory the Great.

[2]Isaiah 28,13.

[3]Cf. Psalm 132 (Latin 131), 4-5.

[4]Cf. Psalm 22 (21), 2.

[5]In chapter 1 of Saint Benedict's Rule, the Sarabaites are the third and worst kind of monks, the pseudo-hermits who reject the community and live according to their own whims and pleasure.

[6]Cf. Lamentations 5,2.

[7]Cf. Psalm 18 (17), 27.

[8]Cf. Job 24,20.

10. WITH TEARS AND SIGHS

Interwoven with typical hagiographic themes (monastic discretion, thirst for martyrdom), the pathos of the brothers' plight colors Bruno's story more and more. Benedict's Neapolitan emotionalism has nothing in common with Stoic "apatheia" or with the "impassibility" and "indifference" exalted in the lives of other saints. And yet, for Bruno, Benedict's inner torment is a sign of his sanctity, of that human integrity which is a fruit of God's grace in those who abandon themselves to the divine will. Benedict is totally himself, totally in touch with his emotions, and totally given to Christ.

Just as Bruno speaks of going on mission as "seeking Christ," so here the practice of discretion, the monastic virtue par excellence, characterizes the way the mission is conducted. At this point it should be abundantly clear that evangelization, from Saint Benedict himself at Monte Cassino, to the first Saint Boniface and Saint Lioba in Germany, to our own Bruno-Boniface, is an integral dimension of early (sixth to eleventh century) Benedictine spirituality and practice. But there is a specifically monastic way to evangelize: with discretion. In other words, it is often more monastic to discard the monastic habit in favor of lay clothing, than it is to preserve the habit for the sake of "identity"; it is always more monastic to sing the Liturgy in the language of the people (in the case of our brothers, the Slavonic Roman rite), than it is to use the Latin, simply because it creates an aura of "mystery." Above all, it is monastic to show delicacy and respect not only towards the persons we are called to evangelize, but also toward their culture, in all its various expressions: this is what Bruno means by "discretion."

Christian martyrs imitate Christ: they do not provoke their "enemies" to kill them, and thus add sin to sin, but they offer their own lives that both the martyrs and the martyrs' slayers may be one in the enjoyment of eternal life. Above all, true martyrs always say, with Jesus, "Father, forgive them, for they know not what they do"; forgiveness and prayer for enemies, rather than "courage" or Stoic fortitude, is the criterion of authentic Christian martyrdom.

Benedict, the citizen of heaven, was in no way like me; he held fast to the truth and kept his promises. Since I was unwilling to come to him, God inspired him to go looking for me. Duke Boleslaw gave him ten pounds of silver for the trip.

Someone had to stay home, and this was John. He was the one best suited to take charge of the monastery and keep it in the service of God and right doctrine, since his first fervor had led him straight to the hermitage. John's desire to enter the third stage[1]—the preaching of the gospel—was less intense than Benedict's, but this was probably because John was by nature more patient. Things that would trouble Benedict's soul he would accept with equanimity, waiting for God to make clear His will. But he understood Benedict's holy restlessness; John shared the hurt his brother's sensitive nature had suffered on account of the wound I had inflicted on our friendship.

I am convinced that if you searched throughout Christendom, you could hardly find anyone equal to Benedict in the love of Christ, and surely no one greater than he. In whatever he did, he sought his Lord's approval and no one else's. He did what he knew to be acceptable in God's eyes, no matter how difficult or painful it was. Benedict could well say, "I do not make my life dearer to me than my self."[2] This alone was the reason for his obsession with obtaining the pope's letter, or with finding me, if I had obtained it. His saintly soul was troubled and in anguish and deprived of all solace. He was all tears and sighs.

Benedict's fellow saint, blessed John, humbly submitted to God's judgments and patiently accepted events as they happened. Thanks to his innate wisdom and God's grace, it was easier for him to restrain his emotions; and if things could not be as he wished, he wished them to be as they were. Benedict, impatient with the slow passage of time, was battered by wave upon wave of emotion. Unable to accept his lot in life, he was at war with himself, afraid that his holy desire might be frustrated and that his hope might fail to attain its crown.

If Benedict had stayed in Italy, he could have borne as much fruit for the gospel there as in Poland. But instead he crossed mountains, rivers, and plains to come to a land whose tongue he did not know. By now, however, he did understand Polish and spoke it well enough. Both he and John wore their hair short and had adopted the sort of clothing worn by the local people, so as to be acceptable to the pagans and not to turn them away by the strangeness of their attire. Benedict wanted to appear like the Polish people in what he wore and the way he lived, so that it would be easier for them to accept the gospel. By creating favorable circumstances and approaching them with discretion— always a necessary virtue—he could then guide them in the way of salvation.

So Benedict left the hermitage where, like a good farmer, he had tilled the soil of solitude. His heart set on finding me, he went forth joyfully, burning the road under his feet. He crossed the Polish border into Bohemia, then a battlefield, and entered its capital, once-noble Prague, where good King Wenceslas the martyr lies buried and where many graces and miracles attest to his holiness. Saint Wenceslas, when worldly cares began to be too much for him to bear, fell in love with heaven; and his evil brother, who served a different lord, slew him like an innocent lamb.

Prague had also had a saint for a bishop: Adalbert, a rare breed of man, whose like today can hardly be found. His disobedient flock would not listen to him and drove him out of the city. So he went to Rome—or "Saint Peter's Garden" as devout pilgrims call it—where he took the monastic habit. When the people of Prague realized that, whether they wanted one or not, they needed a bishop to rule their church, they invited him back. Having promised to change their ways, they did not do so, and Adalbert was compelled once more to flee. Again he returned, but when they finally told him to his face, "We do not want you as bishop," he left for the third and last time, vexed by their evil behavior but happy for a more important reason.

Whatever befell him, Saint Adalbert felt no sorrow, since "all things work together for the good of those who love God."[3] And so he went to preach Christ to the pagans, who slew him with seven wounds. His wounds are the new grace and the great glory of our times.

Adalbert was a good bishop and a better monk, of fair speech and angelic mien, and his worthy life was crowned by martyrdom. The people of Prague would not listen to his preaching or imitate his life, and now, after his victory, they are at war, brother dying at the hand of brother. Having cut off the heads of the innocent, they now are powerless to save their own bodies from the sword. They have repented, but too late; now they wish Adalbert were once more at their head, but they cannot have him. For when he was their bishop they did not want him; their wicked deeds drove him away.

But although they have no merit for it, these evil Christians did perform a good service, when they sent their bishop to preach to others. For Adalbert gave the pagans eternal life by suffering at their hands. "Of great price in the sight of the Lord is the death of His saints."[4]

The just man Benedict entered guilty Bohemia and its ruined metropolis. He planned to continue his journey overland on foot, which would be easier if more tiresome than on horseback, since the main roads were closed on account of the war.[5] His thoughts were of me and of the sweet friendship that united us.

War raged like a winter storm, making travel impossible. Even unarmed messengers, in spite of the traditional law of immunity that protected them, could not reach their destination in safety. For this reason Duke Boleslaw had tried to dissuade Benedict from making the trip, even though he was glad to provide him with money for it. He was afraid that

Benedict might be caught in the crossfire or fall into enemy hands, and thus he, Boleslaw, would lose his most worthy subject. Because of his affection for Benedict, the duke put great confidence in him, and he would sooner grieve Benedict a hundred times than deprive himself of so powerful an advocate before God.

When Benedict saw that all ways to me were cut off, he sank into a deep state of depression (in fact, he was by nature inclined to melancholy). His motive for starting the trip was his love for me, and the bitter tears he shed at not being able to see me face to face were proof of his affection. From his eyes as from a great watershed flowed rivers of tears that furrowed his cheeks.[6]

He thought about the work he had come to do in Poland, and he blamed himself for the straits he was in, since what he desired could not come to him, and he was unable to go find it himself. He told himself that it was his own fault, because he had left Italy without considering the consequences. In his own country, he thought, he might have gained many souls for Christ. He sought and did not find; he lost what he had and bore no fruit. With every good intention he had come to Poland, but his efforts had been all in vain. Instead of disciples to comfort him with their brotherly love, he had enemies and almost total defeat. (He may have quoted to himself these verses of Scripture: "If you rightly offer but do not rightly discern, you have sinned."[7] "I will the good but do not find the way to accomplish it."[8] "Anyone can begin a good work; few are able to bring it to completion."[9])

Benedict's state of mind alternated between anger at Lord Boleslaw for not wanting him to go (after all, Benedict was not afraid, in spite of all the duke's talk about war conditions and enemy troops) and distress at me for my sinful negligence. Since I was then near Prague, I could have fulfilled my promise. (This was true, of course, but at that moment I was just not willing to face him.)

Yes, a sinner always hates to look a saint in the eye! How, then, can I ever face my Master in heaven, since I thought so little of His will and hurried to do my own with all the restraint of a wild horse?! I proposed to render spiritual service in such a way as not to lose earthly advantages. As an untrustworthy servant of Jesus Christ, I sought to win His love without hating this world and all its empty show. (Against myself I can say, "You failed as a statesman and did not succeed as a monk."[10] "Woe to the sinner who follows two ways on earth."[11] "No one can rejoice with the world and reign with Christ."[12])

---

[1]"...to enter the third stage" is not expressed in the Latin, but it is clear that Bruno is alluding once more to the schema *"cœnobium-solitudo-evangelium"* which inspired the mission of Romuald's disciples in Poland and elsewhere.

[2]Cf. the words of Paul at Ephesus, Acts 20,22-24.

[3]Romans 8,28.

[4]Psalm 116 (115),15; the sense of this verse is, "It costs the Lord dearly to see His saints die."

[5]The war, of course, was that waged by the new emperor, Henry II, with his pagan allies against Christian Poland.

[6]Cf. Vergil's *Æneid* 1,465.

[7]Genesis 4,7, according to the Greek (the LXX), most likely cited from Pope Saint Gregory's *Homilies on Ezekiel* 1,11.

[8]Romans 7,18.

[9]A vague reference, perhaps to I Corinthians 9,24 or to some medieval book of sentences which has not come down to us.

[10]Cf. Blessed John Cassian, *Institutes* book 7, ch. 19.

[11]Sirach 2,14, cited from Gregory's *Moralia* 1,36.

[12]Cf. Gregory, *Homilies on the Gospel*, book 1, hom. 12.

11. THE LONG WAIT

"Seeing their hopes dashed to pieces, they became fearful and anxious." Benedict and John have reached the limit of their human fortitude; their only refuge, their only solace, is in faith.

Our two brothers are not heroes. It is only as with a metaphor that the Church speaks of the "heroic charity" of her martyrs and saints. Without their faith, the two would be cowards; with their faith, and by the grace of God which is "made perfect in weakness" (II Corinthians 12,9), they will be able to meet death as martyrs, as witnesses to their Lord, who, in His weakness, cried, "Let this cup pass me by!" and "Why have You forsaken me?!"

Bruno takes the ambivalence of their fearfulness and their faith, the ambiguity of their situation in Poland as missionaries but also as instruments of imperial policy, and gathers it up into the story of Christ and of the apostolic Church. The tale of two tenth-century Italian monks in Poland comes to an end here; the rest of the book narrates a divine history of everywhere and always. The great utopia of the Acts of the Apostles—"Now the company of those who believed were of one heart and soul, and no one said that any of the things which he possessed was his own, but they had everything in common"—is realized once more ("and utopia, once realized, is no longer utopia, but reality," said Lanza del Vasto on his last visit to Camaldoli).

Monastic life, the Church, the "missions" exist for this and this alone: "That all may be one."

Benedict returned to Poland empty-handed, his heart filled with sorrow, his eyes with tears, his soul with great sadness. He and John received some solace, however, in the midst of the fire of affliction. Duke Boleslaw finally granted permission for [Barnabas,][1] one of the Polish brothers, to go to Rome. For the love of God he had become their novice; now he is the spiritual father of the community, having been elected abbot. So Brother [Barnabas] left for Rome, the world's chief city and mother of all the churches. Benedict ordered him under holy obedience to find me, wherever I was, since I was the one who had convinced them to come to Poland. If I had the pope's letter with me, he was to return immediately by the most direct route. If not, he was to ask me to appoint someone to accompany him to Rome, so that together they might request a copy of it. They were not to consider their mission completed otherwise.

When the outcome is certain, the lover's waiting is brief, but when it is not, the lover is filled with fear and the waiting seems long. Benedict tried to temper his sorrow and make this new pain more endurable, by specifying the exact date on which [Brother Barnabas] was to return: either the feast of All Saints [November 1] or at the latest the feast of Saint Martin [November 11]. But I think Benedict forgot—what with their urgent need and his own deep suffering—the teaching of the Holy Rule he had vowed to observe: that a monk should make no plans for the morrow. The same commandment is found in the Conferences of the Desert Elders.

So Benedict stayed in the hermitage and sent [Barnabas] to find me. That wretch, I mean myself, whose delay had caused them such sorrow, was nowhere to be found. Unable to trace my steps, [Barnabas] did the right thing and went straight to Rome to obtain the papal letter.

In the meantime, Benedict settled back into his usual routine and sought to sweeten the bitterness of his soul by renewing his desire for God. Having faced the harsh realities of the moment like a man, he found comfort in the thought of great treasure in the world to come. For him there was one true good among all that is good, one true happiness among all the things that promise happiness to mortals and make them run in vain: that is, the fear of the Lord.[2] This holy fear ruled his life and taught him to call on the living God in the midst of every affliction. It taught him to counter every wrong desire, born of disordered appetites, with the right renunciation, fruit of an authentic vision of reality.[3] Benedict knew that he possessed nothing on earth except his own self, and he had no desire for anything in this world but God. He kept his mind's eye fixed on eternal glory, which is all the wise live for. He dwelt on the night of unending punishment and on the blessedness of the kingdom to come and on the golden rule of discretion[4] and on the other virtues which lead us in the way to heaven.

Benedict and John spent the summer in anticipation of the feast of All Saints, steadfast in the observance of prayer and fasting, waiting like the apostles to be "clothed with power from on high."[5]

The two holy brothers lived in perfect harmony. Whatever one of them wanted, the other—even against his own preference—wanted it as well, whether it was a question of the cell or of work, of clothing or livelihood or prayer. If one of them expressed a desire, the other took care not to disagree with him, for the sake of brotherly love and to avoid all self-will. Together they loved God above every other good. Together they lived an orderly monastic life and gave themselves to prayer with a pure heart.[6] "They were of one heart and one mind."[7] "Behold how good and how pleasant it is, when brothers dwell in unity."[8]

All Saints' Day came and went, and Barnabas did not return. Seeing their hopes dashed to pieces, they became fearful and anxious. But their fear and anxiety were only for their own and others' salvation, not for what would become of them in this world. (They were experiencing what the Wisdom of Solomon says: "The corruptible body burdens the soul, and our earthly dwelling depresses our mind with many thoughts."[9])

Benedict and John were not worried about the uncertain outcome of human affairs. It was rather because of their great love for King Otto and their desire for his eternal happiness that they felt such sorrow, just as it was their affection for [Barnabas] that made them bewail his delay. They were afraid that both of us—[Barnabas] and myself—might have come to grief, and they wondered whether they would ever see us again in this life. In fact they never did.

They blamed themselves for whatever might have happened to Barnabas, and they beseeched our merciful God to hasten his and my return, in the words of the Psalm, "You are my patience, O my God, and my mercy."[10]

Deeply anxious and distressed, they said to one another, "If people trouble themselves for earthly goods which do not last, should we not be willing to endure our troubles, so as to obtain the true good which we shall enjoy for ever in heaven?" On and on they went, tormented by thoughts that allowed them no rest.

Every time they saw each other and shared their thoughts—which was always, since their love for one another made them inseparable—it was the same complaint: Why had I failed in my promise to come, and why had [Barnabas] not returned with the pope's letter? And they said, "All this time we have been waiting in vain. All our efforts have been wasted. We sweated over learning the Polish language, so as to make it easier for the people here to understand the gospel. We threw away our razors and made ourselves miserable by letting our beards grow—we even shaved our heads! We adopted their customs and started wearing their clothing, and we hoped they would accept us as their fellow countrymen, since our external way of life was like theirs.[11] We did all this so that we could either preach the gospel or suffer martyrdom for Christ's sake. (It does not matter which, since the one leads to growth in holiness and the other to eternal salvation.) But now, without the pope's permission, we can do nothing. Everything depends on his approval, and we sinners are obviously unworthy to receive it."

But on the contrary, God "will not forget the needy, and the hope of the poor will not perish for ever."[12]

---

[1]"Barnabas" is the name given to this brother by a contemporary chronicler, Cosmas of Prague. On his journey when the five brothers were slain, Barnabas ensured the continuity of the monastic community founded by John and Benedict. He was a priest when he became their novice.

[2]The biblical sense of this "fear" has often been misunderstood. It is certainly not that passion which is aroused by the proximity of unknown danger. Other biblical expressions, in fact synonyms, are: "to seek the

Lord's face"; "to serve the Lord"; "to wait for the Lord"; these all bear the same fundamental meaning as "to fear the Lord." In the Rule of Saint Benedict, the "fear of the Lord," that is, the sense of His constant presence, is the first of the twelve "degrees of humility" (chapter 7).

[3]"...right renunciation, fruit of an authentic vision of reality" is *"abrenuntiationis perfectum contemptum mundi,"* a highly technical expression which does not bear literal translation. "Contempt for the world" is a Semitic hyperbole, like "hating one's life in the world" in John 12,25. As a "vision of reality" it posits God's primacy over every other good and the world's radical contingency and insufficiency. This "contempt" becomes "perfect," in the gospel sense, when it is a "seeking first the kingdom of God"; then the monk practices "right" renunciation and receives the blessing of the "poor in spirit" (cf. Matthew 6,33.3).

[4]"Discretion" is the monk's "golden rule," and in Romuald's teaching it becomes the sine qua non for perseverance in the hermitage. Its opposite, as we have seen, is presumption, the typical vice of the novice, who in his first fervor takes for granted his understanding of the monastic calling and his ability to fulfill externally what he assumes to be its demands. Discretion, on the contrary, gives priority to a "strategy of perseverance," more demanding than any outward penance, since it requires that the monk continually humble himself, recognizing honestly his own limits.

[5]The Lent of All Saints, September 14 to October 31, is followed by the "recreation of Saint Martin," November 1 to 11, during which fasting is suspended, as in Easter time. It was during these recreation days that Barnabas was to arrive, bringing the authorization of the mission—a new Pentecost, as it were (cf. Luke 24,49).

[6]Benedict and John practice and exemplify "the good zeal which monks ought to have" (Rule of Saint Benedict, chapter 72).

[7]Acts 4,32. We are still in the climate of Pentecost. The image of the apostles, of the women, and of Mary the Mother of Jesus, gathered in the Upper Room, is the preferred model for the monastic community throughout the Middle Ages.

[8]Psalm 133 (132),1. In the eleventh century, there are no more fervent proponents of the cenobitic life than the disciples of Saint Romuald. In his letters to the Abbot Saint Hugh, Saint Peter Damian sings a veritable paean to the glory of Cluny.

[9]Wisdom 9,15, cited from, and in the sense of, Gregory's *Moralia* 20,3,8.

[10]Cf. Psalm 59 (Latin 58),17.

[11]On the inculturation of the gospel and of the monastic life, as practiced by our brothers, see above, chapter 10.

[12]Psalm 9,18.

12. IN THE BLOOD OF THE LAMB

"And what of those for whom heaven and earth are not enough, who cannot live except in anticipation of another heaven and earth? For those whose lives, such as they are, remain a dream, a curtain, a blank mirror, and who cannot accept that they will never understand what it really was all about? They will believe for the simple reason that the consummation of their desire can be expressed in no labile human tongue. Only one language can do justice to the highest claim of the human imagination—that of Holy Writ" (Czeslaw Milosz, The Land of Ulro *[N.Y.: Farrar Straus Giroux, 1984], pp. 267 f).*

There were two novices in the hermitage, blood brothers by the name of Isaac and Matthew. These two Poles were a mirror image of the two Italians, Benedict and John, noble offspring of noble parents.

Isaac and Matthew had sisters who had consecrated their virginity to God in a monastery of nuns. As monks, the two brothers began to experience that deeper bond of brotherhood which is a gift of the Spirit.

In the meantime, thieves were hatching a sacrilegious plot. Having heard about the ten pounds of silver which Duke Boleslaw had given Benedict, and supposing the brothers still had the money, they planned to steal it under cover of darkness. Night time, the friend of wickedness, would conceal their action.

It was the eve of one of the great feasts of the Christian Church, that of good Saint Martin the Almsgiver, and soon the brothers would gather in the chapel to sing the divine memorial—the Psalms of Vigils—and to celebrate the sacrament of salvation—the holy Mass.

The following is the account of one of the monks' servants, whom they sent to town for supplies on the afternoon [of November 10]. That evening their thoughts persecuted them more than usual. Like a couple of Greek poets, Benedict and John sang their endless elegy. "In vain we left our native country, in vain we traveled to a foreign land and spent our energies learning a strange tongue, so as to make war against paganism with the arms of Christ. All this was in vain, because we do not have the pope's letter, and there is no trace of the brothers who were to bring it here." And they repeated the Psalmist's lament: "Will God forget to have pity, or will He in His wrath shut up His mercy?"[1]

"O the depths of the riches of God's wisdom and knowledge and mercy!"[2] They had no way of knowing what was about to take place. There had been no word from Rome, and they had all but lost heart. Their anguished spirit groaned within them. But even if the pope's letter had been in their hands at that very moment, the martyrdom they so ardently desired would have been no nearer. They did not know what the Lord had in store for them. For He who brings forth good from the evil deeds of men, who has promised to heed those who ask in His name, and who never lies to His saints, intended to grant them their heart's desire.

"If He is slow in coming, wait for Him; He shall indeed come, and He will not delay."[3] "Can a mother forget to take pity on the child of her womb? Yet even if she should forget, I shall not forget you."[4] "For a little while I left you, and with great mercy I shall gather you again."[5] Thus says the Lord God, the hope of saints and their mighty fortress, who made all things good, who is great in His works, the Lord bright and fair, wondrous in His saints.

It was the dead of night; the brothers, sound asleep, were resting their weary bones. The band of assassins approached, eager to commit their terrible crime. Their hearts throbbed and their passions rose. Their lips trembled, their nostrils flared, and the blood raced in their veins. With quick feet, chattering teeth, hushed voices, flushed faces, sweaty palms, they brandished their weapons, greedy and eager for the easy fight like dogs for blood or wolves for prey.

They came with intent to do harm, but their very deed turned to the good of their victims. They hoped to gain something from it, but they gained nothing, for what they did was evil, very evil in the sight of God.

They came to do harm for harm's sake, and like the thief in the night they ended the day of life for the brothers, who had done harm to no one. Benedict had in fact accepted Boleslaw's money, but when he realized he could not complete his journey, he returned every penny of it. Benedict had no room in his heart for the love of money. But as for the thieves, "This is all they see in the whole wide world."[6]

All but one of the thieves were Christians, but even a pagan's religion would have made him hesitate to do what they were about to do. Without fear and without hesitation, these "Christians" were ready and willing to slay good men, and they gave no thought to the Scripture which says, "Do not place your hopes in iniquity, and even if riches abound, do not set your heart on them."[7]

Among the conspirators in this heinous crime (which would lead to such a precious death) was one pagan. He was to all intents and purposes their leader—and so expected a larger share of the spoils. He knew the brothers well, having been briefly in their service. He entered the monks' dormitory, careful to keep his weapon hidden. But before this, to overcome the fear which this unspeakable sacrilege aroused in him, he drank two goblets of strong liquor, as it were the devil's sacrament.

Suddenly the assassin appeared before the sleeping saints, a candle in his left hand, a club in his right, and a frightful look on his face.

The brothers sat up in bed. They broke their silence (necessity, in fact, breaks all rules), thinking more of unexpected guests than of anything else, since Christ was always in their hearts and upon their lips.

The following is the assassin's own description of the scene; he later did penance for his crime. "They started to whisper something to each other, but I don't know what they were saying." (Could it have been the verse which is said in the monks' chapter Office, "Of great price in the sight of the Lord is the death of His saints"[8]? But in our opinion, it was probably the Confiteor[9], since they were in immediate danger of dying that precious death.) The repentant murderer continued his story. "But I just stood there, dead in my tracks. I was going to kill them, and I was afraid of doing it."

When the brothers had finished whispering to each other whatever it was they wanted to say, John spoke up. (Patient Brother John, who was about to be sainted as a martyr, had the better command of both Latin and Polish, and he was the one who usually answered the door when visitors arrived.)

"My friend," he said, "why have you come? What is the meaning of all these men with weapons?"[10]

Astonished, the man who was about to kill him (and who now so deeply repents of the good he did by evil means) gave John this answer: "Our Lord Boleslaw sent us to arrest you, and he told us to show you no mercy!"

A smile crossed John's face. "The good prince loves God and us too much for him ever to have given such orders. What use is it to lie, my son?"

His murderer answered, "All right, we're going to kill you—that's why we're here!"

Saint John said, "God help you and us!"

The assassin, pale with fear, drew his sword and struck John twice, adding two wounds to the third, not so noble as the other two, which his body already bore (this was the eye he had lost to smallpox). Then the assassin turned to the other monks, and first among them the pearl of great price Blessed Benedict. With one blow he split Benedict's skull, and the jets of blood colored the walls in the corner where he fell, leaving bright stains which can still be seen today.

"May my soul die the death of the just."[11] As the hour of their death drew near, the brothers' sorrow was deeper than ever before. But even the God-Man Himself—our redemption, our salvation, our mercy—as He approached the Passion which, in His great love for us and for our salvation, He was about to suffer as a glorious sacrifice, declared to His disciples that He was weary and sorrowful unto death. He, the Word who in the beginning already was and who holds every living soul in His hands, to show that He was moved to compassion and was disposed to bear our sins,[12] said, "My soul is sorrowful unto death."[13]

The example of Our Lord is confirmed by that of His saints, and in a special way by the good and true Israelite, whose martyrdom was a ray of light in a dark age, Saint Adalbert. The Prussians would neither listen to him nor kill him, and this misfortune plunged him into the depths of sorrow. He ultimately blamed himself—although in no way was he at fault—for not being able to win their souls. But as Saint Adalbert's companions later testified, he never let his own sorrow be a burden on them, until finally the Prussians, by God's decree and in spite of themselves, turned their malice into a blessing and killed him.

The same thing happened in the case of our brothers. A short time ago they were sad beyond all measure; but God, who is the holy and faithful Friend of humankind, abounding in kindness and mercy, grants us in His own way much more than we can ask or even understand. The brothers were anxious to go out and seek martyrdom, but God gave it to them at home. Although it is highly dangerous to rush headlong into martyrdom or to come upon it unprepared, it is safe and holy to seek it in prayer as a gift of God.

Of the two Polish brothers whom Blessed Benedict and John had trained in monastic life and received into vows, Isaac was the next to be slain. He was a robust fellow, and he did not awake quietly like the others but began to yell, "God, help! God, help!" (A noble cry, according to the verse: "A mighty fortress is the name of the Lord; in Him the just will take refuge and be saved."[14]) Isaac stood up, as if to make a prayer, and he was struck on the shins by the sword; he then raised his hands to shield his body, and they received a second merciless blow ("The eye is drawn to what is loved, the hand to what hurts."[15]) At that moment he realized that Christ, who is the salvation of all who believe in Him, was about to bestow on him at home what he had longed to find elsewhere—death by martyrdom, whereby a sinner lays aside the great weight of sin, which clings so closely. Brother Isaac was filled with joy and cried out, "O happy night and blessed hour! It is not our merits; it is the mercy of the Lord!" (As in the Psalm: "My heart will rejoice in Your salvation; I shall sing to the Lord, who has been good to me."[16]) And then he said to his assailant, "May the Lord bless you for the good you are doing us." (Thus Isaac fulfilled the gospel word: "Bless those who persecute you and forgive them, for they know not what they do."[17]) Having said this, he received a blow on the neck and died.

When his murderers heard him bless them for all the evil they were doing, and when they beheld such goodness, and the gentle and peaceful way Isaac accepted death, only then, too late, did they begin to regret their deed and feel remorse, as if to say, "Woe to us—what are we doing?! We came to kill them, and they rejoice at being killed! No man has ever blessed his murderers as they do. But it is too late to change our plan; we have to go through with it. We must kill them all, or people will find out what we did and make us pay for it."

Here we see the miserable way sinners react to God's patience: since they know He will not punish them physically in this world, they ignore the intolerable sentence their souls may be subject to in the world to come. "It is a terrible thing to fall into the hands of God"[18] the Almighty!

Their next victim was Isaac's brother Matthew. Terrified by what was happening, he tried to get away, but they struck him dead in front of the church, and he fell face down as if prostrate in prayer.

The last to die was Christian, the monks' cook. His own brother was the one who had been sent to town that evening ("One will be taken, the other left"[19]) He took up a stick to defend himself, and he called to the brothers for help, not realizing that they could no longer hear him. Christian was an affectionate and pleasant-natured man, and since he had been generous in serving the monks, it was fitting that he, the fifth, should fall with the other four martyrs, and thus earn the favor of Him from whose fifth wound flowed blood and water[20], for our salvation and the forgiveness of our sins. He chooses to give the same wage to the last as to the first,[21] for He is good, and by His mercy each and all will be saved, regardless of their own merits.

The assassins expected to find money, and when they found none, they were filled with chagrin. So they used their swords to divide among themselves the Mass vestments; the brothers had brought these vestments from Italy along with other gifts from the emperor, such as the well-made books, which, however, the thieves did not touch. But they did take from the altar the antimension, which contained the relics of the saints.[22] They wrapped their booty in an oilcloth, and then they set fire to the walls of the church, in the hope that the flames might spread to the rooms in the enclosure and burn the bodies; so people would not cry, "Thieves! Murderers!" but would say, "The brothers died an accidental death."

But God's thoughts are not as those of men.[23] The church did not burn; the bodies of the saints are buried in peace; and God did not let the guilty remain hidden, even though no one lived to testify against them. Repenting too late, they fled faster than they had come; and to add to the burden of their guilty conscience, they heard, as soon as they were outside, the voices of the saints they had just slain, singing sweetly within the cloister. We know this fact from their sworn testimony, for they are now living in that same monastery as servants, paying their debt as best they can.

So they fought an unfair fight and fled as cowards; and the souls of the martyred brothers, whose noble lives were crowned with a deliverance they did not expect, were presented sinless and holy before the eternal and true God, Jesus Christ.

The martyrs lay, not where they had been sleeping, but where they had fallen to the sword. Except for their servant Christian, no one had tried to resist their attackers, but each of the brothers died a martyr's death, rejoicing in the Holy

Spirit. Matthew lay by the church, where he was fleeing to safety. Christian, while defending the innocent, fell in the middle of the compound. Isaac was rising to meet his martyrdom, and wounded three times by one sword, lay stretched full length on the floor like a penitent. John had fallen from his bed and crumpled to his knees; he looked as if he were praying. Only Benedict, the first among them, seemed to be lying asleep, although he too had yielded his spirit to God in a glorious death.

As the assassins fled the scene of the crime, they heard singing inside the monastery; so they returned to see if anyone was alive. The brothers were all dead, of course, but holy Benedict had pulled his hood over his head and turned over to face the wall. One of the murderers threw open the gate and rushed in, afraid of his own foul deed, afraid of finding them still alive, afraid that he would be punished for his crime. With trembling hand he touched their cold members and looked nervously at their pallid faces, but he could not find the least sign of life. They were, in fact, certainly dead. But just as the great Saint Denys the Areopagite, having been beheaded, was seen carrying his own head as angels sang, likewise, through his intercession, our little Saint Benedict was able, after his death, to turn over in bed and, lest he break the rule of monastic dress, to cover his bloodied head with his cowl.

It was a gloomy day that dawned on frail mortals. When the local villagers arrived for Mass, they found the gate still closed, but no one dared enter the enclosure. As the morning wore on and none of the monks came out, they all began to wonder what was happening inside. One of them, overcome by curiosity, peeked through the hedge and saw Christian lying dead in the courtyard. He was the innocent servant of the innocent,[24] a layman who had gladly rendered his service to the monks, and the merciful God, seeing the faith and love of the holy brothers, allowed Christian to be crowned with a joy equal to theirs.

Astounded, all the villagers rushed in to behold the monstrous spectacle. No one presumed to touch the saints' bodies with unclean hand or sinful heart, until all the facts concerning the crime of the night before had come to light.

It was not until the third day that, the bishop having been informed, word was sent throughout the recently Christianized territory and enough clergy and nuns were present to celebrate properly the funeral of the holy innocents. The forest nearby provided sufficient wood for their caskets, and the bishop ordered that a large grave be dug inside the church, even though there was barely enough room there for the four monks.

As soon as Bishop Unger [of Poznan], an old man rich in good will, arrived with his clergy, they celebrated a solemn Mass and sang the Divine Office. Then the bishop entered the holy place where the brothers lay and offered his heartfelt prayers and supplications. There he saw Benedict, the gem, the star, the ornament of them all, whose unfailing fervor had won them the Lord's blessing and the baptism of martyrdom. Benedict lay in the corner, to your right as you enter the building; he was lying on his side with his face to the wall, having assumed that position after his happy death, as it were to make himself more comfortable. His noble head was toward the south, his venerable feet toward the north (like the winds in the Song of Songs: "Arise, O north wind, and come, O south wind, and blow upon my garden, that its fragrance may be wafted abroad,"[25] as if to say: "Go back, Satan, and come, Holy Spirit, fill my soul, that its sweetly smelling virtues may appear"). Those who had died with him lay where they had fallen by chance, or rather, where they remained at prayer. And from Benedict's head, more precious than gold, came the ruddy tint that colored the walls; even his cowl was found to be soaked with blood ("He has washed his robe in wine, and his cloak in blood"[26]).

So with prayer and song, as is fitting, the bishop devoutly accompanied the bodies of the saints to their grave. They were buried in one tomb, first the two Italians and then the two Poles. It was Saturday, the day Our Redeemer, the Son of God, rested in His tomb, after He had redeemed a lost world by His Passion and, for our salvation, had slain death by His death.

In the middle of the church they buried the noble flower of youth, Benedict, and the admirable child of glory, John. At the back, along the side walls, were the other two, whom the grace of God had recently called to monastic life and had made worthy of martyrdom. ("The virtues hold the central place, but for the disciples there is praise at the end."[27])

Since he had tried to defend himself with a stick, Christian was thought to be less of a saint than the others. So they buried him in the cloister outside the church (thinking perhaps of the verse: "Do not yoke the ox with the ass,"[28] that is, the wise with the foolish). But not very long after the funeral they exhumed Christian's body and found him incorrupt, as if he were still alive, and without the least odor of decay. This discovery was followed by a sudden cloud-burst, and the rain forced the workers to take shelter. So the monks carried him into the church and buried him there, after his elders, that in death as in life he might remain united with them. ("There is no distinction between Jews and Greeks, slave and free,"[29] for we are all one in Christ.) They opened the monks' tomb to place him there, and although considerable time had elapsed, the undecayed flesh of the holy brothers gave off no odor of death, much less the heavy stench that rises from the putrid flesh of sinners, after even one day.

---

[1]Psalm 77 (Latin 76),10.

[2]Romans 11,13.

[3]Habakkuk 2,3.

[4]Isaiah 49,15.

[5]Isaiah 54,7.

[6]A maxim perhaps from some medieval hagiographic text which has not come down to us.

[7]Psalm 16 (15),11.

[8]Psalm 116 (115),15.

[9]The penitential rite which precedes Mass or Compline.

[10]Cf. the words of Jesus in the garden, when they came to arrest Him, Matthew 26,50-55.

[11]Numbers 23,10.

[12]This phrase is from the Latin hymn for the feast of the Ascension.

[13]Matthew 26,38 and Mark 14,34.

[14]Proverbs 18,10.

[15]Not from the Bible, this expression is a common medieval Latin proverb.

[16]Psalm 13 (12),6.

[17]Bruno joins Romans 12,14 with Luke 23,24.

[18]Hebrews 10,31.

[19]Matthew 24,40 and Luke 17,34.

[20]Cf. John 19,34.

[21]Cf. Matthew 20,14.

[22]*"Pallium de altare tulerunt, in quo erant reliquiæ"*: a *pallium* is a pall, a cloth covering, and not an altar stone; hence our translation *"antimension."* This is one of several clues to the liturgical practice of the brothers in Poland. It is likely that they celebrated the Eucharist according to the "Liturgy of Saint Peter" or *Missa glagolithica*, which is the Roman rite of Mass—with the addition of some Byzantine elements—translated into Old Slavonic by Saint Cyril of Thessalonica, co-apostle (with his brother Saint Methodius) to the Slavs. This liturgy was commonly used in Bohemia at the time of Saint Adalbert. In fact, the *Missa glagolithica* was celebrated there, one day every year, up to the eve of the Second Vatican Council. Poland soon lost the privilege of the Slavonic Mass, but Sunday Vespers and other Church rites continued to be celebrated in the language of the people.

[23]Cf. Isaiah 55,8.

[24]Cf. Sirach 44,14.

[25]Song of Songs 4,16; the allegorical interpretation is from Pope Saint Gregory's *Moralia* book 9.

[26]Cf. Genesis 49,11.

[27]Source uncertain; perhaps a lost hagiographic text.

[28]Cf. Deuteronomy 22,10, according to the interpretation given by Saint Gregory, *Homilies on Ezekiel* 2,7.

[29]Galatians 3,28; Saint Paul adds, of course, "there is neither male nor female, for you are all one in Christ Jesus."

13. LIGHTS IN THE SKY

This and the following chapters put our twentieth-century rationalism and pragmatism to the test. Bruno's story fascinated us, as long as his attention was focused on the deeds and the inner struggles of John and Benedict and the others. Now he would have us listen to his account of the miracles that followed the Brothers' death, and our Cartesian-Newtonian paradigm automatically raises its guard. Even as believing Christians, we find ourselves resisting his message.

What can we say? It may help a little to realize that Bruno of Querfurt is exercising considerable restraint; he limits the miraculous strictly to that which eyewitnesses of the events related to him personally, and even then he is selective. It may help a bit more, if we keep in mind the liturgical-sacramental reference of all these "signs and wonders." Eyes and ears accustomed to seeing all things as "sacrament" are more open to synchronicities and psychic events which we would either ignore or attempt to explain away.

There is another theme present in these chapters: we might call it a sort of "liberation theology," a vision of the relation between the saints' gospel witness and certain social realities. As in life, so in death, the Brothers are on the side of the poor, including the "poor sinners" who killed them. All the wonders that follow their death are signs of a divine compassion that pardons every fault and liberates every guilty conscience, while showing unyielding severity toward the superficiality and cynicism into which clergy and religious often fall.

Here is something we must not pass over in silence. It was the darkest hour of the night, and two boys were keeping vigil over the saints' bodies, singing the holy Psalms. All of a sudden, John, who lay beside his brother Benedict, turned over on his side. One of the youths, overcome by panic, fled from the church. But the other, realizing that this was a sign from heaven, kept on singing. (This lad is now a monk and serves as deacon in the monastery church.[1]) So it happened that what Benedict did right after his death, John did in his casket.

This was the first of many signs and graces which God has continued to grant since the re-establishment of the monastic community, on account of the holy brothers' merits.

On Saturday, after the washing of the feet which the monks celebrate as a reminder of the Lord's commandment to love one another[2], the whole community saw a candle burning brightly at the saints' tomb, although no one had lit a candle there. This same light appeared several times thereafter, so as to show how brightly their souls shine in heavenly joy before the glorious face of God, and to make this known on earth in a way that human eyes could see.

If this fact of the candle is not unusual enough, I can tell you about another miraculous light which the saints lit; a number of eyewitnesses still living in the nearby village can testify to it. The Saxon king, [Henry II], was moving with a large and powerful army against the village, and everyone was convinced that the whole countryside was in peril. But at midnight there appeared a large, bright circle of light that hovered over the church and illuminated the entire courtyard; it remained there for no less than an hour. The same prodigy was repeated a year and a week after their martyrdom; the light above the church was fully as bright as the first one.

When the first light appeared, the people understood that the martyrs were protecting their land; in fact, [King Henry's] army passed through without doing any damage. When the miracle was repeated, it became quite evident that under the simple tombstone in the church was hidden a heavenly treasure. No one could doubt that the brothers were indeed saints, and that whenever their intercession was devoutly sought, mercy would flow out from the monastery over the whole land.

On another occasion, one of the monks and a lay person were asleep near the church. They were startled into wakefulness by a great light; to their amazement they heard singing and the voice of one who was reading the passage of the gospel that ends: "Enter into the joy of your Lord!"[3]

---

[1]This is Stephen, spoken of below, chapter 19.

[2]Cf. Rule of Saint Benedict 35.   [3]Matthew 25,21.

143

14. ARISE AND WALK!

In the monastery there was a monk [by the name of Stephen], who now officiates there as deacon. For a long time he had been suffering from a disease of the bones which left him paralyzed, and he was unable to come to church.

Then one night Benedict and John, surrounded with heavenly splendor, came to another member of the community who was catching a few winks of sleep. With shining faces they said, "You must chide Brother Stephen for his long absence from church. Why is he so lazy? He loves his bed too much! He should get up and come to choir with the community."

That morning the monk who had dreamt the dream I just described saw Brother Stephen up and about, while the previous day he lay close to death from his illness. To the amazement of the dreamer, Stephen had been healed while he slept. No sooner had the merciful physicians given their order, than Stephen was healed, rose from his bed, and walked to the church as if he had never lost the use of his limbs. This clearly shows how compassionately attentive the martyrs are to the needs of those who, in their honor, serve God day and night in the monastery. (Remember the Lord's saying: "Seek first the Kingdom of God, and all these things will be added unto you"[1]—that is, whatever you truly need.)

There is no way of knowing—for they are too numerous, thanks be to God—how many persons have been freed from every sort of demonic influence by the brothers' merits. And we are simply too lazy—shame on us—to count the number of prisoners liberated, by their good graces, from every sort of chain and shackle, material or spiritual. It is clear that, although they live in eternity, they care for the temporal welfare of those who serve God as they did, and even of those who are more spiritually than materially needy, since their faith is weak, but who nevertheless rejoice in the belief that now God has five more saints in heaven. (For Jesus said of a great sinner in the gospel, "Great as her sins were, they are forgiven, for her love was great."[2])

---

[1] Matthew 6,33.　　　　　　[2] Luke 7,47.

15. MASTER WOLF

Now to return to Brother [Barnabas], whom our saints, while still living, sent to Rome: when he came with the papal document, he found that the brothers' story had already had its happy ending, that is, they had been martyred and were gone straight to heaven. But I, whom Benedict in his goodness and great affection used to call "my brother," had obtained the same document before all this, although the brothers did not know it.

Our Redeemer's merciful will had been fulfilled in His saints; so Brother [Barnabas] returned to Rome with the news of their martyrdom. The pope, having carefully examined the matter, concluded that the five brothers were without doubt martyrs and ordered that they be venerated in their monastery.

I, the gyrovague[1], was nowhere to be found. In fact, [Barnabas] made his second trip to Rome not only to convey the news of the brothers' death but also to seek information about my whereabouts. The Saxon, [Henry II], was making war on Poland, and when [Barnabas], accompanied by good Bishop Unger, passed through the territory under his control, [Henry] was afraid they were spies and had them arrested. [Barnabas] was sent to Magdeburg under guard and locked up in a monastery. One night his fitful sleep was interrupted by a vision of John and Benedict. They scolded him severely for the few days he had spent in the monastery, even though he was imprisoned there against his will.

They told him, "One of the two men you put in charge of the monastery has left; the other will leave too, if you do not return immediately."

Barnabas had, in fact, entrusted the care of the martyrs' shrine to two clerics in his absence. So he did not hesitate for a minute. Trusting in the saints' help, he fled under cover of darkness. He passed undetected through the thick of enemy troops and arrived home safe and sound (as the angel said of Tobias, "I shall lead him and bring him back in safety"[2]).

The cleric's leaving the shrine was typical behavior for our times, in which people are in love with themselves and "the charity of many grows cold."[3] The young man was unstable and an easy prey for self-deception. He let himself be overcome by homesickness and left the martyrs' shrine without the slightest twinge of conscience. As he was happily on his way home, a wolf crossed his path and turned to face him, growling and baring its fangs. The cleric went pale with fear. He lost his voice, his feet would not move, his limbs shook, his hair stood on end, and his knees started to buckle. Terrified at the thought that his end was near, he began to wish he were back in the monastery, which a short time before he had been glad to leave.

You can see this same attitude in people caught in a thunderstorm. The lightning, whose serpentine flash threatens sudden and ruthless death, frightens them, and they start wishing they had done the good deeds they omitted and done better the few good deeds they did. Now they are willing—too late and for fear of hell—to undergo greater hardships for the love of God.

So our young cleric finally learned his lesson, thanks to his lucky misfortune in meeting good Master Wolf. In the secret place of his heart—where every human conscience is brought face to face with God[4]—he thought, "If only I could escape from the bloody jaws of that terrible beast, how happy I would be to return to the martyrs' shrine!" He called on them by name, not once but many times, and promised that never again—unless, after careful consideration, he saw it was better to do so—would he leave the monastic enclosure.

Because the saints love us, they forgive us; because they desire our good, they turn to our benefit even the threat of death. In order that their servant might behold their power, our holy martyrs sent the wolf back into the woods faster than he had come. ("If God is for us, who shall be against us?"[5] "After such prodigies, tell me, O Nature, where are your laws?"[6])

The wayward cleric did not wait any longer. Like the prodigal son he returned to the monastery and to his spiritual father, [Barnabas,] just back from Magdeburg. The young man made amends and, to the joy of the elder monk, told the story of how the saints had miraculously saved him from the wolf.

"I was on my way to my 'home, sweet home,'" he said, "sure that nothing would happen to me. As I walked along the familiar path, suddenly there appeared before me a ravenous wolf. I was sure I was going to be killed. I called on the saints with all my heart, for I knew that if they helped me, I would get back to the monastery. And so my life was saved, and my soul as well." Barnabas and the lad had arrived together, although by different routes, and together they rejoiced that a son was restored to his father by the grace of the Son of God and for His glory. ("All shall know me, from the least even to the greatest."[7] "As is the life of the father, so also the life of the son is mine."[8])

---

[1]Just as "Sarabaites" (Rule of Saint Benedict, chapter 1) are pseudo-hermits, living "private lives" and doing no one's will but their own, so "gyrovagues" are pseudo-cenobites, staying a while in one monastery, until they get tired of the food or the company, and then moving on to another. Bruno's calling himself a gyrovague is, of course, just his usual breast-beating.

[2]Cf. Tobit 5,15.

[3]Matthew 24,12.

[4]Literally, "where the God who sees weighs every human person": *intus in archano cordis, ubi omnem hominem pensat videns Deus.*

[5]Romans 8,31.

[6]Bruno again cites a source unknown to us.

[7]Jeremiah 31,34.

[8]Ezekiel 18,4.

16. THE SAINTS DO NOT PLAY GAMES

After the saints' burial, a priest was sent to the monastery to celebrate the hours of the Divine Office. One night he invited his altar boys over for a party, and they began to eat and drink in the very room where the brothers had died. Suddenly a noise like thunder or an earthquake shook the house to its foundations. Their hearts leapt to their throats and their blood froze; the boys stopped their game and were silent. But after a moment they got over their fright, and the priest encouraged them to return to what they were doing.

But once more God's wrath was revealed against those who without shame abandoned themselves to joking, laughter, and drunkenness in the very place where angels had sung for joy at the death of the saints. Again came thunder, warning of terrible punishment. The entire building rose from its footing and seemed about to fly off into space, as if it could not bear the outrage of hearing empty chatter in the place where God had fulfilled His word of truth.

This was the first sign of the martyrs' holiness manifested after their burial.

Then one Sunday an elderly priest who had become a novice, Moses by name, made a mistake at Mass as the brothers came to receive the kiss of peace, and did not follow the proper ceremony. The sacristan was standing near the saints' tomb, and when he saw the priest's confused movements, he started to laugh (this is an illness common to monks who do not practice inner discipline).[1] All of a sudden the monk felt a jabbing pain pierce his heart like an arrow. He fell backwards, convinced that his knife had stabbed him, but when he reached for it, he found he was not even carrying a knife. Moaning with pain, he realized that he had sinned against God in the presence of His saints.

The laughter of ridicule is from the devil; the monk who gives himself to easy laughter no matter what the circumstances commits a serious sin, and it is very serious if he laughs during prayer and psalmody, in the sight of the angels of the Lord God.[2] Of the Lord, who came down from heaven to save us, it is often said that He wept, but never that he laughed.[3]

---

[1] One of the "tools of good works" in the Rule of Saint Benedict 4,53, is that a monk "speak no foolish chatter, nothing just to provoke laughter."

[2] The translation depends on the punctuation of the Latin text. If we read *"...cum sit diabolicum irridere, monachum facile ridere omni loco grave peccatum est...,"* then our translation stands. If, however, we place the comma after *"monachum"* instead of *"irridere,"* then we must translate, "Since it is diabolical to laugh at a monk, it is a grave sin to give oneself to easy laughter no matter what the circumstances..."

[3] This is an ascetical commonplace, but it cannot be sustained on the grounds of biblical exegesis. A number of recent authors have pointed out the numerous instances of humor and wit in the Bible and, in a special way, in the gospels (see Elton Trueblood, *The Humor of Christ* [New York: Harper & Row, 1964]).

17. ANDREW'S DREAMS

This chapter has a theological density which the space of a single note does not allow us to elaborate. Enough to say that no more interesting implications for Liberation Theology can be found in any other medieval hagiographic text. The anti-capital-punishment and anti-war stance of Bruno of Querfurt is echoed in Peter Damian as well; the parallelism between two writers separated by a full forty years seems to suggest that these ideas were implicit (or perhaps even explicit) in their common sources, among which were the teachings of Master Romuald himself.

A certain brother by the name of Andrew, when he heard of the martyrs' death, was pierced to the heart with compunction. So he abandoned self-will and entered the monastery which Duke Boleslaw was having built over the brothers' tomb, and for which he had appointed [Barnabas] as abbot. Andrew lived there with great simplicity as a layman, but his intention was to spend his life in the monastery.

One night, when he had been there a year, he was asleep in his cell, and all of a sudden he was awakened, as if someone had pulled the cover off his bed. He jumped out of bed and ran to open the window; there he beheld the following vision. The entire courtyard was bathed in light, and in the midst stood the holy brothers. Then they began to walk; the humble Benedict was preceded by the blessed John, who carried in his right hand a large torch and on his left arm a book. A thurible hung from the ring finger of John's left hand, sending up clouds of incense that filled the courtyard.[1] He heard the doors of the church swing open. Andrew was the one who kept the keys to the church, and his first thought was that the novice master must have come and taken them, and then gone into the church with the saints. Overwhelmed with panic, he groped around for the keys and found them still hanging from his belt. Now more frightened than ever, he went back to bed and hid himself under the covers.

The two saints came to him again. In a dream Andrew saw them just as they had appeared to him while he was awake, with shining faces and robes white as snow, carrying the same torch and censer. They ordered him first to go tell the abbot; then Benedict gave him this message for Duke Boleslaw: "We have already appeared several times, even to lay persons; why do you still not believe? By God's power we have freed many prisoners from shackles and stocks, sometimes even shattering the chains that bound them. These miracles, if not the fear of God, should have convinced Boleslaw to immediately set free those he had cast into prison. Even the men who killed us—who in spite of their malice brought us great happiness—ought to suffer no harm; Boleslaw must not confiscate their goods or drive their wives and children into exile. Let him rather destine these men to the service of the monastery, so that they may repent and live. Say to Boleslaw, 'We did you honor by coming to your land, where we have found the great mercy of our loving Savior. You humbly supplied our needs as long as we were in the flesh; now you must finish the great work you have begun. Do as we tell you: free those you have imprisoned and show mercy to the men who killed us. You may build churches wherever you like; but we command you now to build one over our cell, where our monastic family will gather to worship every Sunday. If you do as we tell you, you know that we shall protect you with our love; and by our intercession you will receive many graces from God during your lifetime.'"

With these words the dream ended; the saints withdrew from Andrew's eyes into the chapel, and from the chapel into heaven.

The abbot, however, realized that Boleslaw was little inclined to believe in miracles and would have given no credence to a dream; so he did not permit Andrew to tell him about it. ("They trembled with fear, where there was nothing to fear."[2])

Andrew had another vision, soon after he had been clothed as a monk. He was working in the garden for the community, when suddenly the cloudless sky resounded with a great thunderclap, and the two saints came walking toward him. Andrew threw down the mattock and fell at their feet like a dead man.

They rebuked him. "Why did you not do as we ordered you? Forget the abbot and go directly to Lord Boleslaw. Tell him exactly what we said to you in the dream." They repeated their previous instructions and admonished him severely to obey them.

Andrew later said that, at the moment of his vision, he understood nothing but what he heard with his ears. Totally confused, he tried to ask them something, but the saints silenced him with a gesture. (Since "praise is unbecoming in the mouth of a sinner"[3]; it is very dangerous for a man of unclean lips to speak to the holy ones.)

Then they said, "Open the church. If the brothers want to sing Mass, we will listen to them." Andrew could not tell where they were; their voices seemed to come from behind him. He turned and saw some guests approaching; they wanted to attend Mass. The martyrs were no more to be seen. Struggling to regain his senses, Andrew unlocked the church for the visitors, and once inside he fell prostrate on the tomb of the saints.

He heard what seemed like the sound of their footsteps behind the altar.

---

[1]An interesting liturgical detail: note that, in the absence of a deacon, the celebrant of the Divine Liturgy of Saint John Chrysostom (the "Byzantine rite") carries the thurible in this manner during the entrance procession with the gospel book (the "Little Entrance").

[2]Psalm 14 (13),5.

[3]Sirach 15,9.

18. AN AROMA OF INCENSE

After this terrifying vision, the priest Christopher was vesting for Mass, and an intense fragrance, like that of the incense used for the Liturgy, began to fill the entire cloister. As he remembered it afterwards, Christopher said that the aroma was so strong that it took his breath away. So with contrite heart and the fear of God he celebrated the Mass, during which was heard once again the thunderclap that heralded the saints' presence; and the stone cover of their tomb seemed to leap into the air.

On another occasion the brothers were at table, but one of them, Paul, remained behind in church, praying. He too saw the same vision as Andrew, according to what is said of the unseen God, "With the simple He is in secret intimacy."[1]

Once more God in His goodness showed how agreeable in His eyes was the life of the martyrs. It happened that the monks were burning some reeds along with the wicker baskets woven by the saints; everything else burned, but their baskets remained intact, as if to say, "You have tried me by fire and found no iniquity in me."[2]

From Hungary there arrived one day a promising novice, ready for every obedience and of great purity and simplicity of life. One night he saw a light as bright as the sun that illuminated the entire church, and he heard voices singing sweetly and softly, "Hosanna, hosanna!" And the church was filled with an aroma that spread throughout the courtyard. Realizing that such wonders had been shown to him a sinner, he wanted to run away and hide.

All the brothers who joined the monastery in the early days are witnesses to these facts, especially good Brother Anthony[3], who saw the first miracle, and Paul, a man of great simplicity and purity, of whom we have just spoken. "But now," the brothers say, "since the community has increased in numbers, we no longer enjoy these favors. Then it seemed that we were in Paradise; our one comfort and our only desire was to go to the chapel and remain there in prayer, forgetting even to eat or drink. Now we no longer see any miracles, on account of our sins; but formerly, by day and by night, we smelled a sweet fragrance everywhere, and we saw thick clouds of incense floating not only throughout the church but in the whole monastery."

Then there was a man in prison, tormented by his chains. One night, during that sleep which makes us momentarily forget our ills and offers us some little relief, two heavenly beings suddenly appeared to him and ordered him to get up. It was the two holy brothers, and with one voice they commanded him to arise and follow them. He sighed and said he was not able to do so. At that, the saints touched his chains with the tips of their fingers; the chains broke into pieces, scattering fragments outside the cell. Fully awake now, the prisoner realized that he could move freely, and he ran off after his liberators, whom he saw before him in bodily form.

In their goodness, the saints are at work in heaven, praying for our salvation. Having freed a prisoner from bodily chains, they sent him on his way, ordering him to go to the monastery and offer thanks to God. And they told him to fear no more, as it is written, "The Lord is my light and my salvation: whom shall I fear?"[4]

---

[1] Cf. Proverbs 3,34.

[2] Psalm 17 (16),3.

[3] Anthony, or Tuni, was a relative and confidant of Boleslaw; he later became abbot of the monastery.

[4] Psalm 27 (26),1. This paragraph offers us another example of Bruno's "Liberation Theology." The text echos a number of passages in the gospels and the Acts of the Apostles (especially Acts 12,1-11).

19. FINISHING TOUCHES

In Bruno's last chapter, Master Romuald appears once more, as it were a literary inclusion, framing the story of his disciples. Brother John recites the master's "Little Rule," a cento of maxims from early monastic writers, striking in its use of metaphor (the monk as a fisherman, the Holy Spirit as a mother bird). Of Brother Benedict it is said that he would never speak ill of anyone, nor listen to others speak ill of those who are absent, as earlier it was said of John Gradenigo, through whom he had met Master Romuald.

It should be noted that every time the saints appeared, only Benedict and John were seen, and not the other three. This is evidently because their common glory, which is after all a gift of God, fell especially on the holy life and even holier desires of these two.

They were martyred on the same day when Saint Menna, uttering sublime prophecies in Greek, endured the same fate; and Saint Martin, the precious confessor of the Lord and gem of the priesthood, who while on earth shared part of his garments with Christ, this day in heaven put on fully the same Lord Jesus, who is the life of the angels and the Lover of humankind. (Even in our own time, Saint Martin continues to bestow on France the fruits of his merits, with countless signs and graces.[1])

The day of our brothers' martyrdom was a Thursday, that same day on which the Lord of glory ascended with great triumph into heaven, leading captivity captive and bestowing on fallen humanity redemption from death and a share in the peace and joy of the angels. This was the day when Our Redeemer gave to us, the redeemed, the cup of salvation, His own Body and Blood, our one hope in the emptiness of our misery. This was the day when the Creator of the world washed the feet of His disciples, showing us, by the great honor of His sublime humility, what love truly is. This day there died in God's love "two united with three, and three inseparable from the other two."[2]

These were the two brothers, John and Benedict, brothers in spirit and in truth. Their virtue was measured not in the quantity of time but in the quality of their fervor: only a short time were they in the monastery, a longer time in the hermitage, but at all times they renounced their vices and passions and their very selves. Equal as regards obedience and humility, they differed one from the other in the practice of patience and charity. Young in years, they were inwardly mature, striving with one accord to live for heaven by practicing brotherhood on earth.

They had no love for power or wealth, and thus they were able to guard their virtues and to endure the sadness and inner pain that were their lot. But if they were sad and in pain, it was not because they were soft and lazy like us, or had accomplished nothing worthwhile; but only because they had done less than ought to have been done by those who, like Mary, had chosen the better part and had girded their loins for labor.[3]

They feared the just judgment of Christ and the wrath of God for not having fought the good fight and become "a spectacle to the world, to angels and to all humanity,"[4] rather than spectators on the sidelines. They feared that, although ready and willing to run, they may have been found unfit for the race, since "it depends not upon human will or exertion, but upon God's mercy."[5]

They desired to raise the pagan Poles from death to life in Christ, convinced as they were that the more souls they gained for God, the greater would be His mercy upon themselves, for in His love for us He spared not His only Son. And if, in realizing this desire, they were to receive the cup of salvation from Him whose every gift is good, they would gladly have drunk it. They did not, of course, want anyone to sin by killing them, but on the contrary, that all might be saved through their labors, and that they might win the favor of their Lord.

When their sorrow was greatest, God came to save them, in a way they had not expected. Weary at heart, regretting

what little they had done and unwilling to take their rest
having borne no fruit, they found great peace after a brief
moment of pain. Their violent guests, arriving with inhuman
intent and with swords, unwittingly brought the brothers a
joy that knows no measure and no end, that cancels every ill
and fulfills every good desire.   Nothing was lacking in
God's gift or in their glory: their Polish novices and their
cook were also killed, innocent victims like them. These
three had not joined them in view of any worldly gain, but
wholly intent upon God's service, they too won the prize
their elders had so long desired. What they were looking for
elsewhere they found at home; what they were ready to work
for came to them as a free gift. This is the way seekers find
what they seek: not as a wage for their labors but as a grace
from heaven while they sleep.[6] How great are God's mercies!

His gifts are not silver or gold, but the good deeds He
enables us to do. His judgments are sung by the angels and
are all of them just, "more precious than gold and sweeter
than honey from the comb."[7]

John and Benedict were both worshipers of Christ, and
His grace was all they desired in this life. They were both
citizens of heaven, and heaven they gained, together with
their three companions. Their age was not to be counted in
years; long life for them was a life without blame. First
among them, Benedict detested all malice as if it were
poison. Never did he utter a word of detraction, and never
would he allow one such word to be uttered in his presence.[8]
Whether a brother was guilty or not, he ill endured self-
justification. He never started an argument himself, and he
could not bear to hear others' arguments, attentive to what
Scripture says, "While there are jealousy and strife among
you, are you not of the flesh?"[9] "The Lord's servant must
not be quarrelsome but kindly to everyone."[10]

Whenever he heard a story of the saints, Benedict always
said, "They lived their lives well; now let us see how we live
ours. Each one will have to bear his own load."[11] As a monk,
Benedict accepted the good times and the bad, especially
after he left his native Italy to seek the kingdom of God.[12]

Always he repeated to himself the words of the Psalm, "Great are the works of the Lord, to be sought in all that He wills."[13] He left us this saying as his spiritual testament.

John, for his part, used to say, "God loves nothing so much as purity of heart. Surely he will not condemn us if our mind wanders at prayer, since we have not been able to study. But those who have done so and still do not want to listen will surely be judged, as in the saying, 'Judgment is for the one who knows what to do and does not do it.'[14]"

ॐ

John had received the following little rule from Master Romuald, and he sought to keep it throughout his life:

"Sit in your cell as in paradise. Put the whole world behind you and forget it. Watch your thoughts like a good fisherman watching for fish.

"The path you must follow is in the Psalms—never leave it.[15]

"If you have just come to the monastery, and in spite of your good will you cannot accomplish what you want, then take every opportunity you can to sing the Psalms in your heart and to understand them with your mind. And if your mind wanders as you read, do not give up; hurry back and apply your mind to the words once more. Realize above all that you are in God's presence, and stand there with the attitude of one who stands before the emperor.[16]

"Empty yourself completely and sit waiting, content with the grace of God, like the chick who tastes nothing and eats nothing but what his mother brings him."[17]

ॐ

Benedict came to the monastery before John and was his superior in the hermitage; his time spent in God's service was more than John's. Benedict was the more fervent of the two and had nothing to envy in his brother, since he received the reward of his labors. But John was greater than Benedict in the practice of patience; if his outward circumstances were favorable or unfavorable, he did not care, and in the midst of his spiritual ups and downs, he kept to the golden mean. Benedict was totally absorbed in the things of the spirit; John always had pleasant words on his lips, and thanks to his gentle and warm personality, he was a man of peace. Benedict's love for God and neighbor—the fulfillment of law and prophets[18]—was greater than John's; but John's inner quiet and his constancy at work made him more stable in the face of changing circumstances.

They were both good men; if one of them ranked lower than the other, he certainly ranked higher than the rest. Dying as martyrs, Benedict and John lived full lives in a short span of time. John was pleasing to God for his patience and hope; both were blessed for their fear of the Lord. Meek and humble of heart, they became fit dwelling places for the Holy Spirit, who said through the prophet, "On him my Spirit shall rest."[19] And on whom shall He rest, but on those who are humble and quiet and attentive to His voice?[20]

In love they were inseparable, in humility they walked, in the truth they lived. If their lives were good, their end was even better. They have inherited alleluia and bequeathed us eleison.[21]

This is the gift of the living God, who made all things good and made them for His glory; it is the gift of Jesus Christ, the Son of God, who redeemed us by His blood; it is the gift of the Holy Spirit, who instructs us all in right speech and right living.

HOLY, HOLY, HOLY IS THE KING OF GLORY, OUR GOD,

WHO HAS UTTERED ONCE FOR ALL THE WORD THAT SAVES US,

WHO IS, WHO WAS, AND WHO IS TO COME,

THE ONE FOR WHOM WE LONG,

FOR ENDLESS AGES OF AGES.

AMEN!

[1]"France" translates *Gallia* for the sake of readability, even though, in the year 1008, the French nation-state had not yet taken form. In Part One of this book, *Gallia* is translated "Catalonia," since the area of the Pyrenees in which the Abbey of Cuixá is nestled did not become French territory until the seventeenth century. You may say I ought to have used "Gaul," but I felt that "Gaul" would be more of a distraction from the story than either "Catalonia" or "France."

[2]In the manuscript, these two lines seem to be verse; their source is unknown.

[3]Cf. Luke 10,42. But note the paradox: like Mary of Bethany they are contemplatives, but like Martha her sister they "girded their loins for labor."

[4]I Corinthians 4,9.

[5]Romans 9,16.

[6]Cf. Psalm 127 (126),2.

[7]Cf. Psalm 19 (18),10.

[8]A virtue cherished by Benedict's first teacher, John Gradenigo: see above, part two, chapter two.

[9]I Corinthians 3,3.

[10]Cf. I Timothy 2,24.

[11]Cf. Galatians 6,5.

[12]Again, we are reminded that the brothers came to Poland not to seek death by martyrdom but the kingdom of God for themselves and for others. This clarity of intention is an integral dimension of their sanctity, and of the holiness of all Christian saints.

[13]Cf. Psalm 111 (110),2.

[14]Cf. James 4,17.

[15]*Una via est in Psalmis:* not, of course, "one way is in the Psalms," but "the one way [for you as a monk] is [meditation on] the Psalms." The Psalter, for Saint Romuald and his contemporaries, did not mean the biblical text by itself, but included the Old and New Testament canticles and those texts with which the liturgy Christianizes the psalmody of the Jewish temple: the antiphons and especially the doxology, the *Gloria Patri*.

[16]We should remember how Master Romuald himself stood before emperors: with the humility of a monk, but also with the freedom, dignity, and *parrhesia* of a child of God.

[17]"Empty yourself completely" translates *"destrue te totum"*; you could also translate it, "Strip yourself naked," but not "Destroy yourself," not even as a paradox, a kind of Christian *koan. De-struo* relates to *con-struo*: we are to "de-construct" our ego-structures (which are always, it is said, tendentially paranoid), in order to experience God, or the grace of God, the Holy Spirit, as "mother," and to know the all-sufficiency of grace. This image is consistent with that of the fisherman, who is always attentive but seems to doze; both evoke the "little way," the opposite of that ascetical machismo and athleticism which have been the typical vices of hermits since the third century.

[18]Cf. Matthew 22,40.

[19]Cf. Wisdom of Solomon 4,13.

[20]Cf. Isaiah 66,2.

[21]That is, they have entered into the heavenly Pascha, the eternal Easter, where all sing "Alleluia," while we are left on this Lenten earth, where we sing *Kyrie eleison,* "Lord, have mercy!"

PART THREE: THE LIFE OF BLESSED ROMUALD
BY PETER DAMIAN OF FONTE AVELLANA

INTRODUCTION

Between the living and the writing of a life there is often so great a difference that what is written about a person gives little help in understanding what his or her life means. Indeed the written life sometimes hinders our grasp of what it meant to live it.

Think of Thomas Merton. At this writing—in December 1993—he has been dead for twenty-five years. Volumes more of his journals and correspondence remain to be published, joining the sixty or so titles printed during his lifetime. Do we understand him better now? If you discover him through *The Seven Storey Mountain*—the autobiography or quasi-novel the young Merton wrote a few years after joining the Trappists—do you finish reading the book with a clear notion of what it means to be born, like Merton, in southern France and to grow up on islands (Long Island, Bermuda, Britain)? Do you understand why he converted to Catholicism after reading James Joyce and visiting the sanitized reconstructions of medieval monasteries in a Manhattan park? Or grasp his reasons for joining Gethsemane abbey in Kentucky, a monastery of the "strict observance" which was then one of the least likely to foster his growth as a writer and a social commentator? In other words: is the reader of Thomas Merton's books faced with a mystery?

Don Anselmo was right, of course. I wanted to call this book *The Romuald Mystery,* but the word "mystery" is not the right label for a human being, however ungraspable he may seem at first. The books by and about Merton of Prades and Romuald of Ravenna may leave me short of the meaning of their lives. But after I close the books, as I reflect on the meaning of my own life, on what it means to believe and to doubt, to love and to fail in loving, I begin to understand them.

I think I understand Saint Peter Damian now—at least, his dilemma seems like my own. He had never met Saint Romuald, although he was twenty when Romuald died. How was he, trained as a rhetorician and gifted as a writer and a thinker, to portray Ravenna's new saint, a man more of action and experience than of thought, who had written little or nothing and expressed himself more through gestures—now eccentric, now playful—than through words? Not only did the two differ in their culture and intellectual formation; they were also men of very different character. Peter Damian had been wounded by life and needed to be alone; Romuald had been challenged by life and needed to be free. The former was a clear thinker who expressed himself in radical dichotomies; the latter was a lover of paradox, who resolved contradictions by uniting them within himself. Peter Damian ended his days in bishop's orders and with a cardinal's hat hanging on a peg in his cell; Romuald was an ecclesiastical superior for no more than one year of his long life, and he chose to die in a monastery hidden behind a circle of hills, about as far from bishops and other potentates as you could get in medieval Italy.

Yet Peter Damian loved Romuald and wanted very much to become like him, and I believe Saint Romuald, from his place in heaven, loved Peter Damian and helped him to live with his own contradictions. So when the monk Peter of Fonte Avellana discovered he had enough in common with "the mysterious master" to see through the mystery of their differences, he wrote a book about him. Peter Damian was then thirty-five years old, and Romuald had been gone for fifteen years. The book became the nearest thing you could find to a best-seller in the eleventh century.

Today if you want to read this book and get some meaning from it, keep in mind three things: 1. The author's intentions, 2. The literary genre of his work, and 3. The sources he drew on.

The Author's Intentions

You find his chief intention in the first word of the book: *Adversum,* "Against!" Peter Damian begins his career as a writer (the *Life of Romuald* is his first published work) lashing out at what he calls the "unclean world" *(inmunde munde),* a phrase we could perhaps translate as "institutionalized meaninglessness": a society and a Church which were stuck in a rut, spinning their wheels, maintaining forms without content, unaware of the real world of the eleventh century, when people on the move were seeking new meanings and new forms. Peter Damian sees a great mass of people "hungry for God's word" (cf. Amos 8,11), hungry especially for a word made flesh in the orthopraxis of saints like Romuald of Ravenna. But Peter Damian intends to do more than satisfy the people's craving for liturgical spectacle and stories about saints; his ultimate intention is to project Romuald's deeds on the wide screen of his project for a renewed Church and a new kind of society.

Deeds, not miracles. It was not skepticism or scholarly scruples which made Peter Damian remind his readers that "John the Baptist worked no miracles." What is of value, in the life of Romuald as in that of the Baptist, are the prophetic implications of their actions. The total existence of a saint challenges the Church's present and prophesies its future.

The Literary Genre

The Life of Romuald is not "historical" in the modern sense of the term; Peter Damian is not Romuald's "biographer." He himself tells us so: *non hystoriam texens sed quoddam quasi breve commonitorium faciens.* He is not weaving history but giving us a sort of brief commonitorium—at one and the same time a "testimony," a "reminder," and an "exhortation."

Like Bruno of Querfurt in *The Life of the Five Brothers,* Peter Damian follows standard patterns derived from texts read and reread in monasteries since the fourth century—those of Athanasius and Jerome, of course, but, among Benedictines, the hagiographic text par excellence: Pope Saint Gregory the Great's *Dialogues,* especially book two, entirely dedicated to Saint Benedict, who for all medieval monastics was none other than the author of their Rule. The Rule itself, although not a narrative text, offered patterns for writers of saints' lives, reminding them in its last chapter that "the fullness of justice is not contained in this

167

Rule" and, by implication, that this fullness is to be sought in the example of those who, seeking God, went beyond every rule, "running, with unspeakable sweetness of love, in the way of God's commandments" (*Rule of Benedict,* prologue).

So once again we see how these saints' lives are in reality commentaries on the Bible: the "memory" they evoke is that of biblical prophecy. In the life of a holy monastic, salvation history is relived; in him or her the people of God once more go forth from their various Egyptian and Babylonian captivities into a desert of freedom and testing that ends at the empty tomb in the garden below Calvary. The Passover mystery—Exodus and Resurrection—has been "sacramentalized," Saint Ambrose tells us, and now it passes over into the lives of those who are willing to leave what is known and secure and to be espoused to the Lamb, to face the Beast (above all, in their own hearts and thoughts) that they may see and enter the City without a temple.

Peter Damian gives us his *Life of Romuald* as a liturgical text, a book to be read in church, from the pulpit, as instruction for the faithful who come to the saint's tomb for his yearly feast. The book was not meant to remain on the hand lettered page but to sound out during the celebration of the Divine Office, at the vigil Hour of Readings, adorned by Psalms. Today, as we read it silently in our rooms or in a library or on a Greyhound bus, we have to make a mental effort to put the words back in the space where they can resonate properly, the space of prayer and song. Only there can they once again become prophecy.

The Sources

The only sources Peter Damian had to draw on were oral, the tales of their master recounted by Romuald's immediate disciples. We know this to be the case, first, because Peter Damian tells us so, and, second, because internal criticism of the text easily demonstrates the fact that he had never read the *Life of the Five Brothers* by Bruno-Boniface of Querfurt.

Historians are aware that oral tradition can be very reliable when it is a question of places and deeds, but is less so with regard to names and dates. The brief note at the head of each chapter will inform the reader whenever Peter Damian's sources failed to give him the precise sequence of Saint Romuald's wanderings. As we stated before, the chief guide to the chronology of Romuald's life is Bruno of Querfurt, whose account is confirmed by the few references to Romuald which we find in contemporary documents. One of the earliest of these dates back to the first or second decade of the eleventh century; this is a Life of Peter Orséolo written by an anonymous Catalan monk, who gives us the first certain date in Romuald's life: Sunday, September 1, 978, when he and Peter Orséolo left Venice with the abbot of Cuixá.

This date is also the key for resolving the question of how old Romuald was when he died. Peter Damian says he was 120. Now the rest of Peter Damian's chronology (in spite of its inaccuracies, which we shall see) fits nicely into the 49 years following that date (Romuald died almost certainly in 1027). This means that Romuald would have been 71 when he left Venice for Cuixá, that he had been with his teacher Marino, fishing in the Venetian lagoon, for nearly half a century, that Marino himself would have been at least 90 and ten years later would have had the strength to hike down from the Pyrenees and over to southern Italy, where he was killed by pirates! All of which is absurd and means that, once again, our Cartesian-Newtonian rationalism must bow aside and let us take numbers as symbols, the way everyone in Antiquity and the Middle Ages took them. Saint Romuald had to have lived 120 years, because he was a new Moses, the captain of a new exodus of monks and nuns toward a promised land of interior liberty, beyond the desert of formalism and rules.

THE LIFE OF BLESSED ROMUALD

Prologue

Against you, a world gone wrong,[1] I must protest! You boast an unbearable horde of moronic sophists, who babble on with you and go dumb before God. You have so many among you, superbly arrogant, who vaunt their vain eloquence and their empty philosophy. But you can find no one who is the least bit inclined to write something useful for God's people now and in the future. Your courts are full of lawyers ready to hold forth at length and defend any case, as long as there is money in it. But the church is empty of anyone with the skill to write about virtues and to narrate the deeds and glories of a single saint. O world, your people know all there is to know about doing evil, but they are too ignorant to do any good.[2]

Fifteen years have come and gone since Blessed Romuald let go of his flesh to fly up to heaven. And we are still waiting to see one of your wiseacres write at least a short story about his long and glorious life. But no one has come forth to answer the needs of those who believe and are devoted to him; no one has provided the church with something to read at the liturgies in his honor, a few words that might be useful for the many.

For me, the most useful thing to do would have been to stay hidden in my hermitage, meditating on my sins, instead of telling a tale about somebody else's virtues. The right thing for me would have been to bewail the darkness of my errors instead of shadowing the splendors of Romuald's holiness with these inept words.

But the fact remains that all through the year and especially on his feast day, crowds of believers from far and near flock to his tomb to see the miracles God works through him. They come eager to hear the story of his life, and they find nobody there to tell it.

A worry has begun to gnaw at me, and not without reason: might it not happen that, as years go by, Romuald's fame will grow dim among the people, and they will forget him?

This worry is not my only motivation; I am also constrained by the requests of my fellow monks and bound by
my love for them. So here I am, sifting through the notes I
have taken from what Romuald's disciples have told me, and
with God's help, I shall try to describe his life's course from
start to finish.

I am not trying to write a biography of Saint Romuald—
this is something beyond my limited skills. All I want to do
is to leave behind a written testimony about him, a brief
promemoria without any literary pretensions.

But first let me inform my readers that I do not intend to
fill up these few pages with miracles.[3] All I want to do is
convey something that people can imitate, that is, the kind
of life Saint Romuald lived. He himself sought protection
from the winds of vainglory behind the shelter of humility;
whatever he did that might have attracted attention, he tried
his best to hide. Had he not worked a single miracle, Romuald
would merit all the veneration he receives, if only for the life
he lived. The Bible attributes no miracles to Saint John the
Baptist, and yet the living Truth itself tells us that none born
of woman is greater than he.[4]

There are always those who think they can honor God and
His saints by inventing lies about them. They forget that our
God has no use for lies; they think He will be pleased with
their tall tales, while in fact they are rejecting the truth, who
is God Himself. The prophet Jeremiah has a word for them:
"They have trained their tongues to lie and devote all their
energies to doing wrong."[5]

How easy it would have been for them to relate simply
the few truths they had received, instead of going to all that
trouble and inventing stories to fill up the gaps in their
knowledge. They think they are promoting God's cause,
while in reality, as false witnesses they are fighting against
Him. Remember what the apostle Paul said: "If Christ has
not been raised, then our preaching is without substance,
and so is your faith. What is more, we have proved to be false

witnesses to God, for testifying against God that he raised Christ to life when he did not raise him."[6]

As I am constrained to write this book against my own better judgment, I choose to preface it with these remarks. Now let me get on with my story; the prayers of him about whom I am writing will obtain God's help for me.

[1]This translates an untranslatable pun: *inmunde munde*, "O unclean world."

[2]Cf. Jeremiah 4,22 in the Latin.

[3]Saint Athanasius says the same thing at the beginning of his *Vita Antonii*, but like Peter Damian, does not entirely keep his promise.

[4]Cf. John 10,41 and Matthew 11,11.

[5]Jeremiah 9,5.

[6]I Corinthians 15,14-15.

1. At the abbey of Classe, Romuald does penance for his father's crime.

In the tenth century of the Christian era, human life was cheap. To resolve their disputes, men usually had recourse to violence; the Church was still far from developing a culture of dialogue and non-violence. Ecclesiastical canons prescribed no more than forty days' penance as reparation for homicide; for us this seems as good as nothing, but the theologians and canonists of the day deemed it sufficient.

Two traits in Romuald's character emerge from this first chapter: he was very sensitive to life values (the beauties of his natural environment, the preciousness of human life itself); and he was extremely impulsive in fulfilling the dictates of his conscience (an upright person may show horror for another's sin but is seldom inclined to expiate it himself). These qualities of Romuald's personality would likely have been considered weaknesses by his contemporaries and even among the clergy. But with these two golden threads, God wove the fabric of Romuald's sanctity.

172

A native of Ravenna, Romuald was born into the highest ranks of the military aristocracy. As an adolescent he felt inclined to the sins of the flesh and fell into all the vices typical of his age and rank.[1] But part of him belonged to God; after every fall he strove to get up and move on to higher goals. For example, when he was out hunting and happened upon a pleasant glade, he immediately felt drawn into solitude and said to himself, "How fine it would be to live like hermits, deep in these woods, how easy to stay quiet and free from the world's turmoil!" Heaven put these thoughts into his mind, like a prophecy, and he began to fall in love with what was to be his life's work.

His father's name was Sergio, a man of the world all taken up with business. Sergio had a feud with a relative who contested his ownership of a piece of land. Romuald refused to take sides between them, fearing they would resolve their contest with the sword. Seeing this, Sergio threatened to disinherit Romuald if he persisted in his refusal.

But why go on? In the end the two decided on a duel. They faced off outside the city walls, blade against blade, and as they fought, Sergio's sword struck home, and his enemy fell dead.

Romuald had wounded no one; yet for the simple fact that he had been present, he took upon himself the canonical penalty for the crime. Without delay he went to the monastery of Sant'Apollinare[2] in Classe, where he remained in penance for forty days, as is the custom for homicides.

[1]Peter Damian speaks of himself in similar terms, in the few autobiographical references in his writings (cf. Opusculum 42, chap. 7).

[2]Apollinaris was the first bishop of Ravenna, who lived in the second century—legends make him a disciple of the apostle Peter; he suffered persecution, but was not, strictly speaking, a martyr. In the apse of the sixth-century basilica, his name is spelled according to the pre-Romance dialect spoken at the time: *Apolenaris,* and this is the way Peter Damian spells the name, rather than giving us its correct Latin orthography, *Apollinaris.* However, although Bruno of Querfurt's spelling of *Romaldus* probably represents the way Saint Romuald himself pronounced his own name, Peter Damian always writes *Romualdus.*

2. Saint Apollinaris appears to Romuald; moved by the Holy Spirit, Romuald becomes a monk.

The basilica of Sant'Apollinare now stands surrounded by farm land, but a thousand years ago it overlooked a vast lagoon, like that of Venice, and Ravenna itself was a city of canals. It was called "in Classe," because in olden times the Roman imperial fleet ("fleet" in Latin is classis*) wintered there. In Romuald's day, Sant' Apollinare in Classe was Ravenna's most important ecclesiastical institution, but the life the monks lived in no way corresponded to the abbey's social and cultural prestige.*

At Classe Romuald was befriended by a certain lay brother. The Latin text calls him a conversus; *the term indicates a man who entered the monastery at an advanced age—a rather rare case at the time. Most of the monks were* nutriti, *whose parents had placed them in the monastery as children; although theoretically free to leave at any time before final vows, most of them chose to remain.*

Romuald at that time was at least twenty, hence much too old to join as a nutritus *and too young to become a* conversus. *Nevertheless the old brother exhorted him to take the robes and gently coerced the youth to make a couple of all-night vigils with him in the great basilica. During those vigils, Romuald had visions of the monastery's patron Saint Apollinaris, but the visions did not convince him. Peter Damian makes it clear that Romuald's motivations for joining the monastery were personal and interior, and were a grace of the Holy Spirit.*

With the recommendation of Onesto degli Onesti, former abbot of Classe and bishop of Ravenna from 971, Romuald was clothed as a monk. Hence his entry into monastic life can be dated between 971 and 975.

At the monastery of Classe, while subjecting himself to rigorous penance, Romuald began to have daily conversations with an elderly lay brother. The brother gave him some good advice, to the extent of his limited knowledge of the spiritual life. And he kept exhorting Romuald to leave the world and embrace monastic life, but he failed to convince him.

One day as they were chatting about many things, the brother, in a humorous vein, threw this question at him: "What will you give me in return, if I make you see Saint Apollinaris in the flesh?"

Romuald answered, "I bind myself on oath: the minute I see the holy martyr, I'll become a monk!"

So the brother told him not to go to bed that evening but to stay with him in church and keep vigil all night. And through the silent hours they remained in prayer.

At cockcrow they began to see the saint rising from behind the Blessed Virgin's altar in the middle of the church.[1] He emerged from the eastern side of the altar, where the porphyry plaque is.

Immediately the church was filled with such a splendor that it seemed the sun had focused all its rays there. The blessed martyr, adorned with his priestly robes, circled the church as if to honor its altars with the smoke of his thurible. Having done this, the bishop returned to the place whence he came, and the light vanished with him.

So the brother began to press Romuald to fulfill his promise, but the more vehemently he did so, the more Romuald resisted. He kept asking to see the vision once more. Again the two kept watch in church, and again they saw Saint Apollinaris.

(In later years, whenever the subject of the burial place of the saint came up, Romuald always insisted that his tomb was indeed in the basilica, and he continued to say so till the end of his life.)

Romuald kept coming to the monastery. At night, after the monks retired to their beds, he would often remain before the high altar to pray, with sighs too deep for words. The days went by, and one morning Romuald was praying with great intensity. At that moment the Holy Spirit set his

175

heart on fire with love, and he burst into tears. He went and threw himself at the feet of the monks and begged them through his tears to clothe him in the monastic robes.

The monks of Sant'Apollinare were afraid. Romuald's father was a hard man, and who knows how he would react if they took his son into the community? So Romuald went and poured out his heart to the archbishop, Onesto degli Onesti, who before his election to the see of Ravenna had been abbot of Classe. To the young man's ardor[2] the archbishop added the stimulus of his own exhortations and ordered the monks to accept him. Now safely under the archbishop's protection, they clothed Romuald in the cowl, and thus began his three years in the monastery.

[1]When the Camaldolese Benedictines came to reconstitute the monastic community at Classe in the twelfth century, they searched for the remains of Saint Apollinaris and found them under the high altar in the apse. Our monks remained there until Napoleon's troops threw them out and turned the great basilica into a gymnasium. In the 1960's, Classe was once more offered to the Camaldolese, but our general chapter did not accept the offer, and at present the basilica is staffed by Valombrosan monks.

[2]*Qui [episcopus] alacer factus castæ concupiscientiæ exhortationis stimulos addidit.*

3. A few monks, reproved by the novice Romuald, plot to kill him.

The tenth century was an age of iron, even among monks. What remained of Greco-Roman culture was but a thin veneer over the barbarian instincts of Ravenna's heterogeneous population, and the spirit of the Gospel had in these thousand years penetrated no deeper. No wonder then that one or another of the monks, annoyed at the presumptuous young aristocrat who was aflame with novitiate fervor, might consider homicide an appropriate way of ridding themselves of the nuisance.

176

Peter Damian clearly suggests that Romuald's fervor was not all virtue. Years later, as a wise teacher of monks, Master Romuald would set his own novices on guard against the vice of presumption—taking things for granted and relying on one's own judgment and will power—as the first and gravest danger a monk must face.

Romuald began to realize that some of the monks were strolling down the broad path to perdition, while his heart was set on the narrow gate that leads to life. Romuald knew he had to follow his heart, but this did not seem possible at Sant'Apollinare. "What should I do?" he asked himself, and a thousand thoughts beat upon his soul like waves of a winter storm.

With hard words Romuald presumed to denounce the easy ways of the monks, and he exposed their faults through repeated references to the Rule. But the more he insisted, the less attention they paid to him. "After all, he is only a young novice," they said. In the end their tolerance was exhausted, and they could bear his reproofs no longer. They set about plotting to kill him.

Romuald was accustomed to rise early, before the monks got up for their nightly vigil Office, and when he found the doors of the church locked, he would say his prayers in the dormitory. Now the dormitory was on the second floor of the abbey and looked out over the cloister. At the devil's prompting, these sons of Cain decided that the next time Romuald started reciting his prayers in the dormitory, they would throw him headlong over the railing to the pavement below.

Hearing them discuss this plot, one of the brothers warned Romuald. So he shut the door of his mouth and began to pray to his Father in silence, in the secret chamber of his heart.[1] And thus he was safe; he avoided being cast down bodily into the cloister garth, and he kept the monks' souls from falling into the abyss of mortal sin.

[1] Cf. Matthew 6,6.

4. Romuald leaves the monastery and goes to live with the hermit Marino.

Having withdrawn from the community, Romuald places himself under the guidance of a lay-hermit by the name of Marino. Only Peter Damian mentions him; there is nothing of him in any other document.

Marino was not a Benedictine monk. His prayers were not a monastic liturgy but consisted in the chanting of Psalms while wandering along the shore of the lagoon. Romuald himself, after three years at Classe, ought to have committed to memory the entire Latin Psalter. Hence when Peter Damian tells us that Romuald had difficulty reading the text of Marino's Psalter, we suspect that the problem was not Romuald's illiteracy, but the language in which the Psalms were written. As we know that Marino was to end his days in Apulia, where Greek was still the common language, his Psalm book may very well have been the Greek text used by Byzantine monks. (On Marino in Apulia, see below, chapter 15.)

Day by day, Romuald's love for the monastic ideal grew stronger, but his heart found no rest. Then he heard that not far from Venice was a man of the Spirit, Marino by name, who lived as a hermit. It was all too easy for Romuald to get the permission of Classe's abbot and chapter to leave the community. He boarded a ship heading north, firm in his decision to ask the man to accept him as a disciple.

In addition to the usual virtues, Marino was endowed with great simplicity and absolute sincerity. No one had trained him in the hermit life; he had simply taken it on by himself, moved by his own good will.

This was how he lived: in all seasons of the year his daily rations, three days out of seven, were half a loaf of bread and a handful of fava beans; the other days he added some soup and a glass of wine. Marino sang the entire Psalter every day. Rising early, Romuald with him, he would wander aimlessly, stopping now and then to sit under a tree and sing twenty Psalms, then moving to another tree to sing thirty more, and so on.

Years later, Romuald would speak of him with a smile: "A rough and ready type he was, without any formation[1] for the solitary life." Romuald himself had left the world unlettered. So it happened that when he opened the Psalter, he could hardly decipher the written words and stumbled over them as it came his turn to sing. Squinting continually at the page gave Romuald a headache, and Marino, who sat facing him, would box him on the ear with a stick. One day he could take no more and said, "Please, master, start hitting me on the other ear, since I am going deaf in this one." Marino, impressed with his disciple's meekness and humility, softened his indiscreet severity and stopped using his stick.

---

[1]This is the point of the whole chapter: without any polemical overtones, Peter Damian (and Romuald) make it clear that without monastic formation no one can live as an authentic Christian hermit.

5. Romuald follows Abbot Garí and the doge of Venice to the abbey of Cuixá.

The events in this chapter take place in Venice, between the years 976 and 978. Peter Damian's account is garbled, and we need to correct it from sources closer to the events.

1. The predecessor of Peter Orséolo as doge of Venice was not Vitale but Peter Candiano IV (whose brother—that is, Vitale—became doge after Orséolo left office). Peter Candiano was the one who married Waldrada, daughter of Hubert marquis of Tuscany and sister of Hugh, who inherited their father's title.

2. The documents closest in time and space to these events do not implicate Peter Orséolo in the plot to overthrow Peter Candiano. In fact, the "plot" was a popular uprising against the dictatorial powers Candiano had assumed, sure of the support of the Tuscans and of the imperial court.

3. Peter Orséolo did not possess the duchy of Dalmatia (the coastal regions of present-day Slovenia and Croatia). It was his son, Peter Orséolo II (successor of his father's successor, Vitale Candiano V) who conquered the territory for Venice.

Peter Orséolo was in reality only a witness to the assassination of Peter Candiano, like Romuald at the duel between his father Sergio and their relative. As doge, Orséolo—a man of great meekness, who after the birth of his one son and heir had made a vow of chastity—sought to make peace between the contending parties, guaranteed freedom and immunity from prosecution to Candiano's Tuscan wife Waldrada, and attempted to cancel all the physical effects of the revolt. From Constantinople he summoned architects and craft workers to begin construction of the Byzantine-style basilica we see today in Saint Mark's Square, as well as the famous campanile, which fell and was rebuilt in the same style early in this century.

It was of course Abbot Garí of Cuixá who resolved the political problem, accepting Peter Orséolo as a postulant. Romuald's own role in this—however minor it may have been—won for him the gratitude of the Tuscans, and the Marquis Hugh would later finance Romuald's monastic foundations in his territory.

At that time the duchy of Dalmatia was ruled by Peter Orséolo, who had obtained this title by favoring the assassins of his predecessor Vitale [Peter] Candiano. I hope I shall not go too far off the subject if I say a few words about this murder.

Candiano had taken as his wife the sister of Marquis Hugh the Great, and wishing to imitate his brother-in-law, had formed a militia of Tuscan and Lombard mercenaries, paying their wages with public funds. The Venetians could not endure this and plotted an armed assault on the doge's palace, in which he and all his family were to be slain. But

Candiano had informers; so he doubled his guard day and night and foiled his enemies' plan. Having failed various attempts, the conspirators hit upon a simple idea: set fire to the Orséolo palace, which stood next to that of the doge, and let the flames chase him out of hiding and cremate his family.

To effect this project, they needed Orséolo's consent. So they agreed that, in exchange for the loss of his property, he would become the lord of all Venice; with his rival out of the way, Peter Orséolo would be the next doge. It was in this way that Orséolo obtained the duchy of Dalmatia, but as soon as he had satisfied his every ambition, Peter's heart was touched by God's grace, and he repented of what he had done.

Then from the county of Barcelona[1] arrived a venerable abbot, Garí of Cuixá. He was accustomed to go on pilgrimages, and he had traveled to many holy places throughout the world. When the abbot came to call on the new doge of Venice, Orséolo immediately asked his advice on how he might avoid the dire consequences of his grave crime. They also took counsel with Marino and Romuald, who agreed with the abbot that Orséolo's only hope was to abandon the world, and not only resign from an office he had usurped by a criminal act. "Having unjustly assumed an authority that was not your own," they said, "you must now submit yourself to another man's power."

However, since the office of doge was of such political importance, Orséolo could not publicly announce his decision to become a monk. So he thought it prudent to follow a secret plan. There was soon to be a festival in honor of the patron saint of one of the private chapels on his mainland properties. On the eve of the feast, he sent his wife to oversee the church decorations and the preparation of the banquet for his invited guests, who were to accompany him there the following day. As soon as his wife had left, he took what money he had on hand and set out, like the great penitent he was, for Garí's abbey in Catalonia, accompanied by his relative John Gradenigo (who had also been involved in the revolt against Candiano), and by the three holy monks. Peter Orséolo and John Gradenigo entered the novitiate at Saint Michael of Cuixá, and Marino and Romuald set up their hermitage close by the abbey. A year later, Peter and John joined them there and shared the same austere cell.

[1]*Ex ulterioribus Galliæ finibus.*

6. Romuald and Gradenigo live by the labor of their hands.

Saint Peter Damian fleshes out his story of Romuald's years at Cuixá—about which his informants could tell him very little—by borrowing from hagiographic literature. One of his sources is the Life of Hilarion *by Saint Jerome (342-420):*

> Hilarion sustained his weary members with nothing but vegetable broth and a few dried figs, three or four days out of each week. He prayed often and sang Psalms as he tilled the earth, so that his physical labor might double the fatigue of his fasting.

Another source is the Institutes *of Cassian (365-435):*

> At the end of the Office of prayer, each one returns to the cell he occupies, either alone or in the company of another monk, with whom he is united by having the same trade or who studied with the same teacher or who received the same kind of education, or whose virtues are similar to his own.

We often find Romuald sharing his hermit's cell with a brother; for a good part of his life this seems to have been his normal custom. First with Marino by the Venetian Lagoon, then with John Gradenigo at Cuixá, and later with Blessed William of Pomposa near the latter's abbey, Romuald dwells in solitude but is almost never alone.

While at Cuixá, Romuald's ardent quest for God and his growth in virtue made him an example of monastic living for the brothers. Soon everyone in the hermitage took to asking Romuald's advice in all matters practical and spiritual, and they willingly accepted his decisions. Even Marino was glad to become a follower of the young hermit, who a short time before had been his disciple.

For a whole year, the only cooked food Romuald took was a handful of boiled garbanzo beans. And then for three years running, he and John Gradenigo lived by their own labors; they tilled a field and harvested grain, all the while doubling the severity of their fast.

7. Romuald is tempted by the devil.

Once again Peter Damian fills the gaps in his information with pages from the classics of hagiography, like the following phrases, taken here and there from the Life of Antony *by Saint Athanasius (296-373):*

The devil could not stand to see such virtue in a mere youth, and he assaulted Antony with attacks worthy of a veteran. The devil's initial skirmishes tempted Antony to leave his chosen path by reminding him of the wealth, high social status, and comfortable existence he had abandoned. But when the devil realized he was impotent in the face of Antony's prayers, he turned to night-time incursions. First he tried to keep him awake with numerous demonic apparitions and to frighten him with horrible sounds. But even by day he fought with Antony, so there could be no doubt that the soldier of Christ was engaged in combat with the devil himself. Thus he thanked the Lord, and filled with daring against the enemy, he said to him, 'How miserable, how despicable you are! Henceforth I shall pay you no mind. The Lord is my help; I shall rejoice in the presence of my enemies.' And as he sang this verse, the demonic form dissolved before him.

The devil made war on Romuald, especially during the early stages of his monastic journey. Various and sundry temptations he aroused in Romuald, and he distracted him with many temptations to self-indulgence. Now he made him think of all the wealth a courageous man like himself might have laid hands on. Again he reminded Romuald that he had left property which was rightfully his to greedy and ungrateful relatives. At times the devil made him feel that whatever he did was petty and useless, and at other times he filled him with horror at his hard labors and promised him that a very long life lay ahead of him.

How many times he knocked on Romuald's door and awakened him soon after he had fallen asleep, and then kept him awake all night with the thought that it was just a few minutes before daybreak! For five years the devil came and sat on Romuald's legs while he was in bed, and with this illusion of weight made him feel he could not easily turn over on his side. What should we say about all the vicious animals whose appearance Romuald had to endure? Or about the many times he had to utter invectives against the demons that presented themselves to him?

It even happened once or twice that a brother, for some necessity, approached Romuald's cell during the night silence; the soldier of Christ, always ready for battle, would think it was the devil and would call out, "Now what do you want, repulsive creature? They have cast you out of heaven; what do you expect to find in a hermitage? You dog, you serpent, begone!"

When the brother who had come to his cell heard him say these words, he knew that Romuald was always in the thick of battle with the forces of evil, countering their onslaughts with the arms of faith.

8. Romuald studies the lives of the Desert Elders, and Peter Orséolo prophesies the destiny of his son.

Marino, the self-taught hermit, had invented his own rule for fasting, psalmody, and vigils. Romuald chose instead to base his way of life on objective criteria garnered from the study of books, which he found in great abundance in Cuixá's rich library. Later, as a monastic teacher, Romuald would

*always refer his disciples to monasticism's written sources,
especially those listed in the last chapter of the Rule of Saint
Benedict. For the communities he founded or instructed,
Romuald never wrote a "rule for hermits." The words of
John Gradenigo—recorded by Bruno of Querfurt—sum up
Romuald's teaching method: "Romuald is the greatest her-
mit of our day, yet he lives this beautiful life humbly and
without presumption. He does not take for granted his own
understanding of the life, but follows the Conferences of the
Desert Elders; theirs was the doctrine he taught us."*

*Romuald's compassion for others' weaknesses, exempli-
fied here by his treatment of Peter Orséolo, became the
norm in the communities inspired by his teaching. In his rule
for Fonte Avellana, Peter Damian narrates the discipline
observed there:*

> 'All mitigation of rules in favor of the weaker brethren is
> left to the Prior's discretion. He is to consider each monk's
> capacity for fasting, and in a spirit of charity grant him all
> the food he needs. We make our own these words which
> Blessed Romuald often repeated to his disciples: 'Lest a
> brother abandon the hermitage, let him even be allowed to
> eat meat, if this is what he really needs.'

*In this teaching, Romuald was much closer to the discreet
and balanced spirit of Cluny than to later forms of monastic
life, with their greater insistence on the "letter" of the Rule.*

Once, while he was reading the Lives of the Desert
Elders, Romuald came upon the passage about the brothers
who used to fast in their hermitage from Monday through Friday,
and then on Saturday and Sunday would come together for
common meals, at which a greater variety and quantity of
food was served. So from then on, for fifteen years or so,
Romuald followed this practice without interruption.

But the doge Peter, long accustomed as he was to a rich
diet, found this regime of fasting too heavy, and his health
almost failed. So he went and humbly cast himself at
Romuald's feet. Romuald made him stand, and Peter, with
great embarrassment, revealed his need for a more generous

diet. "Father," he said, "I do want to do penance for my sins, but with my heavy build, I can't get by with half a loaf of dry bread." Romuald, moved by paternal compassion toward Peter, gave him another quarter loaf from his own supply of bread.

Thus he held out a hand of mercy to a brother who was failing on the way, so that with renewed strength, he might more easily follow the path he had chosen.

Once Orséolo's son—who was also called Peter—came to visit him. The younger Peter was a man of great experience in the ways of the world. His father, whether by a gift of prophecy or by natural insight, I do not know, foretold the young man's future: "My son, I know beyond a shadow of a doubt that you will be elected doge and will enjoy success. But you must take care to safeguard the rights of Christ's Church. And practice equal justice toward all your subjects, friend and foe alike."

9. In later years, Romuald teaches the way of discretion to his disciples.

With this chapter, Peter Damian abandons chronological order and takes us at least 15 years into the future (see the preceding chapter). We are at the time of Romuald's full maturity, between 993 and 998, while he is at Sant'Apollinare in Classe or someplace nearby (see chapter 19).

The contents of this chapter nine are taken almost entirely from the great sources of monastic spirituality. In John Cassian's Conferences we read: "It is good to take food and sleep regularly, at the appointed times, even if one feels repugnance for them. ... The fall that results from immoderate fasting is more serious than the consequences of overeating. The latter can be remedied by a healthy sense of regret, and one returns to the practice of moderate austerity, but there is no remedy for the effects of indiscreet

fasting....Our prayers ought to be frequent but brief. If they
go on for too long, some spy [i.e., the devil] will have time
to slip in a distracting thought. This is indeed the true
sacrifice: 'God's sacrifice is a contrite heart [Psalm 50,19
in the Latin Vulgate].'"

Some years later, Romuald read that Saint Sylvester,
bishop of Rome, had introduced fasting on Saturday as a
vigil of the paschal feast of Sunday. So Romuald immediately changed the day when fasting was to be interrupted: no
longer Saturday but Thursday. He did this to favor his
weaker brothers, so that, with a more discreet practice of
fasting, they might be able to continue it for longer periods
of time. Hence he established the following norm for those
who live in the hermitage: fasting means to abstain from
cooked food for three days running and then for two, while
on Thursdays and Sundays they may give thanks and sit
down to a meal of cooked vegetables and soup. Exception
was made for the two Lents, when most of his disciples
joined him in fasting the whole week through.

It was fitting that a man like Romuald, who loved to sing
God's praises "with choirs and drums," would arrange all
his practices musically, that the God of infinite light might
hear the harmonious intervals of the octave, the fifth, and
the fourth.

Regarding total fasting—eating nothing all day—although
he himself often practiced it, he absolutely forbade it to his
disciples. "If you want to grow continually in your monastic
commitment," he said, "then the best kind of fasting means
eating every day and feeling hungry every day. If you
practice fasting with discretion, what seems hard at first will
become easier." Romuald had no use for monks who started out
doing heavy penance, and then weren't able to keep it up.

About staying up at night to pray he was very cautious.
What he did not want anyone to do was to stay up and then
fall asleep at dawn, after the night Office of prayer. He had
no patience for those who couldn't stay awake in the morning. If someone confessed he had gone back to sleep after

the Vigil of Twelve Psalms or worse yet at sunup, Romuald would not let him sing Mass that day.

"Better to sing one Psalm with feeling," he said, "than to recite a hundred with a wandering mind. But if you haven't yet received the grace of singing from your heart, do not give up hope. Be constant in your practice, and one day He who gave you the desire for the prayer of the heart will give you that prayer itself.

"When your heart's intention is fixed on God, it will keep lit the incense of your prayer, and the wind of distraction will not put it out. Do not worry about stray thoughts; they may come and go, but they will not take your attention away from God."

10. Romuald befriends a poor farmer and sustains his cause.

Here we return to Romuald's years in the hermitage above Cuixá. The chapter gives us two important themes: an authentic hermit always stands on the side of the have-nots, against those who hold economic and political power over them; and God is revealed to us whenever we see "the hungry filled with good things and the rich sent away empty" [cf. Luke 1,53]. Peter Damian recounts similar episodes about Romuald in chapters 36, 43, 54, 65, and 71.

While at Cuixá, Romuald developed a close friendship with a local farmer. This kindly and generous man, richer in good will than in material possessions, provided Romuald with tools and other useful items for the hermitage.

Now the poor farmer had a cow, but a wealthy and greedy count, acting like a barbarian, had his servants take the farmer's cow and send it to the butcher, to satisfy his gluttonous palate. The poor man ran to Romuald's cell and, weeping loudly, told him the story, and how his family had lost its sole wealth. Romuald immediately sent word to the count, humbly asking him to give the cow back, but the count laughed at Romuald's request. "The cow has already been slaughtered and roasted," he replied, "and today I'm going to enjoy eating it."

At the dinner hour the table was set and the roasted meat was brought out and placed before the count. But the time had come for God's justice to prevail. When the count took his first bite, he choked on the meat, and for all he tried, he could not spit it out or swallow it. So unable to breathe, he died a horrible death in the sight of his guests. The glutton who had despised a monk's request was, by God's just decree, sent to his grave fasting.

11. Another count, repenting of his sins, makes his confession to Romuald.

Oliba Cabreta, whom Peter Damian calls "Count Olibano", was the son of Miro, count of Barcelona, and the father of Abbot Oliba, Garí's successor at Cuixá. Count Olibano goes and makes his confession to Romuald, who by now, in his last year at Cuixá, has been ordained a priest. The count is mentioned in a document dated February 988, with a list of his donations to the monastic congregation headed by Abbot Garí.

In those parts there was another count, Olibano by name, whose domain embraced the monastery of Abbot Garí. However high-ranking by earthly standards the count might have been, the weight of his many sins had brought him spiritually to a very low estate.

One day he came to visit Romuald. He ordered those with him to wait outside Romuald's cell, while he went in alone and told him everything he had ever done, as it were a general confession. Having listened attentively to the count,

Romuald said, "If you would be saved, you have no option but to leave the world and enter a monastery."

These words came as a surprise to Count Olibano. "I have many churchmen with me," he said, "and they know all my deeds. Never have I heard them say such a thing, nor have they ever imposed on me such an intolerable penance." So he went out and had all the bishops and abbots in his entourage come forward. He asked them whether his spiritual state was as Romuald had said. All of them with one voice confirmed Romuald's advice, and they apologized for never having spoken in these terms, saying, "We were afraid of how you might have reacted."

Once again Count Olibano sent everyone away, and with Romuald's help he formulated a secret plan: they would organize a trip to Monte Cassino, saying it was only a pilgrimage, but once there he would consecrate himself irrevocably to the service of God in Saint Benedict's monastery.

12. Sergio, after his exodus from sin, wants to return to his former slavery.

Romuald's father also decides to become a conversus *and enters the abbey of San Severo near Ravenna. The underlying metaphor of this monastic choice is the exodus of the Israelites from their slavery in Egypt; the monastery is thus a desert of privation and testing, but like the wilderness of Sinai it also represents the experience of freedom and intimacy with the God of the covenant.*

In the meantime Romuald's father Sergio had entered a monastery, but a short time later, at the devil's prodding, he repented of his conversion and wanted to return to "Egypt." The monks of San Severo Abbey—not far from Ravenna, where Sergio had taken up residence in the body, if not in the spirit—found a way of getting a message to Romuald. The news of his father came as a shock, and he concluded that he could not take Count Olibano to Monte Cassino. Abbot Garí and John Gradenigo would have to accompany him, while Romuald ran to save his father from perdition.

Peter Orséolo had already reached the happy end of his life's journey. Romuald entrusted Count Olibano to the abbot and especially to John Gradenigo; and as he was John's senior in monastic life, Romuald enjoined on him by obedience never to let Olibano out of his sight, even if Abbot Garí were to travel on after reaching Monte Cassino.

13. Romuald pretends to be crazy, so as to avoid getting killed.

What you might call "devotional murder"—killing a saint in order to have his relics—was not uncommon in those days. If you remember the story of the Five Brothers, you might have more than a slight suspicion that Duke Boleslaw himself spread the word about the money he had given to Benedict and John, in the hope that somebody would give Poland a few more martyrs to add to Saint Adalbert.

The year is 988, shortly after Peter Orséolo's death in January—perhaps during Lent. Romuald's feigned insanity is compared with that of King David (I Samuel 21,13-14). In book 17 of his Conferences, *Cassian cites this story, but not as an example to be imitated, while pretending to be a glutton is seen as an expression of humility in* Conferences *17,24 and in the* Vitæ Patrum *8,4.*

When they heard that Romuald was planning to leave the country, the local people were deeply grieved. They debated among themselves the best way to keep him there, and at a certain point their warped devotion led them to the conclusion that the best thing would be to kill him. If they couldn't keep him there alive, then at least his dead body would provide them with sacred relics to protect their homes and lands.

But Romuald was told of the plan. So he shaved his head completely, and one day after sunup, hearing some people approach his hermitage, he started stuffing food into his mouth. When the villagers saw this, they thought he had lost his mind. "He is touched in the head," they said, and so they did not touch his body. Thus the shrewd insanity of this spiritual David defeated the insane shrewdness of those wise according to the flesh. He kept them from sinning and, fearless of his own death, held death at bay, thus increasing his merits.

So at last he was free to act. He left not on horseback or by ox cart but on foot with a stick in hand, and he walked all the way from the Pyrenees to Ravenna. There he found his father threatening to take off the robes and go back to the world. Romuald had him put in stocks and chains and gave him a good beating. Thus a son's severe love tamed his father's body, so that God's healing touch might bring back his mind to a more healthy state.

14. Sergio sees the Holy Spirit.

After telling us about Romuald pretending to be crazy, Peter Damian gives us this anecdote about Sergio's holy dementia. Ravenna's hagiographic tradition puts apparitions of the Holy Spirit—under the form of a dove—in quite a different context: these apparitions are said to have accompanied the election of the first twelve bishops of the city.

Once Sergio had regained his sanity, he began to make rapid progress in monastic living, and he corrected those faults of his which were driving him back to the world. Among other things, he acquired the habit of stopping frequently to pray in front of an icon of the Savior, where— if no one else were present—he would pour forth his prayers with abundant tears and great compunction of heart.

One day his concentration was greater than usual, when something happened which is unheard of in our days. It seems the Holy Spirit appeared to him—in what form I do not know. Immediately he dashed out of the chapel and started running around the cloister asking everyone, "Where did he go? Which way did he leave? Did you see him come this way?"

"Who?" they asked.

"The Holy Spirit. I saw him! I saw him!"

They laughed. "You must be mad!" they said.

"No, no! I saw the Holy Spirit!"

A few days later he took to his bed and died. As the Lord said to Moses, "No man can see me and live." Even Daniel, who never claimed to have seen God but only a vision of what seemed like God, said, "I lost consciousness and was ill for several days."[1] Thus Sergio, having seen eternal life, that is, God, had to leave this life of space and time.

[1]Cf. Daniel 8,27.

15. John Gradenigo becomes a hermit at Monte Cassino.

Oral tradition among the monks of Monte Cassino was obviously the common source of the stories about John Gradenigo which we have from Peter Damian and Bruno of Querfurt (cf. Life of the Five Brothers, *chapter 2).*

As at Cuixá, so at Monte Cassino, there is a hermit colony close by the abbey. Not far from John Gradenigo's cell is that of a former abbot of the monastery, and this fact shows how much in harmony with the reformed monasticism of the tenth century (generically termed "Cluniac spirituality") is Romuald's synthesis of the anachoretic ideal with the Rule of Saint Benedict.

In the meantime, Count Olibano deeded all his lands to his son. Then he loaded fifteen mules with everything of value they could carry, and with Abbot Garí, John Gradenigo, and Marino he left for the abbey of Saint Benedict. After they arrived at Monte Cassino, Olibano bid farewell to the members of his court who had accompanied him. At this, they shed bitter tears; up to that moment, in fact, no one had suspected it was his intention to stay there as a monk.

Marino remained with them only a very short while, and then he left for Apulia, where he continued to live as a hermit. But he had not been there long, when he was slain by Saracen pirates.

Another few days went by, and Abbot Garí announced his intention to leave for Jerusalem. Garí was fond of going on pilgrimage—"to pray at the holy shrines," he said—and John also felt the urge to follow his example. Garí agreed to have John accompany him, but when Olibano heard of their plans, he was desolate. Tearfully he begged them, "Do not abandon me here! You gave me your word that you would assist me during my novitiate. These were Father Romuald's orders." And he added, "At least you, John, must remember that your Father Master entrusted me to your care. Didn't he say you would be a disobedient monk, were you to leave me here alone?"

But John and the abbot were unmoved; they took leave of Olibano and set out on their pilgrimage. Having reached the foot of the mountain and before taking the road across the plain, they stopped to talk. At that moment Garí's horse, startled by something, reared up, and the abbot could not rein him in. The horse struck John with his hoof and broke his thigh bone.

Howling with pain, John fell to the ground. All too late he remembered Romuald's injunction and loudly acknowledged, "This is all on account of my disobedience!" His broken leg reminded him that he had broken his promise. Like a dumb animal who rebels against its rider, so he, although endowed with reason, acted against the will of his teacher and even against his own better interests.

There was nothing for John to do but return to the abbey. He eventually asked permission to build a cell nearby and there he remained for some thirty years—that is, until the end of his days—living as a hermit.

He was a man of great charity, of admirable humility. He practiced fasting with great rigor, of course, but with such discretion that no one in the monastery knew what foods he abstained from and what foods he ate.

Among his many virtues there was his strong aversion to gossip. "Whenever you speak ill of someone," he taught, "the words you utter come right back at you, like an arrow that bounces off a rock and returns to strike the archer."

After John's death, God worked a number of miracles through his intercession.

16. Romuald, living as a hermit near Classe, overcomes his fear of the devil.

Once again, Romuald does battle with demons. These accounts are all built around the framework offered by traditional hagiographic texts, like Athanasius' Life of Antony; *see also Gregory the Great,* Dialogues 2,8.

Once he had set his father back on the right path, Romuald built himself a hut in the wetlands near Classe, in a locality called Peter's Bridge. But after some time there he moved to a chapel, Saint-Martin-in-the-Woods, on land belonging to the abbey. This change was prompted by his concern lest his health fail and he be unable to fast as before—not that Romuald was afraid of being ill or that he minded the nauseating smell of the swamp!

The chapel stood next to an abandoned cemetery. One evening, as he was singing Compline, it happened that his mind wandered, and he thought: the cemetery! Horrible images started to dance in his head. And as he dwelt upon them, some wicked spirits broke into the chapel and threw him to the ground. His body, weakened by fasting, felt it was being beaten and battered by them. Under their blows, Romuald's mind turned to God's grace, and he cried, "Dear Jesus, beloved Jesus, why have you forsaken me? Have you delivered me into the hands of my enemies?"

As he uttered these words, God's power scattered the evil spirits. And immediately a great flame of love for God rose up in Romuald's breast and melted his heart like wax. He poured forth his soul in tears, and he felt no more pain.

After a few minutes he regained strength, pulled himself to his feet, and, his wounds still bleeding, sang the rest of Compline. When the demons had entered the chapel, the window next to where he had been standing blew open and hit him on the forehead. Romuald was left with a scar, visible evidence of the wound.

17. Romuald drives away the evil spirits.

Made strong by frequent battles, the soldier of Christ daily confirmed his commitment to grow from strength to strength. As he got the better of his weakened enemy, he had less cause to fear their attacks.

At times, when he was in his cell, evil spirits appeared to gather around, but they were held at bay, like hideous vultures and crows unable to approach a well-guarded body.

On other occasions, the demons presented themselves under some other guise, human[1] or animal, and he who had won the victory in Christ mocked them: "Here I am—what are you waiting for? Show your valor, if you have any! Do you admit defeat? Have you no weapons to hurl at this poor monk?" Shaming the spirits with such words as these, as with sharp-pointed javelins, Romuald put them to flight.

But then the devil, seeing he could not prevail against God's servant directly, tried more devious means. Wherever the saintly monk went, the devil stirred up trouble among his disciples. If the enemy failed to dampen Romuald's ardent love for God, he would try to discourage his concern for his neighbor's salvation. Unable to make Romuald surrender, at least the devil might impede his victory in defense of others.

[1]Peter Damian says "as Ethiopians" here, and it is hard to defend him against the charge of racism, except to say that his color prejudice is a fruit of "invincible ignorance."

18. Romuald builds a monastery, but the monks beat him up and drive him away.

To illustrate the point he has just made, Peter Damian narrates the story of Romuald's first attempt at being a "founder," which resulted in total failure.

Around the monastery which Romuald built, a village grew; it is called Verghereto. Among the populace the memory of Romuald is still alive, and oral tradition has handed down an account of these events similar to that of Peter Damian, but with a few interesting particulars. Note that the monastery at Verghereto is dedicated to Saint Michael, as was the abbey of Cuixá, and in fact the Apennines near Bagno di Romagna closely resemble the gentle slopes of the eastern Pyrenees, where Garí's abbey stands.

Romuald himself was not the superior of the monastery at Verghereto—he lived as a hermit a short distance away; this was his habitual practice in the communities he initi-

*ated or reformed. Only once, in the year 998, did he over-
come his reluctance to govern others and by way of exception
let the monks of Classe elect him their abbot. Even there, it
did not last. Hardly a year had gone by, when Romuald,
failing to save the souls of his monks and fearing to lose his
own, renounced the office and went off to Monte Cassino.*

*Peter Damian sees Romuald's preoccupation with his
own soul as a grave temptation. The hermit isolated from
others and centered on self is on the road to damnation;
penance and prayer, silence and solitude are then nothing
but fuel for the flames of a private hell.*

At that time, Romuald moved to a place called Bagno, in
the foothills of the Apennines. Settling in for a good long
time, he built a monastery, had it dedicated to the Archangel
Michael, and then set up his hermitage a short distance away.

For Romuald's work there, the Marquis Hugh sent him
seven pounds of silver coins. Romuald accepted them with
an eye to distributing the money among the poor. He soon
heard that fire had destroyed the abbey of Palazzolo near
Ravenna, and so he sent the homeless monks 60 coins,
keeping the balance for similar works of mercy.

The monks of Saint Michael's were furious. Like a herd
of wild oxen they turned their rage on him, first because he
did not go along with their way of doing things, and second
because he donated part of the money he received to others
instead of turning it all over to them. So they got together
and headed for the hermitage with sticks and clubs. They
beat him up, took the money, and hurling insults at him,
drove him out of town.

Bruised and depressed, Romuald turned his back on
Bagno and started walking. "Never again," he promised
himself: "never again. From now on the only thing that
matters is the salvation of my soul. I am going to save my
own soul and not bother any more about anyone else's."

He turned these thoughts over and over in his mind until,
at a certain point, a deathly terror flooded his brain, and he

knew he had come close to the edge of damnation. Had he continued obstinately in the direction his thoughts were leading him, he would have fallen into the abyss of God's judgment.

Meanwhile, the monks of Saint Michael's were enjoying their vendetta. For some time they had wanted to rid themselves of that hermit, whom they regarded as a dead weight. Proud of their accomplishment, they started making jokes about Romuald and laughed themselves silly. Then they had an idea: "Let's celebrate," they said; "this is an occasion that deserves a banquet with all the frills."

Now it was winter, and the chill of the season reflected the coldness of their hearts. One of the monks—the one who had treated Romuald with the greatest cruelty—suggested they fix a hot drink of wine and honey for dessert. And so he set off for town to buy the honey, but as he was crossing the river, he tripped on a loose board, fell off the bridge, and was swallowed up by the raging waters. Thus God's just judgment was satisfied, and death came upon him who had thought to celebrate with a honeyed drink a deed for which he ought to have wept.

That night all the other monks went to bed as usual, and while they were sleeping, the first heavy snow of the season made the roof cave in over their heads. Everyone was injured: one had a fractured skull, the others a broken leg or arm or other injuries. One monk lost an eye, and rightly so, since by dividing himself from his neighbor, he had extinguished one of the two lights of love, even though he preserved the other.[1]

[1]Cf. Matthew 22, 37-40.

19. Saint Apollinaris orders Romuald to return to Classe.

The year is almost certainly 993 (see below, chapter 22). This dream or vision of Ravenna's patron saint initiates Romuald's second vocation and a new phase in his mission of monastic formation and reform—a mission begun unsuccessfully at Verghereto.

At this point it would be good to read chapter 9 once again. Returning to Classe and to the community which had received his vows and clothed him in the black cowl of Cluny, Romuald rediscovered his Benedictine origins and at the same time broadened his monastic culture with new readings (for example, the Homilies of Saint Sylvester *mentioned in chapter 9). The man remained what he was, with his hypersensitive and impulsive character, but the monk acquired that virtue which monastic tradition considers the mother of them all: discretion.*

There was a time when Romuald dwelt near Mount Catria. After he had been there for some time, Saint Apollinaris appeared to him and with great authority ordered him to return to his monastery at Classe and stay there. Romuald told himself, "I must not disobey this vision." So without a moment's delay he abandoned the hermitage where he had been living and set out for the place to which he had been directed.

20. Romuald dwells in the Vales of Comacchio.

Rather than tell us about Romuald's arrival at Classe and his stay in the abbey or nearby, Peter Damian gives us two stories out of chronological order, situated in the wetlands north of Ravenna.

Well into middle age now, Romuald can no longer bear the humid climate and falls ill. The illness is probably acute malaria; he will have a number of attacks of it throughout his life (see chapter 26).

Most of the land in this area has been drained and reclaimed for farming, but here and there remain patches of wetlands which can give you an idea of the natural environment Saint Romuald knew and loved. A local legend tells us that he planted roses near his hermitage, which continued to grow and bloom for centuries after his death.

For a certain period of time, the venerable Romuald dwelt as a recluse in the Vales of Comacchio, at a place called Origario. He had not been there long, when the humid climate and the swamp gas made his face swell up and his hair fall out. He didn't even look like the same man who went to live there a short while before. His skin had a greenish tinge to it, like that of a lizard.

21. Romuald puts out a fire with prayer.

The "island" of Peréo, once a patch of dry land between the river Po and the swamps, is now a village called Sant'Alberto (from "Sant'Adalberto"), surrounded by farms and orchards. Here Romuald will set up a short-lived hermitage, and the emperor Otto III will have a church and a cloister built, from which he will send missionaries up to Poland (see chapters 30 and 28, in that order).

The monk William who shares Romuald's cell is most likely Blessed William of Pomposa. Elected abbot of his monastery, William will add a hermitage to it, in accordance with the practice at Cuixá and Monte Cassino.

Then there was a time when he was living on the island of Peréo, twelve miles north of Ravenna. At Peréo he shared his cell with a venerable monk and disciple named William.

Once a fire started in a corner of the small house where they were living; it quickly spread to the roof and became uncontrollable.

The holy monk Romuald immediately turned to his usual means of defense. Rather than do what people usually do in these cases—start moving furniture outside, strip the tiles off the roof, throw water or sand or what not on the flames to quench them—Romuald just recited a prayer. Instantly God's power suffocated the roaring blaze.

22. Romuald offers hospitality to the emperor and in exchange is made abbot of Classe.

Otto III makes his second foray into Italy in the year 998; he is eighteen years old. Holding court briefly at Ravenna, he finds the city without an archbishop and its principal abbey in need of a new abbot. So to fill the see of Ravenna he summons the most learned man of the day, the great Gerbert of Aurillac, a Frenchman who had not long been abbot of Bobbio in northern Italy. Now Gerbert was a good friend of Abbot Garí, and during a visit to Cuixá in the early years of the decade, he may have heard Garí speak of the hermit Romuald. So it is not unlikely that Gerbert himself suggested that Otto name Romuald abbot of Classe.

As abbot, Romuald recalls his brothers to "the strict discipline of the Rule." In what sense? The "discipline" which Romuald evokes is the common life, the apostolic koinonia which unites the monks and makes them all equal. In the context of feudal society it was inevitable that distinctions of birth and learning be maintained even in monasteries. And this is precisely what Romuald can not tolerate.

Imposing the fellowship of equals upon a community accustomed to a complex system of rank and privilege ingratiates him with no one. But Romuald is obeying his conscience and cares not for anybody's opinion of his behavior. In a different context, Bruno of Querfurt says the same thing: "Romuald's personality, as a contemplative and a true servant of God, had one outstanding characteristic: whatever people would have liked to see him do, he tried at all costs to do exactly the opposite. Only when he could get them to insult, taunt, and slander him (provided he did nothing against his own conscience), would he consider himself worthy of esteem and capable of preserving his virtue. Romuald was always totally consistent with himself."

Romuald's failure to reform his community and his resignation from the office of abbot after little more than a year are certainly historical facts, but Peter Damian narrates them in terms borrowed from Pope Gregory the Great's account of Saint Benedict at Vicovaro.

At Ravenna, Gerbert will remain only a few months. On February 4, 999, Pope Gregory V dies—or is poisoned—at the age of twenty-seven. He was Otto's cousin and the first German pope, and now Otto gives the See of Peter its first Frenchman, Gerbert of Aurillac. As pope, Gerbert takes the name Sylvester II and thus implies that the young Otto is destined to be a new Constantine. Now with the archbishopric of Ravenna once more vacant, everyone begins to ask whether Romuald will be the one to fill the post, thus giving him another good reason to resign.

While Romuald was staying at Classe, the young emperor Otto, wishing to reform the abbey, gave the monks the faculty to freely elect whomever they would choose. Without hesitation and unanimously they asked for Romuald.

However, the emperor doubted whether this holy hermit would accept an invitation to court from a mere messenger. So he decided to go see him personally. Otto arrived at Romuald's cell close to sundown. Romuald, finding such an illustrious guest at the door of his hermitage, offered the emperor his own bed for the night. Otto accepted the invitation, but he would not take Romuald's blanket, finding it much too rough.

The next morning, King Otto brought Romuald to his palace in the city and pleaded with him to accept the office of abbot. Romuald was reluctant to reply; Otto failed to extract a yes from him. So the emperor tried threats: "If you do not accept the office, I shall call a synod and have all the bishops and archbishops and the entire council excommunicate you." At this, Romuald surrendered to the inevitable and gave his consent. But then he added, "This is not news to me; God already told me it would happen, five years ago."

Romuald governed the monks according to the strict discipline of the Rule. He allowed for no special privileges; no monk—be he high-born or learned—dared commit any illicit action that would take him off the straight path of the common life. In other words, Romuald's heart was set on heaven and his one concern was to please God in all things, even when this was displeasing to men.

The monks whose abbot he had consented to be realized too late the kind of abbot he was. First they threw accusations at one another, for having suggested the name of Romuald, and in the end they turned their wrath against him, spreading gossip and inventing scandals about him.

23. Romuald leaves Classe; he makes peace between the emperor and the people of Tivoli.

The Life of the Five Brothers *helps us establish the chronological order of the events which follow Romuald's resignation as abbot.*

1. Romuald resigns: December 999. Bruno of Querfurt says Romuald addresses his resignation only to the emperor and not also to the archbishop.

*2. He leaves Classe and goes directly to Monte Cassino:
Peter Damian tells of this journey in chapter 26, but compare*
The Life of the Five Brothers, *chapter two. At Cassino
Romuald finds his friend John Gradenigo, whom he had last
seen in 988, at the latter's departure from Cuixá. Romuald
remains at Monte Cassino for at least ten months; he falls ill
in September-October of the year 1000 and is nursed back to
health by a young monk, Gradenigo's disciple Benedict of
Benevento (see chapter 28).*

*3. October 1000: Otto III arrives in Rome and sets up his
court on the brow of the Aventine Hill, next to the monastery
of Saints Boniface and Alexis (Sant'Alessio), a community
which unites a group of Greek monks with Cluniac
Benedictines. One of Otto's confidants, Tammo by name,
becomes a monk there, taking the name Thomas (chapter
25), and with him Otto's personal chaplain, Bruno of Querfurt
(chapter 27). Bruno's monastic name is Boniface, taken to
honor the great English monk and missionary, Wynfrith-
Boniface (675-754), "apostle to the Germans."*

*4. Before the end of the year 1000, most likely in early
November, Romuald arrives in Rome. He meets Otto on the
Aventine and invites Bruno-Boniface and Tammo to join him at a
temporary hermitage which he establishes outside the city,
perhaps near Saint Benedict's first monastery at Subiaco.*

*5. Contemporary documents inform us that the siege of
Tivoli opens the year 1001 (hence certainly after Romuald's
retreat at Monte Cassino); on February 16, Rome itself
rebels against Otto III. The emperor retreats to Ravenna
with his German troops and Pope Sylvester II; Romuald and
his disciples retire to the island of Peréo (see chapter 30).*

Romuald realized that as abbot he had ceased to grow as
a monk, while his monks' behavior was going from bad to
worse. Without a moment's delay he went to see Otto. The
emperor and the archbishop of Ravenna tried to talk him out
of it, but Romuald threw the abbatial staff at their feet and
abandoned Classe.

On a later occasion, King Otto lay siege to Tivoli. The townspeople had taken the much-decorated commander of his troops, Duke Mazzolino, and had killed him; then they barred the city gates to the emperor himself.

Without question it was God's providence that Romuald happened to be in the vicinity of Tivoli. He obtained an agreement of clemency for the townsfolk and thus further bloodshed was avoided. The pact imposed the partial destruction of the city walls, while the king held their leaders hostage, and the duke's assassin was to be delivered in chains to Mazzolino's mother. But in her presence Romuald uttered a prayer that moved her to pity; so she halted the man's punishment, forgave him, and sent him on his way home, unharmed.

24. Romuald corrects the hermit Venerio.

To the hermit Venerio, Romuald repeats the message that he himself received when, in the solitude of Mount Catria, Saint Apollinaris appeared to him: that he must live his solitary life not against, but in communion with, his monastic community (see chapter 19).

Romuald wants to see hermits trained and supported within the framework of the Benedictine cœnobium, not as an alternative to the latter but as the completion and crowning of the cenobitic experience. We can compare the present chapter with an episode recounted by Saint Gregory the Great (Dialogues 3,16): Saint Benedict comes across a hermit who has bound himself to his cave by a chain; he tells him, "If you are a servant of God, do not bind yourself with a chain of iron but with the chain of Christ's love."

While at Tivoli, the venerable Romuald bore another good fruit, which I must not pass over in silence.

There was a holy man who at one time had been living in a monastery. So great were his humility and simplicity, that his brother monks despised and derided him, thinking him insane. One of the monks came to blows with him, another threw the dirty dishwater at him, while a third never ceased to find fault with everything he did.

Considering that he would never find peace under such treatment, Venerio fled the monastery and retired to a solitary place. For six years he lived there, fasting to excess and abstaining from wine and all cooked food.

Romuald asked him, "To what monastic authority have you submitted your rule of life? As a hermit, whom do you obey?"

Venerio answered, "I am under no particular authority; I am free to do what seems best to me."

"If you are bearing the cross of Christ," Romuald told him, "you must not forget Christ's obedience. Now go, ask your abbot to give his consent, and then come back here, but as his humble disciple. Thus the house of your holy life, which your good will is building, will rest on the foundations of humility and will have the strong support of obedience."

This and other counsels Romuald left him, and he taught him how to control his thoughts and defend himself against the assaults of evil spirits. Venerio felt strengthened now, and enlightened, and he was eager to continue his search for God.

So he joyfully accepted Romuald's advice and went to his monastery, received the abbot's consent, and came back to his beloved solitude. However, he decided he ought to live on land which belonged to the abbey. So he found an inaccessible site high on a cliff, where he could remain unknown. Here he arrived with three small loaves of bread from the monastery, and for the next four years he lived alone, without the comfort of human companionship, without eating bread or cooked food, and without ever drinking wine. He gathered roots and berries to eat, and a cleft in the rock collected enough rain during winter to provide him with water throughout the summer.

In the end it came to be known that a servant of God dwelt on that cliff, and many persons came to him and offered him food and other necessities. But he felt no need for it all and gave it away to the shepherds and beggars.

Then the bishop took an interest in him, and he had to let them build a chapel on his cliff. A short time later he died. Some people hiked up to the chapel one day and found his body in front of the altar bent double, as if he had been praying on his hands and knees. At that altar the Lord deigned to work a number of miracles.

Venerio was indeed good earth, which having received the seed of God's word from the mouth of Romuald, rendered a hundredfold.

25. Tammo becomes a monk, and the emperor promises to take the cowl.

The events in this chapter are well documented; they take place in 998, before Romuald's coming to Rome and before the events recounted in the last two chapters.

We need to complete Peter Damian's story, which is partial and not entirely just in its judgment of Otto and his cousin, the young (26-year-old) Pope Gregory V. Otto's involvement in papal politics is to a certain extent justifiable: by forcing the election of his cousin, Otto seeks to loosen the stranglehold on the papacy by two or three patrician families, who generally installed their least worthy relatives on the papal throne. If Gregory V is "too young" to be pope, at least he is of canonical age for ordination; one of his predecessors was barely 18 (!) when elected to the See of Peter.

At the end of 997, the patrician Crescentius takes steps to drive Gregory V from Rome. In February of the following year Otto and the imperial troops escort the pope back to the city. Crescentius takes refuge in Castel Sant'Angelo near Saint Peter's Basilica. Although it is a military fortress, the "castle" is also a sacred place, having been Hadrian's tomb and now papal property—hence a "sanctuary" from which no one may be taken by force of arms. For this reason, Crescentius has to be made to leave voluntarily. He does so, believing himself safe, and is slain.

In chapter three of his Life of the Five Brothers, *Bruno of Querfurt gives his own, slightly different account of Otto's vow to become a monk.*

While in Rome, blessed Romuald converted a German by the name of Tammo. It is said that this man was so dear to the emperor that they used to wear each other's clothes and, as often as they were at table together, would eat out of the same dish.

The Roman senator Crescentius, having incurred the emperor's wrath, fled to Castel Sant'Angelo, which, being an impregnable fortress, guaranteed he could resist the imperial troops.

Tammo went to him at the emperor's orders and promised him safe passage. Crescentius fell for the lie and, with the pope's consent (for the pope also considered him an enemy), underwent capital punishment for *lèse majesté*. The emperor took his widow as concubine.

Now since Tammo had been an accomplice and had sworn a false oath, Romuald ordered him to become a monk. When Tammo asked the emperor's permission, Otto not only granted it readily, but was overjoyed at Tammo's decision. In fact, Otto was accustomed to show great benevolence to the monastic order, and he was excessively fond of the company of monks. Having confessed his crime to blessed Romuald, the emperor imposed upon himself the penance of walking barefoot from Rome to the shrine of Saint Michael on Mount Gargano.

On another occasion he spent an entire Lent at Sant'Apollinare in Classe. While at the abbey, Otto, attended by a very small retinue, followed the monastic regime of fasting and prayer as best he could. Under the royal purple he wore a hairshirt next to his skin, and instead of using his cushioned and blanketed bed at night, he preferred to sleep on a rough mat. He even promised Romuald to abdicate his imperial crown for a monk's cowl. Thus a man who enjoyed power over so many of his fellow mortals submitted to Christ, the Poor, to whom he owed his very existence.

26. Romuald leaves for Monte Cassino and then settles at Peréo.

Peter Damian reverses the directions of Romuald's journeys. From the Life of the Five Brothers *and other contemporary documents, we know that, after his resignation as abbot of Classe, Romuald goes directly to Monte Cassino, where he spends several months (and is ill, as Peter Damian also tells us). Then he goes to Rome, pays his respects to the emperor at Sant'Alessio on the Aventine, and retires for the pre-Christmas Lent (12 November to 24 December) at or near the abbey of Subiaco, accompanied by the two newly-professed monks from Otto's court, Tammo-Thomas and Bruno-Boniface. Finally, in mid-January of the new year 1001, begin the series of popular rebellions (at Tivoli and in Rome itself) which will force Otto to retreat to Ravenna.*

The rest of Peter Damian's account of the relations among Romuald, Otto III, and Romuald's disciples is also hopelessly tangled. Here is the chronological sequence of the events:

1. See Peter Damian's chapter 30: the young emperor has a cenobitic monastery built at Peréo, dedicated to Saint

Adalbert (martyred in northern Poland, 997), for the purpose of forming missionary monks. Romuald gives his consent to this project, bringing down fierce criticism on his own head. This takes place during the late summer and early fall of 1001.

2. See chapter 28: Otto asks Romuald to allow two of his disciples (Benedict of Benevento and John of Ravenna) to leave for Poland (November 1001).

3. Shortly before the departure of Benedict and John, Bruno-Boniface, troubled by the presence of Otto and his court in the hermitage of Peréo, moves to another hermitage, perhaps that of William of Pomposa (cf. chapter 21). This fact gives Romuald himself motive to leave, and he sails across the Adriatic to his ancestral lands in Istria, modern-day Croatia.

4. That same year, at Christmas, Pope Sylvester II presides over a synod at Todi, where it is decided that Bruno-Boniface shall be ordained archbishop and sent to the newly-evangelized lands of Eastern Europe (Hungary and Poland especially). In January 1002 we find Otto laying siege to Rome; the citizenry rout him, and he retreats to the castle of Paterno near Mount Soracte. There he falls ill of small-pox and dies at the age of 23 (see chapter 30). Pope Sylvester dies the year following.

5. See chapter 28: news of the emperor's death reaches Benedict and John in Poland. By this time they have a few Polish novices, and they are anxiously awaiting the arrival of Bruno-Boniface with the papal license for their mission. On November 11, 1003, they are attacked in their sleep by a band of robbers and die a holy death; the local church and eventually Rome recognize them as martyrs.

6. See chapters 34 and following: it is now 1005, and Romuald returns to Italy, where he begins the most prolific phase of his career as a monastic reformer. His new communities are at Biforco in Romagna, at Val di Castro in the Marches, and at Orvieto in Umbria.

7. At last we come to the events of chapter 27: on March 9, 1009, Saint Bruno-Boniface of Querfurt meets death at

*the hands of the Prussians near the modern-day border
between Lithuania and Poland. News of his martyrdom
reaches Romuald at Orvieto.*

Leaving Tivoli together with Tammo and his most famous disciple [Bruno-]Boniface (whom the Russian church
now venerates as her own martyr), as well as a few other
German novices, Romuald went to Saint Benedict's monastery at Monte Cassino. There he became seriously ill, but
soon, by God's mercy, he returned to health.

As a gift he received a fine horse from the son of Duke
Boleslaw of Poland. Romuald had guided the young man
toward a monastic vocation. Now you see a saint's humility,
for he made a deal with someone—what a shrewd busi-
nessman Romuald was!—and got himself a donkey in
exchange for the horse. So much did he desire to imitate our
Redeemer, who rode into Jerusalem on the foal of an ass,
Romuald preferred a jenny to a stallion.

With all his disciples he returned to Peréo, where he had
been living as a hermit. Many came to join them, and he
provided each with a cell. Great was the rigor of their life in
the hermitage, and their example aroused great admiration
among the people. Who could doubt the wonders God had
wrought, when they saw men accustomed to silk garments,
gold ornaments, fawning lackeys, and whatever could delight
the eye or palate, now content to live alone, wear a rough
robe and go barefoot, exhibiting the severity of their fasts by
their gaunt faces and wasted limbs? Furthermore, they all
worked hard: some carved wooden spoons, others did
weaving or made fish nets.

27. Bruno-Boniface witnesses to Christ among the Prussians.

This chapter, the longest in his Life of Romuald, *contains Peter Damian's most serious historical error, when he calls "King of the Russians" the pagan ruler of the* Prussian *tribes in northern Poland, where Bruno-Boniface is slain.*

In 1988 the Christian Churches celebrated the thousand-year anniversary of the baptism of Vladimir, the holy prince of Kievan Rus''. In part one of this book we quoted at length a letter written by Bruno-Boniface to Henry II, in which he tells of his visit to the court of Saint Vladimir and the hospitality he received there. The friendship between these two saints of the undivided Church—only a few decades before Rome and Constantinople will excommunicate each other—is a prophecy for our times, as we struggle to heal our divisions.

When Bruno-Boniface dies as a martyr (March 9, 1009), Romuald is at Orvieto. At the news of his disciple's death, he leaves for Rome and petitions Pope Sergius IV for permission to go on mission himself (see chapter 39).

One supposes you will be reading this chapter after having read the Life of the Five Brothers; *if not, please go back and read at least the prologue and the last chapter. You will find a very different Bruno-Boniface there: a gentle soul, a man of tormented conscience but of great warmth and affection, anything but the cold and frugal fanatic described in this chapter. Saints often do not deserve the reputation they acquire after their canonization.*

To be fair to Peter Damian, we must recognize that he is doing in this chapter what everyone expected him to do. He takes a few sketchy lines from one or two eyewitnesses and then paints a portrait around them with the broad brush of hagiographic commonplaces and allusions to Pope Gregory's Dialogues *and Jerome's* Life of Hilarion. *The end result does not look much like the Bruno-Boniface we know from his own writings. In fact, it bears more than a passing resemblance to Peter Damian himself, at least to a darker side of his character which occasionally overshadows his gentle humor and his wisdom. Keep this in mind as you read the chapter, and you may find it interesting.*

In his life as a monk, the blessed [Bruno-]Boniface excelled over all his companions. The emperor, to whom he was related by blood, was so fond of him that he always called him "my soul."

At an early age he began his study of the liberal arts, but he was especially gifted in music. Once as an imperial chaplain he visited a church dedicated to the Roman martyr Boniface. Immediately he felt a desire for martyrdom, like that of his patron saint. "My name is Boniface," he said; "why then should I not also bear witness to Christ with my blood?"

Later, when he had become a monk, his abstinence was so frugal that often he would take food only on Sunday and Thursday. Whenever he passed a clump of nettles or even a thorn bush, he would throw himself into it and roll around. For doing this, a brother once corrected him. "You hypocrite!" he said; "you are doing this to draw attention to yourself." His only reply was: "Your saints are the confessors; mine are the martyrs."

After a long period of hermit life, he began to prepare himself to preach the gospel. First he went to Rome, where the pope ordained him archbishop. An elderly monk who had accompanied him there from Ravenna told me that, throughout the journey, the venerable man proceeded on foot, chanting Psalms with his companions. He was always several paces ahead of them, although he walked barefoot. Only on account of the toilsome journey did he take food every day—that is, half a loaf of bread and water—while on Sundays and feasts, still eschewing cooked food, he would add some raw fruits or vegetables to his usual rations.

Ordained a bishop, he began to celebrate a double Office, adding the canonical to the monastic psalmody. When his travels took him across mountainous terrain, he did mount a horse. But I heard them say he never wore stockings or leggings, so that his feet would freeze to the stirrups, and he could hardly get them out without pouring hot water on them.

Once he had arrived in pagan territory, he began to preach with such intense fervor, that no one could doubt that he desired martyrdom. Now after the martyrdom of blessed Adalbert and at the sight of all his miracles, many Slavs had converted to the faith. So for this reason the pagans, with calculated shrewdness, would not lay hands on Boniface. Their not wanting to kill him was to all effects an act of cruelty toward one who so longed to give his life.

This venerable man finally reached the presence of the king of the [Prussians] and preached to him in strong and ardent words. The king looked at his tattered clothing and bare feet, and concluded that all this talk of religion was just leading up to a pitch for money. So to get him to stop his raving, the king promised to make him a wealthy man. At this Boniface went straight back to his lodgings, changed into his finest pontifical vestments, and returned to court. At the sight of his splendid garb, the king said, "Now I know that it is ignorance of the truth and not material poverty that makes you mouth such nonsense. However, if you really want me to believe your teachings, you must submit to this test: let two stacks of wood be set up close together and put to the torch, and when they are both as one flaming mass, you must pass through the midst of them. If you come out with the slightest burn, we shall throw you back into the fire. But if it happens—although I don't believe it will—that you come through unscathed, then none of us will hesitate to believe in your god."

This pact was pleasing both to Boniface and to the pagans there present. So Boniface put on Mass vestments, honored the bonfire with holy water and incense, passed through the midst of the flames, and came out with not even a hair on his head singed. At that, the king and all the other spectators cast themselves at his feet weeping and begging pardon, and they all earnestly asked him to baptize them.

Crowds seeking baptism began to gather; they were so numerous that the holy archbishop had to take them to a large lake, in order to find water sufficient to baptize them.

The king issued a decree ceding the kingdom to his son and promising never to leave Boniface's side for the rest of his life. In the king's household, one of his brothers refused to become a believer; so the king had him put to death while Boniface was absent. Another brother, who did not live at court, had been unwilling to listen to Boniface from the very moment of his arrival. Moreover, when his brother converted to Christianity, he could not contain his rage against Boniface. Realizing that, if he let Boniface live, the king would take him into his protection, he had the saint beheaded in his own presence, surrounded by a great crowd of men and women. But instantly he was blinded, and upon all those present there descended such a great stupor that no one was able to speak or hear or perform any human act. Everyone remained rigid and immobile as stone.

When the king heard of this he was overwhelmed by grief, and he decided he must put to the sword not only his brother but also everyone who had applauded his crime. Immediately he went to the place and found the martyr's body lying before his brother and the crowd, who stood there senseless and unmoving. At the sight, the king and his men decided that first they must pray for them, that God in his mercy might restore them to their senses, and then, if they accepted the faith, the king would grant them pardon and allow them to live; otherwise they would be put to the sword.

When the king and all his Christians had prayed for a considerable time, not only did the stupefied men and women regain their senses, but they all decided to seek the grace of eternal salvation. Thereupon they broke into tears and asked to be punished for their crime. With great earnestness they received the sacrament of Baptism and began work on a church to house the holy martyr's body.

If I should try to enumerate all the virtues of this admirable man Boniface, I might run out of breath, but certainly not out of material. However, since his life and virtues have yet to be put into writing, it has been our wish to remember them here, along with the deeds of Romuald's other disciples, that by praising them we might show how great was their teacher. As long as the sublime deeds of the disciples, who are his crown, echo in the assembly of the faithful, all will know through them how sublime was the one who taught them.

28. John, Benedict, and their Polish companions bear witness to the forgiving Christ.

In his Life of the Five Brothers, *Bruno-Boniface tells the story of the two Italian monks who together with two Polish novices and a handyman shed their blood after having forgiven their assassins. The book is a hymn to friendship and is full of human warmth and great zeal for Christ's gospel. The discrepancies between Bruno's account and Peter Damian's are evident at first reading: for example, the novices Isaac and Matthew become "serving-boys," the monks absolve each other but do not address words of forgiveness to their assailants, and the brothers are said to have been in Poland for six years, while in fact they had been there just two years, when they met their death in the predawn hours of Thursday, November 11, 1003.*

While Romuald was living at Peréo, King Boleslaw petitioned the emperor to send spiritually-trained men who would assist in bringing his people to the faith. The emperor immediately went to Romuald and entreated him to make a few of his disciples available for this mission. However, Romuald did not wish to use his own authority to impose this on anyone. He allowed each monk the freedom to choose whether to go or to stay. In a matter so heavy with risks he did not know what was God's will; hence he preferred that the choice be that of each individual monk and not his own. So the emperor began to interview them one by one, to see if at least two might spontaneously volunteer to go on mission. These two were John and Benedict.

They set out for Poland, and when they arrived at Boleslaw's court, they found him ready to provide them with all the support they needed in their hermitage, so that they could devote their time to the study of the Slavic language and then to preaching. After six years, having mastered the language, they sent one of their monks to Rome, to request the pope's authorization for their mission. They also told him to ask Romuald to allow other well-trained hermits to come to Poland with him.

Boleslaw desired to obtain a king's crown from Rome. For this reason he earnestly begged our brothers to take along gifts for the pope and to bring back the crown from the Holy See. But they adamantly refused to honor his request. "We are in holy orders," they said, "and it is not permitted us to become involved in worldly affairs." With this they left the king's presence and returned to their hermitage.

Some individuals were aware of the king's project but knew nothing of the holy monks' reply. Hence they imagined that the brothers had taken back to the hermitage a large sum of money, to be delivered to the pope. So they met and plotted to break into the hermitage at night, kill the brothers, and take the money.

When the blessed martyrs heard men breaking into their cell, they realized immediately what their intentions were. They confessed to one another and armed themselves with the sign of the cross. Close by the monks' cells were two serving-boys, whom the king had sent to help them. With all their strength they tried to protect the holy monks and resist the thieves. But once the thieves were inside, they put everyone to the sword. Then they tore the house apart in a frantic search for the money, but they found nothing.

At that point, in order to hide their crime and make it appear that the brothers died by accident and not by the sword, they tried to set fire to the hermitage and thus consume the martyrs' bodies. But the flames lost their natural prerogatives. However long they held their torches to the walls, nothing took fire. The buildings seemed of stone rather than wood.

Frustrated in their every attempt, the thieves then tried to run away. But divine Providence would not permit even this. For all their trying, they could not find the path through the woods; all night they wandered through thicket and fen. Not even could they sheave their knives; their hands continued to grip them as if paralyzed.

Over the place where the saints lay, an intense light shone until morning, and sweet songs of angels were heard.

At dawn, news of the crime reached the king. He went straight to the hermitage, accompanied by many others, and lest the thieves get away, he had the woods surrounded by his troops. They were found and immediately recognized as the culprits, since by divine sentence their hands could not let go of their swords.

The king examined their case and reflected on how to punish them. In the end, he did not decide for the death penalty they deserved, but rather he decreed that they be chained to the martyrs' tomb. There they were to remain and to suffer for the rest of their life, had the martyred saints not decided differently: it was their merciful will that the assassins be set free.

As the king's order was about to be executed and the thieves were being led in chains to the saints' shrine, immediately, by God's mysterious power their bonds were broken, leaving them free. Later a church was built over the tomb, where God has worked and still works innumerable miracles.

29. A Polish monk, imprisoned by Henry II, is freed by an angel.

As he tells this story, Peter Damian is obviously thinking of his own namesake, the Apostle Peter—see Acts 12,1-11. So if the Polish monk (whose real name, we know from other sources, is Barnabas) is another Peter, then Henry is Herod.

As for Boleslaw's attempt to bribe the pope for a crown, we know nothing of this from other documents, and it would be totally illogical, given the political situation of the moment. The Holy See can offer no help to the Poles, who will be fighting for the next 25 years to resist the imposition of Germanic hegemony over their lands and their churches. In 1005, Bruno-Boniface will succeed in convincing Henry to suspend his attacks on Polish and Bohemian territory, so that he (Bruno-Boniface) can reach the place of the brothers' martyrdom and begin his own missionary work in Poland.

The emperor Henry was not unaware of Boleslaw's project and set up guards on all the roads in order to capture any emissaries Boleslaw might send to Rome.

Thus the monk whom the saints had sent a short time before their death was intercepted and taken straight to a prison. But that night an angel of the Lord came to him and said, "Your mission is concluded; those who sent you have attained their end." Immediately the doors of the prison fell open by God's power, and the angel told him that a boat would be waiting for him on the banks of the river he would have to cross.

The monk hurried out toward the river and found that what the angel had promised him was true.

30. Otto III builds a monastery at Peréo.

This chapter takes us back four years, to the fall of 1001 (see the chronological note at the head of chapter 26). With the building of a cœnobium dedicated to Saint Adalbert alongside the hermitage at Peréo, Otto attempts to realize a complete monastic project, according to the spirit of Romuald's teachings and example, in which the one monastic calling will find three different ways of expressing itself: the community life in the cœnobium, the contemplative experience in a more solitary environment, and finally itinerant evangelization culminating—God willing—in martyrdom.

In the days when Romuald was living at Peréo, at his suggestion the emperor Otto had a monastery built in honor of Saint Adalbert. To this new abbey Otto assigned some lands belonging to Sant'Apollinare in Classe, to which, in exchange, he granted other crown lands in the territory of Fermo. A disciple of Romuald was named abbot, and a number of candidates joined the community. Romuald kept close watch over them and taught them to live under the common discipline of the Rule. He directed the abbot to retire to a cell in the hermitage during weekdays, while on Sunday he could come to the monastery and visit the brothers.

This abbot, however, held Romuald's command in contempt. He began to live like a feudal lord; having taken a wrong turn, the abbot moved farther and farther away from the road to holiness. Seeing that he could no longer work with all the ardor of his heart, Romuald went to the king and reminded him of his promise: "Now you must become a monk," he said. The king assured Romuald that he would do so, but first he had to go to Rome and put down a rebellion; having accomplished this, he would return to Ravenna.

Romuald said, "If you go to Rome, you will never see Ravenna again." Thus he openly foretold the king's death. But he failed to dissuade him, and since he had no doubts about the outcome, after the emperor's departure Romuald left by ship for the city of Porec.

221

As the blessed man had prophesied, the emperor became ill on his way to Rome and met an untimely death near Paterno.

31. Romuald gains perfect compunction of heart and the understanding of the Scriptures.

The mystical experience of Romuald is here presented in ideal and theological terms. But in the context of Peter Damian's narrative, we are near the town of Porec (Parenzo) in present-day Croatia, and the year is 1004. The daily chanting of Psalms brings Romuald to perfect compunction of heart and a prayer which today might be called "pentecostal"—a wordless jubilation like the melismatic "Aaa..." which prolongs the liturgical chant of the "Alleluia." But the most important fruit of this prayer in the Spirit—"too deep for words"—is a profound understanding of the words of Holy Scripture in relation to his personal human reality and to the social and cosmic realities within which he lives.

Romuald dwelt in the territory of Porec for three years, one of which he dedicated to the building of a monastery and the other two to seclusion. Here God raised him to the heights of holiness, from which, by the grace of God's Spirit, he was able to see future events and penetrate with deep insight into many hidden mysteries of the prophetic and apostolic writings of the Bible.

While at Porec Romuald used to worry about his inability to shed tears during prayer. However hard he tried, he could not wring a single drop of compunction from his heart.

Then one day, as he was singing the Psalms in his cell, his eyes lit upon the verse: "I will instruct you and teach you the way you should go; I will counsel you with my eye upon you."[1] At that instant tears began to pour from his eyes, and many mysteries of the Bible came clear to him. From that day forth, whenever he so desired, he could shed abundant tears, and the spiritual meaning of Scripture was no longer hidden from him.

Often thereafter he was so taken up in divine contemplation, that he felt he was melting away in tears, and the fire of God's love burning within him made him cry out, "Jesus, dear Jesus, sweetness beyond compare, desire of my heart, joy of the saints, delight of the angels...!" As the Spirit descended upon him, his prayer went beyond words into a jubilation the human mind cannot comprehend. "We do not know how to pray as we ought," says Saint Paul, "but the Spirit himself intercedes for us with sighs too deep for words."

Romuald never liked to celebrate the Mass in the presence of many people, on account of the gift of tears which would at times overwhelm him. He eventually grew accustomed to these states, and believing, in the simplicity of his soul, that all his disciples shared this grace, he would often remind them: "Be careful not to weep too much, because excessive tears harm the eyes and damage the brain."

Henceforth, wherever the saint lived, he would have them build a chapel with an altar in his hermitage, so that he would not need to go out for Mass and people could not have access to him.

[1]Psalm 31,8 [Psalm 32 in the Hebrew].

32. Romuald sees guests arriving from afar.

This event takes place toward the end of his stay near Porec: Romuald has built a monastery, appointed an abbot named Anso, and settled not far away in a grotto overlooking the sea. Abbot Anso comes to visit him one day, and in the middle of their conversation Romuald announces the arrival of visitors at the monastery gate. It turns out that they are from a group of hermits living in the mountains of Romuald's native region of Romagna; the place was then called Biforco, now San Benedetto in Alpe, near the confluence of two streams.

Once a group of hermits lived at a place called Biforco. They sent messengers to Romuald, asking him how to organize their life in the hermitage and how to fend off the attacks of devils. The messengers had just arrived at the monastery gate, when Romuald—whose hermitage was well out of sight of the abbey—perceived their arrival in the spirit and told Abbot Anso, who has with him, "Go have some lunch prepared for your guests; they are brothers who have come a long way."

Anso took Romuald's words as a joke and laughingly told him, "It can't be—you're a false prophet!"

Romuald insisted, and Anso felt obliged to go down to the monastery. There he found a group of men praying in the church, just as Romuald had said.

Romuald shared his salt of saving doctrine with them, and conferred on them the weapons of virtue, to defend themselves against their enemy's ambush. Having answered in detail their every question, he sent them on their way, full of enthusiasm.

33. While sailing back to Italy, Romuald calms a tempest by prayer.

Accepting the invitation from the brothers of Biforco, Romuald leaves Porec; the year is probably 1005. With him is the monk Ingelbert, who appears again in chapters 41, 56, and 57.

Later, the brothers of Biforco sent other messengers to Romuald, more eager than ever to hear his answers to their questions. Romuald told them, "I am now writing a book entitled *On Fighting Demons;* the next time you come I'll have it ready for you, or I may even go back to Italy with you."

On hearing this, they fell on their faces in front of Romuald and overwhelmed him with entreaties to come to Biforco with them. The next day he gave his consent. "Certainly I'll come with you; now go and book passage for us on a ship to Italy."

When the news reached the bishop of Porec, he was deeply grieved. Happening on the monks as they were making arrangements for the ship, he lashed out against them and called them every name in the book. Then he promulgated a decree threatening with exile anyone based in the port of Porec who offered Romuald passage; whoever took him on board his ship would have to emigrate to Italy with him and would never be allowed to return.

Without delay they sent an urgent request to the bishop of Pula: "Book immediate passage for Romuald." This bishop had in fact often asked Romuald to come preach and win souls in his diocese, and not to remain a recluse in the grotto outside Porec. "Do not hide your fire under the ashes," he told him; "instead, set your light on a lampstand, to shine on all the people in God's house."[1]

After Romuald had waited a while for the messenger to return from Pula, he said to the brothers who had come to his hermitage, "You must know that the brother will get back too late; we shall already have left on another ship before he arrives."

On the Sunday following, just after daybreak, Romuald was standing by the sea with Ingelbert, a brother who later would be ordained archbishop *ad gentes*. Romuald said to him: "Look out to sea. You will see two ships still far from shore, coming toward us at the same speed. One of them will finally take us back to Italy."

Ingelbert looked carefully, straining his eyes and sweeping the entire horizon with his gaze, but he could not see even the wake of a ship. Then as the day grew brighter, he could just barely glimpse the two ships on the horizon, but they were still so far out they seemed rather like birds.

When they arrived in port, Ingelbert asked the captains if they would be willing to take Romuald and his disciples on board. They were overjoyed at the unexpected opportunity and placed themselves, their ships and their crew at his complete disposal. "We consider ourselves lucky to be able to carry such priceless cargo," they said. "However, there's a storm brewing; we're afraid we can't leave today."

Romuald insisted: "Put your trust in God's grace. If you start your return voyage today, I guarantee that none of you will face any danger." But they chose to wait in port all day, and after nightfall they put out to sea.

At dawn the following day they met strong winds, and a storm broke, whipping the sea into a fury. The waves swept over the heads of the crew, tossing the ship to and fro until it began to break up. You could see some of the men stripping to be ready to swim away from the wreck, while others were lashing themselves to mast or rudder, or were hanging on to their oars or anything of wood that could float. At that moment there could be no doubt that shipwreck was imminent, and all hope seemed lost.

But Romuald had recourse to his usual line of defense and started praying. He pulled up the hood of his cowl, put his head between his knees, and in silence poured forth his prayer to the Lord. Then he looked up and addressed Abbot Anso, who was sitting in front of him: "Tell the crew to fear no more. We are out of danger and every single one of us will reach home unharmed."[2]

A few minutes later, when all seemed lost and without any effort on the part of the crew, the ship righted itself and, severely damaged as it was, sailed smoothly into the port of Caorle. Everyone on board rendered worthy thanks to God the Liberator who, in answer to Romuald's prayers, had freed them from the jaws of death.

[1]Cf. Matthew 5,15.
[2]Cf. Acts 27,21-26.

34. Romuald tries to correct the hermits of Biforco.

This chapter conveys an important message. For Saint Romuald, the hermitage does not signify simply living alone (solitude as "privacy"), but rather living in the greatest simplicity and poverty, in order to give oneself totally to the prayer of the heart.

Romuald tries to get the hermits of Biforco to accept the basic norms of the common life, in accordance with the Rule of Saint Benedict, but he fails, in spite of the warm friendship that binds him to them.

When Romuald reached Biforco, he examined all the brothers' cells. As he found them too large and comfortable, he chose to dwell with the eldest of his disciples there, Peter, a man famous for his practice of abstinence and for his extreme simplicity. Peter's cell was built according to the example of Saint Hilarion, who hardly ever allowed himself a cell more than four cubits by four.

This venerable monk later told us that, while Romuald was living with him and they would pass the night singing Psalms, Romuald would excuse himself three times or more, saying he had to pass water, whereas in reality it was because he could not hold back his sobbing and his tears.

Romuald spent a rather long time at Biforco. In addition to instructing the hermits in spiritual practice, he also tried to convince them that they should elect an abbot and live a full community life. But each of the hermits had his own benefactor to provide for him, and they were all accustomed to privacy and the freedom to do as they wished; so they gave little heed to Romuald's advice.

35. At Val di Castro, Romuald bears much fruit for the kingdom of heaven.

With this chapter, Peter Damian introduces and summarizes the most "apostolic" phase of Romuald's life.

The Father of reasonable hermits is sterilitatis impatiens, *"he cannot bear to remain sterile." The hermit life as an end unto itself, reduced to the bare fact of living alone, is radically incompatible with the gospel. In the Church, the Temple of the Spirit, there is a great variety of charisms: one person enjoys the gift of prayer, another that of preaching, still another the gift and privilege of serving the poor, etc. But all can and must bear fruit for the salvation of the world. Other chapters in the* Life of Romuald *also speak of Romuald's preaching and of the popular following he acquired thereby (37, 43, 52).*

The foundation of Val di Castro, in a hidden valley amidst the mountains near Fabriano, dates probably from the fall of 1005. Close by this community for men, Romuald founds a women's monastery (see also chapter 63). Throughout the history of the Camaldolese Benedictines, women monastics have played an important role. There have even been some "double monasteries" of monks and nuns, at times ruled by the mother abbess alone, or for alternate terms by the abbess and the monks' prior. In our small monastic congregation today, the numbers of men and women are about equal.

Romuald could not bear to remain sterile. He felt a deep anxiety and a longing to bear fruit for souls, and kept searching for a place where he could do so. He sent messengers to the count and countess of Camerino, who were overjoyed the moment they heard the name "Romuald" and were eager to offer him his choice of their properties, not only hills and wooded areas but also farm land. After touring their holdings, he found a place suited for the hermit life, a valley surrounded on all sides by wooded hills. In the midst was a broad, level area well suited for cultivation and abundantly watered by several springs.

From Roman times the place was called Val di Castro— "valley of the encampment"—but now its only inhabitants were some reformed prostitutes who were living in common and had a small chapel. They ceded the place to Romuald, who had hermit cells built and began to live there with a few disciples.

Neither pen nor tongue can avail to describe the fruits of souls which the Lord harvested through him. From every part men and women came to him for confession and penance, while he distributed their offerings to the poor. Some of them—the most fervent—he accepted as candidates for the monastic life. For them, Saint Romuald was beyond compare, like one of the Seraphim, all aflame with the love of God. Wherever he went, his words would set others on fire as well.

It often happened that, as he was preaching, his intense emotions would provoke him to tears, so that he would immediately interrupt his sermon and run out of church like a mad man. On other occasions, while traveling on horseback with some fellow monks, he would lag behind, because— just as when he was alone—he kept singing the Psalms, which would inevitably bring tears to his eyes.

In his sermons, Romuald frequently lashed out against secular priests who had gotten their ordination for money. "Unless you are willing to resign from the priesthood," he told them, "you are lost and are nothing but heretics." Some of them, considering him a revolutionary, plotted to kill him.

Others were hardly aware that simony—buying and selling ordination and church offices—was in any way a sin, since up to Romuald's time, the practice had been the common custom throughout the region.

Speaking to a group of priests, Romuald asked them to bring him all their books of church law. He showed them the canons that condemned simony. "Now you know that what I have been telling you is true," he said. When they had read the texts for themselves, they acknowledged their crime and shed tears of repentance. Saint Romuald had them live in community as canons; no more were they to dwell alone or with wives and children, but they were to submit to a superior and live together as brothers.

Even some bishops, who had obtained their sees by payment of money, came to make their confessions to Romuald. In his presence they made a solemn commitment to resign from their sees and take monastic vows. But I doubt whether Saint Romuald, as long as he lived, ever succeeded in converting a single bishop. The commerce in ecclesiastical honors, especially if it is a question of bishop's orders, is so pernicious and hard to stamp out, that no bishop has ever kept his promise to resign; he always puts it off till tomorrow, and tomorrow never comes. It is easier to convert a Jew to the faith, than to get a bishop to give up his thievery and his trading in church offices.

In the same zone, Saint Romuald also built a monastery for young women.

36. A burglar breaks into a monk's cell, but Romuald sends him away free.

This chapter begins a series of fioretti—*humorous and thought-provoking anecdotes about Romuald and his disciples. Many of them are inspired by similar stories in the classics of hagiography. It is practically impossible to set these episodes in a definite place or time, but it is certain that they take place between two precise dates: the papal audience in the spring of 1010, when Romuald asks Pope Sergius IV for permission to go on mission in Hungary; and his meeting with the emperor Henry II of Saxony, which took place at Lucca on Wednesday, July 25, 1022 (see chapter 63).*

Here and in chapters 53 and 55 we find the monk Gregory, said to be the same Gregory who, together with Ingelbert, receives ordination as a bishop from Pope Sergius.

One feast day, Romuald was seated with his brothers in the chapter hall and was nourishing them with saving doctrine. Suddenly he interrupted his sermon. "Hurry!" he said. "There's a burglar breaking into Brother Gregory's cell!" (Gregory, you know, was later ordained as a missionary archbishop.)

The monks rushed out of the chapter hall and found the thief trying to knock down the wall of the cell. They grabbed him and dragged him off to Romuald, who was waiting for them with a big smile on his face.

They asked him, "What do you want us to do to this guy? He is guilty of sacrilege."

Romuald answered, "I really don't know. Should we poke out his eyes? But then he won't be able to see. Or cut off his hand? But then he won't be able to work and may even die of hunger. And if we hack off his foot he won't be able to walk. Anyway, take him inside and give him something to eat. Then we can decide what to do with him."

When the burglar had eaten, Saint Romuald, rejoicing in the Lord, gently corrected and admonished him with a few kind words and sent him on his way in peace.

37. Romuald builds a monastery at Orvieto.

At Orvieto, as later at Sitria, Romuald seeks to involve the whole People of God in his monastic reform (cf. chapter 52). For him, monastics are not to be or consider themselves an "elite," a higher caste of Christians separate from the laity. Rather are they to live hidden with Christ in God and among the faithful, a measure of yeast that leavens the whole mass of dough.

Finally, leaving Val di Castro in the hands of the numerous disciples he had gathered there, Romuald went to Orvieto and built a monastery on land belonging to Count Farolfo, thanks to the generous help offered by the count and numerous other benefactors.

Saint Romuald's ardent desire to bear fruit was so intense, that he was never satisfied with anything he did. While he was busy with one project, he was already planning the next. You would think he was trying to turn the whole world into a hermitage and to involve the entire People of God in his project of monastic reform.

In Orvieto as well he received many candidates, so many that he had to divide them into several distinct communities.

38. A young disciple of Romuald dies a holy death and then heals a blind man.

In Umbria, popular oral tradition has handed down a legend regarding a saintly boy named "Guidino," son of Farolfo, count of Orvieto. He is probably the same as the young disciple of Romuald spoken of in this chapter.

Numerous young noblemen renounced their titles and family privileges, and placed themselves at the service of Blessed Romuald. One of these was the son of Count Guido,

232

who joined the monastery while still a boy. He had not been there long, when death came to take him. Romuald was at his bedside, assisting him, when the boy said, "I see two evil spirits like a pair of coal-black vultures. They are looking at me—their eyes are so terrible!" He called out to Romuald, "O Father Master, now I see many ugly men[1] entering my room. The whole house is full of them!"

Romuald told him, "If you have any sin, you should confess it now."

With great terror this innocent sinner confessed his only sin: "Father Prior told me to take the discipline, but I haven't done so."

Romuald said, "Oh, what a great crime! But God is very indulgent, and you are sure to be forgiven."

Hearing these words, the lad found peace, and he died.

The very next day, a blind man, whom the count supported as an act of charity, came to the boy's grave. He cried out, "O my little master! If you are now with God, as I believe you are, pray to Him for me, that my eyes may see the light of day." The instant he said these words, his sight was restored.

Many other sick people came to his tomb and went away healed. Sweet fragrances kept rising from his grave, as if it were filled with perfume. Thus after death he received great honor from God, for whose love in this life he had renounced the honors of his family title.

[1]Once again, the demons are described as "Ethiopians."

39. Romuald founds three monasteries and leaves for Hungary.

The year is 1010.

From earliest times, Christian monks have seen martyr-dom as the model and mirror of that love which they strive to live by their monastic practice. But many monastics also crowned their practice with actual martyrdom. Romuald's disciples were not the first among Benedictines to join the two expressions of total love: Saint Wynfrith-Boniface, the eighth-century "apostle to the Germans" was one of them; Bruno-Boniface sought to imitate his example, having adopted his name.

For all the fruits he has borne in his work as a monastic reformer, Romuald still "cannot bear to remain sterile." He too must go on mission, and he chooses Hungary, where Bruno has already preached the gospel. Poland is inacces-sible, because Henry II is still waging war against the Christians there and in Bohemia.

Romuald never will arrive in Hungary; a mysterious illness impedes him. What is the meaning of this illness?

We know that in these early years of the eleventh century, Hungary's saintly king Stephen would have preferred to follow Saint Vladimir's example and entrust the evangeliza-tion of his people to Byzantine missionaries; however, he also welcomed Latin-rite missionaries from Rome. The latter were a help to him, since they also offered a certain protection against political interference from the West. This ambigu-ous political and ecclesiastical situation was quite sufficient to make an oversensitive soul like Romuald become physi-cally sick.

Romuald's hypersensitive and impulsive nature emerges also in his relations with the superiors of his communities. He does not wish (as Bruno-Boniface tells us) to be "an abbot of bodies"; so he has his communities nominate one of their members to be superior. Unfortunately, Romuald is

almost always unsatisfied with the choice; he gets into an
argument with the new abbot, and then packs up and leaves.
So it happens at Orvieto (this chapter), at Classe (chapter
41), Val di Castro (45), Sitria (64), and at the abbey on
Mount Amiata (65).

While he was at Orvieto, word reached Romuald that his
disciple the blessed [Bruno-]Boniface had received martyrdom. From that moment Romuald could not contain his
burning desire to shed his blood for Christ, and he set about
organizing an expedition to Hungary. In the meanwhile,
remaining firm in this intention, he founded in a very brief
period of time three monasteries. One was the cœnobium at
Val di Castro, the other was near the river Ésino, while the
third was in the province of Áscoli.

Once the Holy See had granted its permission and consecrated two of his disciples [Gregory and Ingelbert] as
bishops, Romuald, together with twenty-four companions,
began his journey. In all of them the ardent desire to give
their life for Christ was so strong, that Romuald could
hardly have asked any of them to stay and not join the
mission.

Now they were almost at the Hungarian border, when
suddenly Romuald fell ill and could not continue. As long as
he was there, his fever would not abate, but the moment he
decided to return to Italy, he suddenly got well. So he
attempted once more to enter Hungary. At that very instant
his face started to swell up, and his stomach refused to hold
any food.

Romuald called his brothers to council and told them, "I
have thought it all through, and now it seems that it is not
God's plan that I go any farther. But I am well aware of how
you all feel about the mission, and so none of you should feel
obliged to come back with me. We are not the only ones to
whom something like this has happened: many Christians
have sought to attain martyrdom, but divine Providence
disposed differently and compelled them to remain in their
ordinary state of life. Now, although I do not foresee martyr-

dom in store for any of you, I leave you all free either to continue your journey or to come back with me."

Fifteen of the group chose to enter Hungary, and of these some underwent torture, others were sold as slaves, and several became vassals of the local gentry, but no one died a martyr, in accordance with Saint Romuald's prophecy. As for the rest, two had already parted company with the group, and only seven returned with Romuald.

On the way back, Romuald converted a number of Germans, among them a high-ranking nobleman, a relative of Duke Adelbehrn, who became a monk and persevered in that holy state until his death.

Romuald finally reached Orvieto and retired to the monastery he had built there. Just as he had not gone on mission for superficial motives, so he did not return with a sense of failure. In his heart he had already undergone martyrdom and had accomplished his mission of saving souls by bringing people to the monastic life.

At the abbey of Orvieto, Romuald was vexed by a number of scandals. The problem was the abbot: Romuald wanted him to be a true monk, a lover of simplicity, totally detached from worldly matters, and that he not spend the monastery's funds for useless ornaments but rather to provide for the personal needs of the monks. The abbot turned a deaf ear to Romuald's recommendations and showed him nothing but contempt. So Romuald took his disciples and left. They settled at Preggio, on land belonging to Duke Rainier, the future marquis of Tuscany.

40. Romuald strikes terror in the heart of the rich and the powerful.

Romuald, like most saints, "comforts the afflicted and afflicts the comfortable." The mighty are terrified in his presence, while the poor—even petty thieves (see chapter 36)—are quite at ease with Romuald, because they know that his "preferential option" is always for the humble and the needy.

Duke Rainier, under pressure from his family, had divorced his first wife and married another man's widow; this man, a relative, had been seeking vengeance against Rainier, but Rainier killed him—involuntarily, it seems.

Romuald did not wish to be in any way implicated in his crime. So rather than accept Rainier's offer to live on his property rent free, Romuald paid him one gold crown for water rights and another for a supply of firewood. At first Rainier would not take the money, but then, to keep Romuald from leaving, he accepted.

After he had acquired the duchy of Tuscany, Rainier used to say, "Neither the emperor nor any other human being makes me feel the terror that comes upon me whenever I am in Romuald's presence. When I see his face, I do not know what to say, and I can't defend myself—I am totally without excuses."

In fact, God gave Saint Romuald the gift of making sinners—especially the rich and the powerful—tremble with fear, as if they were in the presence of Almighty God Himself. It was the Holy Spirit, dwelling in Romuald's heart, who struck terror in the hearts of those who practiced injustice.

During this same period, Romuald built another monastery not far from the castle of Massiliano.

41. The abbot of Classe tries to strangle Romuald.

Romuald is again in conflict with ecclesiastical authorities. At his side is Ingelbert, whom we suppose is the same Ingelbert who received bishop's orders and went to Hungary with Romuald. However, the episode recounted here may have taken place before the mission to Hungary (see chapters 39, 56, and 57).

When he heard that a man from Venice got himself elected abbot of Classe by simony, that is, by purchasing the office, and who furthermore was a rake, Romuald went there immediately and spared no effort in his attempt to rid the community of the man.

But that reprobate, afraid of losing the abbacy, had no fear of perpetrating homicide.

One night during a thunderstorm, while Romuald was asleep in bed, the man sneaked up on him and tried to strangle him to death. But the saint, still able to draw a little breath, let out a hoarse cry. The faint sound of Master Romuald's voice woke his disciple Ingelbert, who grabbed a smoldering log from the fireplace and prevented that devil's minion from committing his ghastly crime.

42. Romuald makes another trip to Porec, but the pope orders him back.

This is Romuald's last voyage outside Italy.

After these events, Romuald once more sailed across to Porec. But the Holy See and the Roman citizenry sent a delegation to make him return. "If you come back with us," they said "we promise to follow your teachings; if not, we shall have you excommunicated."

His disciple Italy risked losing her teacher, but in this way she got him back.

43. Romuald builds a hermitage near the abbey of San Vincenzo.

The ancient road from the Adriatic Sea to Rome, the Flaminian Way, crosses the Apennines south of the hill town of Urbino, where a natural tunnel (furulum) *gives the mountain pass its current name:* la Gola del Furlo. *To this day a sober, Romanesque basilica stands guard over the pass; this is San Vincenzo, where Peter Damian wrote* The Life of Blessed Romuald.

The geographical references have little bearing on the episodes narrated in this and the following chapters. We are now reading a text beyond particular dates and places, a form of religious storytelling that anticipates the more famous Fioretti *or "Little Flowers of Saint Francis."*

Once again, as in chapter 36, we see Romuald's gentleness toward a poor man compelled to steal in order to survive.

In those days, Romuald stayed for a certain period of time among the high valleys of the Apennines above Cagli. He then moved to Pierced Rock, not far from the monastery of San Vincenzo, which stands by the Candigliano River.

Wherever Saint Romuald went he bore fruit for souls, gathering more and more men and women into the monastic life. He was like a living flame, and he set his hearers on fire with desire for heaven.

Now Romuald was looking for a fit place to build a hermitage. He met a priest and told him, "On your way home, bring along some food for me and for my companions." And he continued his search through the mountains.

Finally he happened upon a solitary monk living near a small chapel. Romuald ordered him, "Come along with me, and show me a place where there is plenty of water."

"I can't," he replied. "If I leave the house unattended, thieves are sure to break in."

Romuald promised him, "If that should happen, I guarantee you that whatever is stolen will be replaced."

With Romuald as his insurance against loss, the monk led him to the place. Meanwhile, the priest came along with the food Romuald had ordered, and he found a burglar breaking into the monk's dwelling. He caught him and kept him there until Romuald got back.

When Romuald returned and saw the man, first he scolded him with fatherly severity, and then with a gentle admonition and without punishing him, he sent him on his way.

By divine Providence, all that had been entrusted to Romuald's care was kept intact, even in his absence.

44. Romuald's prophetic spirit foils two thieves.

While Romuald was building the hermitage there, he went off and left his sack hidden behind a rock. All of a sudden, he sent a brother back: "Hurry! Go check on the sack!" The brother surprised two thieves, who already had their hands on Romuald's sack, but when he opened it, he found nothing missing.

From this fact we can conclude that Romuald's prophetic instinct made him send the brother hurrying back, so that he got there in the very instant the thieves found the loot.

45. Romuald tries to correct the abbot of Val di Castro.

Then Romuald returned to the monastery of Val di Castro. He immediately started telling the abbot, "While you're busy giving orders to others, don't forget about yourself!" He also wanted him to stop using his administrative duties as an excuse for never spending time in his cell. "Stay there and do your spiritual work," he told him; "on feast days you can come out and give talks to the brothers."

The way we see abbots living today was so odious to Romuald, that he was almost as happy to get men like this thrown out of office, as to see some count or duke enter the monastery.

But as Solomon said, "Like vinegar on nitre are songs to a perverse heart."[1] Romuald's preaching only made the abbot of Val di Castro go from bad to worse. As sacrilegious as he was shrewd, the abbot went to Countess Sibyl and her daughter and got their permission to have the lumber they donated for Romuald's cell chopped up into firewood.

Thus the monks at Val di Castro made Romuald leave; in their midst he was like a cedar of Lebanon in a briar patch.

[1]Cf. Proverbs 25,20 in the Latin.

46. Romuald cures a priest of his toothache.

Romuald went on his way and came to place called Acquabella near Mount Apennine; there he made his abode.

Some lay workers were helping the novices finish building their dwellings. Romuald himself was by now too old for manual labor, and so he took charge of the guest house. A priest who was helping with the work reluctantly had to leave his job on account of an unbearable toothache. He excused himself to the brothers and started home groaning with pain. On his way out, he passed Romuald, who asked him why he was leaving; the priest told him he was suffering from a toothache. He opened his mouth to show him, and Romuald touched the tooth with his finger. Then Romuald said, "Go take a small coal from the fire, put it on a twig so it won't burn your lips, and touch the tooth with it. This will stop the pain."

The priest had not gone another fifty paces, when he was freed of all pain. Completely cured, he went back to his job, proclaiming with a loud voice, "We give you thanks, almighty God, for sending such a bright star to shine on our land! He is a true angel of God, he is a true and holy prophet, a great light hidden to the world, who has appeared in our little valley!" He kept on praising God with such a loud voice, that Romuald's disciples had a hard time getting him to stop. They knew that whenever Romuald heard people praise him like that, it pained him to the core.

47. A beech tree defies the law of gravity.

One more of a series of "building stories" without time or place. But a thirteenth-century legend identifies this episode with the building of the Eremo of Camaldoli, which would put us in the year 1025 or thereabouts.

On another occasion he ordered the workers to cut down a big beech tree which was near his cell. The tree was leaning at a dangerous angle over the cell, and anyone could see that it was ready to crash right through the roof. The workers wanted to obey his orders, but they were afraid of which way the tree would come down. Romuald said, "Do it, and don't be afraid!"

So they started carefully chopping into the trunk all the way around. But they had hardly cut through the bark, when it was obvious it was going to fall straight onto Romuald's cell. So they started yelling, "Come out! Come out!" And they said, "If you don't care about the cell, at least save yourself!"

Romuald ignored their cries. "Just finish cutting down the tree," he said.

Finally the tree fell with a great noise. But God's power made it fall to one side, and to their amazement it left the cell intact. At first they were bewildered, but then they cried out, "A miracle!" and started thanking God and singing praise to heaven.

48. An oak falls on a farmer, and he remains unharmed.

But why should we talk about the divine protection which surrounded Romuald, when we know well how many times he saved other people from harm by his mere presence?

Let me tell you just one story, and you can imagine all the rest.

Once near Mount Petrano he was with his workers, and they were trying to cut down an enormous oak. The tree was on the brow of a cliff, and as it started to fall, a farmer came on his way, passing underneath. The tree began to roll down the incline, struck the farmer and dragged him down to the foot of the slope.

The workers were grief-stricken and cried out, "He's gone for sure! His body must have been torn to shreds!"

But great was the power of the Lord! They found him there alive and well, as if not an oak, but an oak leaf had fallen on him. Romuald's presence must have had great weight in God's sight, to have so lightened the weight of a heavy tree.

49. Romuald is accused of sexual abuse by the hermits of Sitria.

The case of an actively homosexual monk must not have been unheard of in Peter Damian's time. In fact, the Church was moving away from previous attitudes of tolerance with respect to same-sex bonding, and Peter Damian's voice is only one of those raised in condemnation of physical expressions of affection, either within same-sex communities or between priests and nuns (see the famous case of Abelard and Héloise). The reader will immediately sense the difference of climate between this chapter and The Life of the Five Brothers.

Peter Damian expresses amazement at these hermits' readiness to imprison an aging Romuald on grounds of sexual abuse. We too are amazed, when in chapter 64 (see below), we hear Peter Damian exalt the extreme ascetic rigor observed at Sitria.

But on the other hand, perhaps we ought not to be so amazed. We do not need very much psychiatric knowledge to see how an indiscreet mortification of the body can lead to strong reactions in the direction either of sadomasochism or of judgmentalness and intolerance.

Perhaps this unhappy experience marks Romuald's departure from his previous custom of sharing his hermit's cell with another brother or a novice. In fact, in the Charter of Camaldoli, the bishop of Arezzo expressly requires that each hermit live singly in a separate cell.

At a later date, Romuald came down from the Apennines and went to live at Sitria.

Now let me warn the reader not to misinterpret Romuald's movement from place to place. In his case, this was no vice but a virtue, as his intention was always to do the Lord's work. Of course, one of the reasons for his continual change of location was the fact that, wherever he lived, vast crowds of men and women would gather. Hence, as soon as he had filled one place, he would have them elect a superior, and then he would go off to fill some other place.

At Sitria, Romuald had to face innumerable insults and accusations on the part of his disciples. I shall put down only one of them here and leave aside all the others, lest I go beyond the limits of this book.

Romuald had a disciple by the name of Romano, a man of noble birth but of altogether degenerate behavior. Romuald tried to correct his sins of the flesh not only by words, but even by severe corporal punishment. This diabolical individual dared turn the same accusation against Romuald himself, the temple of the Holy Spirit. He opened his sacrilegious mouth and, barking like a dog, said, "Our holy teacher committed the very same sin with me!"

Immediately all of Romuald's disciples, filled with rage, turned against him. Some of them said, "That old libertine should be hung!" Others declared, "He deserves to be burned alive in his cell!"

It amazes me that spiritual men, like those at Sitria, could ever believe that a decrepit old man well past the hundred-year mark could commit such an unspeakable indecency. Even had he wanted to, his frigid blood and dried-up body would have prevented him from doing it! But we ought not hesitate to believe that heaven itself allowed this terrible affliction to befall him in order to increase his merits. In fact, Romuald himself had told the disciples in the hermitage where he had been living previously that this was going to happen, and that he would willingly go to face such a dishonor.

As for that reprobate Romano—a sarabaite who had accused a saint of such a crime!—he eventually bought his way into the bishopric of Nocera in Umbria and held the see for two years. But he received what his deeds deserved: in the first year, his cathedral burned down, with all the books, bells, and vestments; in the second, he lost his see and his life.

50. The hermits at Sitria suspend Romuald's priestly faculties.

Again we see an instance of Romuald's oversensitive conscience, which leads him at times to illogical behavior. He does not defend himself, nor does he care what his disciples think of him; he takes upon himself the stigma of a sexual offender and submits to a punishment he did not deserve. This is hardly logical behavior, but a truly free conscience, like the wind or the Spirit, does not follow either human or ecclesiastical logic.

However, Romuald does sometimes go too far. In this case, his inner voice reproves him for his "indiscreet simplicity," and orders him to return to a normal monastic existence. In the end, he experiences a silent ecstasy, which we can compare with his "pentecostal" jubilation at Porec (see chapter 31).

Romuald's disciples imposed on him a penalty, as if he had indeed committed a crime, and completely withdrew his faculties to celebrate Mass. Romuald gladly embraced their prejudice against him, accepted the penalty like a guilty man, and for nearly six months did not presume to approach the altar. In the end, however—as he later told his disciples— he sensed that he would lose God's grace if he did not give up his indiscreet simplicity and trustingly go back to celebrating the Eucharist.

The next day he started the Mass, but he got no farther than the *Sanctus*. He was taken up into ecstasy and stood there silent for a long time, until those present began to wonder what had happened to him. After Mass they asked him why he kept pausing at odd moments during the liturgy. He answered, "I was taken up into heaven and presented before God, and immediately God ordered me to comment as best I could on the Psalms. He told me not to worry about my limited intelligence but to write down whatever came to me. I was overwhelmed with an unspeakable terror and could not answer except to say, 'Yes! Yes!'"

Eventually Saint Romuald did expound all the Psalms and canticles of the Bible, and although the grammar was all wrong, his meaning was clear.

51. Romuald's ecstatic experience in God's presence.

A saying of Saint Romuald, linked to the preceding chapter by the reference to ecstasy. He speaks of this experience in the third person, as does Saint Paul in II Corinthians 12,2-4.

His disciples asked him, "Master Romuald, when the soul appears on judgment day, how old will she seem to be and what form will she have?"

He answered, "I know a person in Christ whose soul was taken up to God, splendid as fresh snow but in the form of a full-grown human being."

So they asked him, "Who was he?"

Romuald became indignant. "Do not ask me that!", he said. "I don't want to say any more."

The disciples started repeating his words among themselves, attributing the experience to Romuald, as was indeed the truth. "We knew from the certitude with which he spoke," they said, "that he was referring to himself."

52. Romuald imitates the austerities of Saint Hilarion.

Of Hilarion, as of Romuald, it is said that he lived tacente lingua prædicante vita, *"keeping silence with his tongue and preaching with his life." In fact the entire chapter is nothing but a series of allusions to, and quotations of, the hagiographic work of Saint Jerome.*

The Vitæ Patrum, *book 4, speaks of an old hermit who wanted to eat a watermelon; so to cure himself of the vice of gluttony, he bought one, hung it up in the middle of his cell, and looked at it but never ate it.*

At Sitria, Romuald lived as a recluse for seven years, never breaking his silence. Although his tongue was silent, his life was a sermon, and he continued to work as never before, drawing men and women to monastic life and sinners to repentance.

He lived with excessive austerity, in spite of his advancing age, when even perfect monks might ease their practice and concede themselves some relaxation.

For an entire Lenten season, imitating Saint Hilarion, he took no food or drink except a porridge of wheat flour and greens. For another period of five weeks he limited himself to a soup made from garbanzo beans and nothing else. By means of these and similar practices—now trying one, now another—Romuald was continually testing his mettle. Thus as a soldier of Christ, but with discretion, he kept himself ready for new battles, but whenever he realized that his health was failing, he would immediately show himself mercy, that his body might regain its strength. On account of the importunities of his aging body, he had two or three changes of underwear—all of rough sackcloth—but he never allowed anyone else to wash them; he would just hang them out in the rain for a month, in order to have a clean change. He never let anyone shave him, but now and then, when his hair and whiskers got too long, he himself would use scissors to cut them.

Sometimes his palate would tease him with a yen for some tasty dish. So he would have his disciples carefully prepare it for him, and then he would just savor its aroma and say, "O my gluttonous palate, how much you would enjoy this rich and tasty food—but alas for you! You shall never taste it." And he would send the dish back to the pantry.

53. Romuald cures Gregory's headache.

Romuald always has a smile on his face, like Saint Antony of Egypt—see Athanasius' Life of Antony, chapter 40.

Here and in chapter 55, Peter Damian mentions "Brother Gregory"; we suppose him to be the same Gregory who, with Ingelbert, received ordination as a bishop for the mission in Hungary (chapter 39). It may seem unlikely that both of them (see Ingelbert in chapters 56 and 57) returned to Italy to live as simple monks. Thus the episodes in which they appear may have taken place before 1010, that is, before the departure for Hungary. As for the locale, it was certainly not Sitria; it may have been Val di Castro or Orvieto.

The healing miracles attributed to Romuald have a strongly sacramental character. Gregory's ills are cured either by the breath of the Spirit (the allusion is to the risen Jesus who appears to his disciples and breathes on them— John 20,22) or by water (alluding to baptism). Even the madman in chapter 54 feels a "strong wind" blowing through his brain, like a personal Pentecost (see Acts 2,2).

For all his austerity of life, Romuald always had a twinkle in his eye and a ready smile on his lips.

One day Brother Gregory had a terrific headache. Moaning with pain he went up to the window of Master Romuald's cell, where a group of monks were standing, and said, "I can't endure this headache any longer."

Romuald realized that the cause of the headache was not physical but rather came from the Tempter. He leaned out the window and breathed on Gregory's forehead, and had the other monks do the same.

After this treatment, Gregory never had a headache again, and he even forgot what a headache feels like. Romuald's gesture, I am sure, had this meaning: since he was convinced that the devil, the cause of all pain, could only be driven out by the Holy Spirit, Romuald did not want to draw attention to himself—hence he pretended it was a game, and had the other monks join in. But in fact he was imitating Jesus, our Redeemer, when he breathed upon the apostles, as Scripture says, and they received the Holy Spirit.

54. Romuald cures a madman with a kiss.

For a madman cured by intercession of Saint Benedict, see Pope Gregory's Dialogues *2,38; Romuald cures others afflicted by insanity and diabolical possession in chapters 59, 60, and 70.*

Then there was the time they brought a crazy man to Master Romuald. When the man had one of his fits, he would say and do the wildest things and couldn't remember any of it afterwards.

Romuald took the man's head in his hands and gave him a kiss.

This gesture of peace restored peace to his troubled mind and heart. Later, recounting his cure, the man said, "As soon as his lips touched me, I felt as if a strong wind were blowing all over my face and through my skull, and it put out the fire in my brain."

55. Gregory is cured of a serious illness by cold water.

On another occasion, the same Brother Gregory had scabies on his leg, a tumor which oozed foul-smelling pus; they were afraid it was elephantiasis. Romuald's prescription was to bathe the leg for three days in cold water; he promised Gregory that he would be completely cured.

Gregory did as he was told, more out of obedience that out of confidence in the effectiveness of Romuald's therapy. The results were miraculous and could only be attributed to the power of God: the swelling went down, the tumor dried up, the fever disappeared, and Brother Gregory was completely restored to health.

I think we have every right to believe that Romuald, who ordered his disciple to bathe three times in cold water, had received the same Spirit as the prophet Elisha, who ordered Naaman the Syrian to bathe seven times in the Jordan.[1]

[1]Cf. II Kings 5,10-14.

56. Ingelbert refuses to acknowledge Romuald's prophetic spirit.

The Ingelbert we meet in chapters 56 and 57 is the perfect example of a hermit who, with all his fasting and penance, remains a "man of the flesh." By separating himself from Romuald, the man of the Spirit, Ingelbert falls into the vice of presumption, taking for granted his ability to teach others, while lacking that humility and discretion which are the signs of the true hermit.

Some carnal individuals did not hesitate to express malicious judgments about Romuald, attributing his words and deeds to an unsound mind or a depraved character.

There was once a disciple of his, who was living in another hermitage. Some relatives of this hermit were in need of help; against his better judgment and only out of pity for them, he agreed to leave the hermitage during Lent and take their cause to Rome.

Romuald's spirit immediately became aware of this, and he wrote an angry letter to a brother who lived nearby, asking why that good man was so presumptuous as to go to Rome for such futile motives. When the brother received the letter, he was amazed. "How could Master Romuald have known this," he asked himself, "since no one from here has been to see him?"

The brother investigated the matter, and found it just as Romuald had said in the letter. So he went to ask the advice of another disciple, Ingelbert, who was living as a recluse. He told him, "Master Romuald was able to see what was happening at a distance—he must be a prophet!"

Ingelbert rejected it all out of hand and scoffed at the brother for believing such nonsense. "To prove that Romuald's spirit is diabolical and not prophetic," said Ingelbert, "I swear this oath: if what he wrote you is true, may almighty God not allow me to stay a day longer in reclusion."

No sooner said than done. Only a few days had gone by, and Ingelbert left the hermitage without Master Romuald's permission. They told me that he never saw Romuald again in this life.

57. The hermit Gaudenzio prefers fasting to obedience.

Peter Damian gives us another lesson about the virtue of discretion and the vice of presumption, or "taking things for granted." The events take place at and near the abbey of San Vincenzo (see chapter 43), where he is writing his Life of Romuald.

Another brother, Gaudenzio by name, whose son is now abbot of this monastery of San Vincenzo, left the world with great fervor, and with even greater ardor served God as a monk. He asked Romuald's permission to renounce all cooked food, and to take only bread, water, and raw fruits and vegetables. Having received permission, Gaudenzio followed this practice faithfully.

A fellow hermit, Tedaldo, indiscreetly concerned about Gaudenzio's welfare, went and told Romuald, "This fasting is too hard for an old man like him. He is too stubborn; you must order him to stop."

Romuald, like the simple person he was, took Tedaldo's word to heart and withdrew his permission for Gaudenzio's fast. Gaudenzio could not bear the humiliation, nor could he stand to share the same cell with Tedaldo any more. So he went to live with Ingelbert, who by then had parted ways with Romuald. At Gaudenzio's request, Ingelbert allowed him to resume his fast.

A short time later, Gaudenzio died. (He lies buried in the cemetery here at San Vincenzo, next to the grave of Romuald's other disciple, the venerable Berardo.) Romuald, considering the fact that he had died in a state of disobedience, would not allow prayers to be said for Gaudenzio.

A short time later one of the monks here at the abbey was celebrating Morning Prayer with his brothers. Suddenly he was struck with such a toothache, that he could not sing another note and had to leave choir. He ran to the cemetery and threw himself across the graves of Berardo and Gaudenzio. He lay there, moaning and praying, and then he fell asleep. At once he saw Berardo, resplendent in his priestly robes, carrying a gold-lettered book as he stood at the altar and celebrated Mass. Then he noticed Gaudenzio standing behind Berardo with bent head and sad face; he remained at a distance and like an excommunicate did not dare come forward for Communion. Then Gaudenzio spoke and said, "Do you see Brother Berardo there, with his marvelous golden book? I would have all that too, had it not been—alas! alas!—for the monk Tedaldo, who took it away from me."

The brother awoke and stood up. He was well now; his toothache was gone. He went and joyfully recounted his vision to the brothers. When Romuald came to hear of it, he ordered the brothers of San Vincenzo to show Gaudenzio their fraternal love and offer prayers for him. We have every reason to believe that the book he lost when he abandoned Romuald's company, was now restored to him, along with Romuald's favor and the brothers' prayers. Tedaldo had stolen Gaudenzio's book by the hand of Romuald, and Romuald gave it back to him through the prayers of the community.

58. The devils attack a monk who goes to sleep in Romuald's bed.

Chapters 59 to 63 form a group of anecdotes related to the theme of evil spirits as enemies of Romuald, the man of God and lover of peace. In chapters 59 and 60, we see a sacramental (bread blessed by Romuald) as medicine which cures a madwoman and a possessed boy.

There are no indications here of either place or time.

There was a time when the venerable Romuald was leaving on a journey. He entrusted his own cell to the care of a disciple and told him to stay there until he returned. But this thoughtless lad was lacking in respect for his teacher, and he did not hesitate to lie down on Romuald's own cot. That very night the evil spirits fell upon him, battered and bruised him and threw him to the ground half dead. The disciple's sin was his lack of humility toward a great man, and it was fitting that proud spirits took revenge on him. He did not reverence a gentle teacher, and so he received punishment from hard and cruel taskmasters.

A similar situation occurred when Romuald left on another trip. This time he entrusted his cell to another disciple. But the young man replied, "Father Master, I don't want to sleep

in your bed. I am afraid that what happened to the other
novice might happen to me."

"Don't worry, my son," Romuald told him. "Go ahead
and sleep in my bed. The brother who slept there before fell
into enemy hands, because he didn't bother to ask me—not
that I am so important! But you have my consent; so trust in
God and don't let fear keep you awake."

So the novice did as he was told. While he was sleeping
in Romuald's bed, no harm whatever befell him.

59. A piece of bread blessed by Romuald calms a woman's fury.

A layman by the name of Arduino placed himself under
Romuald's care so that he might become a monk. Before he
took the cowl, he went home to settle his affairs. When his
wife saw him coming, she flew into a fury typical of a
woman scorned and screamed at him, "So, my good husband,
you've become the disciple of a heretic! You let that old
man seduce you, and then you come home only to leave
again and abandon me in misery—no money, no companionship!" In a rage beyond words, she started to tear the
house apart, as if she were indeed vexed by a demon.

Now it was Saint Romuald's custom to give some little
gift to brothers who went on a journey—some blessed bread
or an apple or something. And his disciples knew by experience that if they gave anything Romuald had blessed to a
sick person, he or she got well. Even the water he used for
washing his hands had healed a number of people. But his
disciples had to be very careful about this, because whenever Romuald discovered what they were doing, he was
profoundly displeased.

After a while, one of the brothers who had accompanied
Arduino, seeing his wife in such torment, took some of

Romuald's blessed bread and gave her a piece. No sooner had she eaten it than she returned to her senses and was freed from all her anger. Immediately she began to express thanks for her healing to almighty God and to Romuald his servant, and she gave Arduino her full permission to become a monk.

60. Romuald's blessed bread frees a boy from a demon.

On another occasion a possessed boy was brought to Romuald, who did nothing but give him a piece of blessed bread. The moment the boy ate the bread, he was freed from his demon. Rightly so: Romuald's blessing entered the boy's body, and like fire it burned the devil and drove him out.

61. The devil threatens to kill Romuald.

As long as Romuald was around, the devil found himself constantly under fire. No longer could he hide his presence from the saint; so he kept manifesting his virulent malice visibly.

Once Romuald was in his cell, and the evil spirit showed himself as he truly is: ugly, disgusting, abhorrent. He started trying to terrify Romuald and with great fury threatened him with death. Romuald, unmoved, asked God to come to his aid; confidently he called out, "O Christ, come help me." Immediately the enemy turned and ran, forcing his way out through the wall with such fury, that he cracked a heavy plank more than a cubit wide. Thus Romuald's dwelling was left with a visible sign of the devil's cruel and burning rage against him; like writing on the wall, it revealed the evil one's secret intention.

62. The devil appears to him as a dog.

There was a time when Romuald was making a journey on horseback with his disciples. Lo! the evil spirit showed himself under the appearance of a red dog. The dog ran toward him with such speed that Romuald's horse took fright, and he was barely able to remain in the saddle.

Romuald asked his disciples, "Did you see anything?"

They replied, "We saw your horse rear up, but we don't know what frightened him. We didn't see anything strange."

So Romuald told them about the dog. "How miserable is that spirit, who once was a shining angel but now shows himself shamelessly in the form of a vile dog!"

63. The devil tries to prevent Romuald from building a women's monastery.

There are many places in Italy which are called, or were once called, Valbona *or* Vallebona. *So we are not sure of the location of this women's monastery, only one of several which Romuald built; another is mentioned in chapter 35.*

On another occasion, Romuald had again decided to build a monastery for women; it was to be at Valbona.

At once his disciples took sides: some were against it, while others vehemently insisted it must be built. In Romuald's presence both sides marshaled their respective reasons pro and con, and as they argued they began to hear a loud noise, as if someone were hammering on the rain barrel in front of Romuald's cell. It was the devil. His blows got louder and louder until they were thundering all through the woods.

Then, the very instant they reached a consensus in favor of the monastery, they heard the evil spirit let out a howl and a series of faint groans. Finally, as the brothers left Romuald's cell and were on their way to their respective dwellings, the enemy unleashed his fury, and there arose such a tempest that it seemed the winds from all four corners of the world had come together to uproot the forest. One of the brothers rebuked the devil, saying, "Unclean spirit, in the name of the Holy Trinity I order you to stop following us." And he was gone.

It is evident that the author of discord was making known his pleasure while the argument was heating up, but when the matter was resolved peacefully, he could do nothing but wail and weep. At first the devil tried to break up an empty barrel and scatter its staves far and wide, but when the bonds of peace and love had reunited the brothers, he gave up and left.

64. Romuald builds a monastery alongside the hermitage at Sitria.

In this chapter we hear Peter Damian sing the praises of the austere brothers of Sitria, while in chapter 49 we heard him bewail all the "insults and accusations" these hermits hurled at their teacher Romuald, including the allegations of sexual abuse.

The contradiction here is in the mind of the author, and there is nothing we can do to resolve it. But we can still find a positive message in this chapter, for it gives us the image of a monastic community that invites the whole surrounding population to take part in its spiritual practice (see also chapter 37). Later piety turned Romuald into a founder of ecclesiastical institutions, but in reality he was an animator of communities whose membership boundaries were often vague and whose duration may have been intentionally brief: no more than a generation or a single Lenten season.

Sitria itself endured until Napoleon came suppressing monasteries throughout Europe, but it remained as an independent Benedictine community, never joining either Camaldoli or Fonte Avellana. At Sitria as elsewhere, Romuald wants there to be a cœnobium governed by an abbot, but when the one he chooses for the office conforms to the usual behavior of ecclesiastical superiors, Romuald returns to Biforco, preferring the anarchy of hermits who do not want to be governed by anyone (see chapter 34). At Biforco, however, the cycle repeats itself: too many people want to become monks; Romuald has them organize a community and choose an abbot; then the abbot starts to persecute Romuald.

In 1967, the first time I saw what remains of the abbey of Sitria, the church, the chapter hall, and one side of the cloister were still standing. Since then burglars have carried off the marble columns of the altar, and the current owner of the property has torn down part of the ruins of the cloister to make himself a summer cabin. But the Italian government has had the church splendidly restored, and it remains a jewel of provincial Romanesque architecture.

Sitria compared well, in name and in fact, with the early Christian hermitages at Nitria in Egypt. Everyone went barefoot, no one ever bathed, all were pale as ghosts and content with little or nothing at all. Some of them locked themselves into their cells, and as far as the rest of the world was concerned, they might as well have been dead and buried. Wine was unknown; they wouldn't touch a drop even if they were seriously ill. Am I talking about the monks? No, even the monks' servants, even the shepherds that cared for their flocks observed the fasts, kept the silence, scourged each other with the whip of cords, and did penance for the least idle word!

This was the golden age of Romuald—no one was persecuting Christians any more, and yet self-made martyrs abounded! Yes, it was a golden age, when citizens of the Jerusalem from on high kept company with the beasts of the forests and the beasts of the hills.

At a certain point, however, the forests and hills were full of hermits, and it was impossible to live there. So Romuald had them build a monastery and elect themselves an abbot, and then without saying a word he withdrew to Biforco.

But not even at Biforco could he get the abbot to live like a spiritual person and stay on the straight path. The abbot took to persecuting Romuald, adding insult to injury.

65. Romuald rebukes Henry II.

Once again Romuald, the friend of the poor and power-less, condemns first with his silence and then with his words the misdeeds of an emperor.

Romuald meets Henry II at Lucca in Tuscany, on July 25, 1022. Upon receiving the emperor's invitation to court, Romuald's initial impulse is to reject it. He is well aware of the fact that Henry—with the help of his pagan allies—has been making war against Christian Poland and Christian Apulia. He also knows how fond the emperor is of meddling in ecclesiastical affairs and what little fondness he shows the poor. In no way—not even in exchange for a hundred monasteries—will Romuald let himself be implicated in these crimes (see chapter 40).

After repeatedly offending court etiquette by his silence, Romuald finally consents to speak with the emperor. But the conversation is all one-sided; Romuald has "a great deal to say," and Henry cannot get a word in edgewise, except to say yes to Romuald's request for a monastery.

Henry must eventually have gotten into heaven, because the Church canonized him in 1146.

Meanwhile the emperor Henry II came down across the Alps into Italy. He sent Blessed Romuald a delegation to ask whether he would grace the imperial court by his presence.

In exchange for an audience with Romuald, the emperor promised to honor his every command.

Romuald absolutely refused to break his silence.

At that point, his disciples got together and went to him. "Master Romuald," they pleaded, "don't you see that crowded together as we are here, we cannot live as we ought? So please go ask the emperor to give you some large monastery, where there will be room enough for the whole multitude of your followers."

Romuald's answer, which he gave them in writing, was prophetic—whether by natural insight or by divine inspiration, I do not know. "I hereby inform you," he wrote, "that you shall have the abbey on Mount Amiata. You must only decide whom you wish to be your abbot." Romuald then went to the imperial court, still refusing to say a word.

As soon as he saw him, King Henry stood up and emotionally blurted out, "Would that my soul were in your body!" Not a word could he get out of Romuald, although he spent the whole day begging him to speak.

The next day, when Romuald returned to court, a whole crowd of Germans ran to see him. As they bowed down before him, they tried to pluck tufts of fur from the leather cloak he was wearing, to take home with them as sacred relics. Romuald was so grieved at all this, that he was about to go straight back to his hermitage. But his disciples stood in his path, and he had to acquiesce.

Face to face with the emperor, Romuald had a great deal to say: about restoring to the churches what was rightfully theirs, about the violence of those endowed with power, about the oppression of the poor, and about many other things. Finally he requested a monastery for his disciples.

Henry eventually gave them the abbey on Mount Amiata. The reigning abbot was guilty of a number of misdeeds, and so the emperor had him deposed. But on Mount Amiata Romuald had to contend not only with the former superior but even with the new abbot he himself had consecrated from among his disciples. Romuald had enough patience to put up with everything, but I do not have enough words to tell you everything he had to put up with!

Let me now give you one example of how God was always there to help Romuald; the rest you can imagine for yourself.

66. Romuald saves the life of a monk who wanted to kill him.

Romuald, filled with the Spirit, "the giver of life," is totally transformed into an image of Christ, "who, when he was reviled, did not revile in return; when he suffered, he did not threaten" (I Peter 2,23). Saint Romuald forgives and protects a monk who sought to take his life.

As a sign, a memorial of his love, Romuald provides his disciples with bread (chapter 67) and with a fish (chapter 68). And as he lies dying, he bids his disciples come "join him in prayer at sunrise the next day" (chapter 69). The final stages of his life's journey are resplendent with the paschal light of Christ's resurrection.

A certain monk became insanely angry at Romuald. Secretly he sharpened a knife and hid it away until such time as he could use it on him.

One night, as sleep came upon him, he saw an evil spirit lunge at him and twist a noose of twigs around his throat. So fiercely did the devil press upon his throat, that the monk was nearly unable to breathe, but with his last bit of energy he begged Romuald to come to his aid.

In his dream the monk beheld Romuald flying towards him and tearing him out of the enemy's grip.

At that point he awoke. He ran to Romuald and fell at his feet. "Look at the bruise on my throat," the monk said, but he was ashamed to confess the sin of his own malicious intentions. In the end, he thanked Romuald for saving his life, and accepted a fitting penance, for although he had planned to take a saint's life, he was given back his own, and the one whose death he had desired rescued him from the grasp of death.

67. Romuald and his disciples, freed from the waters, break bread on the Lord's day.

A number of biblical events echo through this chapter. As it was at the exodus of Israel from Egypt, so now once again the people gone forth from slavery into the desert risks death by water but is saved. The day is Sunday, the weekly Easter, and God's children must not go hungry. "The Lord has given food to those who fear him; he is ever mindful of his covenant" (Psalm 110 [111 in the Hebrew]), as in the monastic order of Sunday Vespers.

Our holy father Benedict himself, as a young hermit, is alone one Easter Sunday, but a priest unexpectedly brings him dinner; to him Benedict says, "I know it is Easter, because you are here" (Gregory the Great, Dialogues 2,1).

It was Saint Romuald's custom, whenever he was observing the cenobitic life, to share meals with his brothers every day, unless he was fasting from all food. He would take one cooked dish, and then he would sit and listen to the reading, or he would watch the others eat, but he would take no other food. In Lent, however, unless some unavoidable necessity demanded his presence, he would remain in his cell.

During the period he had charge of the monastery on Mount Amiata, he went with his disciples in search of a place on the surrounding slopes where they could spend Lent. During their hike they stopped for a long time in a place between two streams. Unexpectedly the streams over flowed, and they found themselves surrounded by water on every side, too deep to wade through. So they could neither move on nor send word back to the monastery.

The only supplies they had with them were some chestnuts. That morning, which happened to be Sunday, they started to peel the chestnuts, doubting whether this might not be their very last meal.

Romuald, however, was his usual, cheerful self. He declared that, since today was Sunday, he was not going to eat anything unless somebody brought him fresh-baked bread for dinner. His disciples were puzzled at his words. "Isn't this presumption?" they asked one another. "How can he hope to eat bread today?" But they knew that Master Romuald never spoke at random, and they decided to trust that somehow they would have a feast-day meal. Around noon, in fact, three men appeared on the opposite shore with bread, wine, and other food in their packs. They had come a great distance, they said, and with much labor they were able to reach the monks.

So with great joy they thanked God and ate their Sunday dinner. The brothers realized that heaven had revealed these events to Romuald, and they doubted no more.

68. At Sitria, a monk finds a fish for Romuald's meal.

At the end of his life, Romuald is reconciled with the communities which had mistreated and unjustly accused him. At Sitria, the sign of reconciliation is a fish, the ICHTHYS *which signifies the Eucharist and the Savior Himself. Then he will conclude his journeying at Val di Castro; there he will leave his body, which the Spirit has transformed into Christ's own flesh.*

A short time later Romuald returned to Sitria. He had taken no food, and the brothers wanted to serve him fish, but in those rugged mountains fish could hardly be found. Embarrassed and dismayed, the brothers asked themselves,

"Where can we get food for our venerable guest?"

One of the brothers—by divine inspiration, I am sure—ran out to the nearby creek, which was almost dry. No one ever went there to fish. The brother started to pray: "Lord, you gave water to the people of Israel from a dry rock[1]—now grant me to find a fish in this stream!" Then he put his hand into the shallow water and caught a fish large enough for a generous meal. Here on the rocky slopes of Catria, God provided food for his servant, and gave him a fish like those which swim in the rivers of thevalley below.

Of the many events which marked the life of Blessed Romuald, I have narrated only a few, but let them suffice. Now I shall tell you of his passing from this life.

[1]Cf. Exodus 17,1-7.

69. Romuald becomes a living stone in the heavenly Jerusalem.

At this point, we should say something about Camaldoli, about which Peter Damian is silent.

Either at Sitria or at the abbey of Monte Amiata, Romuald receives an invitation from Tedaldo, the new bishop of Arezzo. The year is no earlier than 1023, more likely 1025. Bishop Tedaldo has five priests, fervent men of prayer, who desire to establish a monastic-eremitical community at the service of the local church. He invites Romuald to come and form them for their monastic life and their mission to the people. Romuald will spend no more than a year or two with them, and then, sick and bent with the weight of his years, he will make his last trip to Val di Castro. Fifteen years later, as Peter Damian is writing The Life of Romuald, *Camaldoli's Eremo still gives no signs of being other than one of Romuald's many small, temporary communities. A few candidates come to join the original hermits, but they do not persevere. Only with the building of the Cenobio, around the year 1080, will Camaldoli begin to grow, and then other Benedictine hermitages and monasteries— including some*

*founded or reformed by Romuald—will begin to join with it,
thus forming the Camaldolese Congregation of the Order of
Saint Benedict, a religious institute of which Saint Romuald
never even dreamed.*

Saint Romuald lived in many other places, suffered many
other ills chiefly from his own disciples, worked many more
miracles than those few I have permitted myself to recount.
But I prefer to avoid long stories.

After all his sojourning, when he felt his end drawing
near, he returned to his monastery at Val di Castro. As he
awaited death, free of all doubts, he had the monks build him
a cell with a chapel, where he could stay and keep silence
until death came to take him.

Twenty years previously he had informed his disciples
that Val di Castro would be the monastery where he would
eventually retire. And that he would require no assistance at
his death nor any elaborate burial.

When the cell was ready, and his spirit was intent on
living there as a hermit, his body began to suffer more and
more ills and his strength declined, rather from his great old
age than from any disease. For the last six months his lungs
had been severely congested, and he was vexed with a
constant cough. Still he would not take to his bed, and
insofar as possible, he tried to maintain the rigor of his fast.

One day his strength began to ebb, and he could no longer
bear the weight of his illness. The sun was setting, and he
ordered the two brothers who were assisting him to leave
and close the door after them. "Come back at sunrise," he
said, "to sing Lauds with me."

Concerned that he might die in their absence, they were
reluctant to go. They eventually went out, but they did not
retire to the monastery. They remained hiding nearby, as if
to keep watch over a priceless treasure, listening carefully
until they could no longer hear any movement or voice from
within. They knew the end had indeed come. They forced

open the door and lit a lamp. Romuald was lying face down on his bed, having given his life back to God.

Like a pearl that had by chance fallen from heaven he lay there, soon to be put back in the treasury of heaven's King. He had died as he said he would, and he had gone where he hoped to go.

Blessed Romuald had lived one hundred and twenty years—twenty in the world, three in the monastery, and ninety-seven in the hermitage.

Now he shines with unspeakable brightness among the living stones of the heavenly Jerusalem. He rejoices with the throngs of flaming spirits, clothed in the white robe of immortal life and crowned with glory by the King of Kings himself.

70. A scrap of Romuald's hairshirt frees a man from demonic possession.

Romuald is buried at Val di Castro, and his grave immediately becomes a place of pilgrimage. The monks and the people venerate him as a new Saint Benedict: see Pope Gregory the Great's Dialogues *2,38.*

After the venerable Romuald's holy death, God worked many miraculous signs through his intercession. But who would want to read about miracles that have occurred already, when you can see new ones happening every day? Since the wonders which take place at his tomb are so many, I feel it is better to say nothing than to say too little about them. However, two miracles took place elsewhere, and these can suffice for all the rest.

A brother who had been a disciple of the saint donated a small chapel to the monastery, where prayers were to be offered for his soul. He sent a piece of Romuald's hairshirt, cut from the hem of the sleeve, and ordered that it be placed beneath the altar as a sacred relic. The servant who brought it there, however, neglected to place it where it belonged, but rather hid it in the space between two stones in the wall.

Later it happened that they brought a possessed man to the chapel. As he stood there, he started to turn his head from side to side, as if looking for something, until he focused his angry gaze on the wall where the scrap of hairshirt had been hidden. At that he started yelling again and again, "He's driving me out, he's driving me out!" And with a loud cry, the evil spirit left him.

How, then, can the merciful God refuse to answer Saint Romuald's prayers, if a piece of his shirt is sufficient to drive out a demon? And if Romuald is so powerful when he is absent, how much more power does he show in the presence of his mortal remains?

71. By Saint Romuald's prayers, a poor woman gets her cow back.

As a young hermit near Cuixá, Romuald showed himself a friend to the poor, especially to the farmer whose cow was stolen (see chapter 10). On that occasion, he did not succeed in getting the cow returned, but in this case, he did.

On another occasion, a landlord did violence to a poor woman by taking her cow. She wept and cried and begged and supplicated him, but he turned a deaf ear. So she ran back home, took two roosters from her hen coop, and carried them to the church of Val di Castro, where she threw them on the altar. Weeping and wailing, she cried, "Saint Romuald, if you can hear this miserable woman, do not abandon me! My cow was like a mother to me—let me have her back again!"

A miracle happened! The villain with his ill-gotten gain was no more than a stone's throw from her house, when he had a heart attack, left the cow there, went home and died.

72. Saint Romuald's body remains intact five years after his burial.

The body of Saint Romuald was enshrined beneath the altar of Val di Castro until the year 1481. At that time, two monks from Ravenna felt it their duty to rob the grave and take his relics back to his home town. On their way they stopped at an inn, where a strange light coming from their room led people to discover their sack full of the sacred bones. These were taken to the nearest Camaldolese monastery—Saint Blaise in Fabriano—where they were placed in the crypt of the church; they are still there today.

The monks and the bishop of Fabriano opened the tomb in 1980. The skeleton was found to be almost complete, except for those relics venerated in the various Camaldolese communities. The bones of the feet were missing, but later these were discovered in the church at Val di Castro.

Five years after Saint Romuald's death, the Holy See granted permission to erect an altar over his tomb. At that time the superior, Brother Azo, went out to the woods to gather material for a small casket, just big enough to hold a few bones and ashes.

Later that same evening, one worthy monk fell asleep and dreamed of an old man, who came to him and asked, "Where is the superior of this monastery?"

The brother answered, "I don't know."

The old man told him, "He is out in the woods making a box, but it's going to be too small to hold the saint's entire body."

The next day Azo came back with his box, and the brother who had had the dream asked him where he had gone.

Azo answered, "I'm too tired. I'll tell you later."

So the brother himself told Azo where he had been and why he had gone there.

When they opened Romuald's tomb, they found his body intact, almost the way it was when they buried him, except that there were some patches of mildew on his skin. So they threw away Azo's box and prepared an urn big enough for the saint's body, held services to honor the sacred relics, and built a consecrated altar over them.

The day of Romuald's passing was the nineteenth of June, [1027] in the reign of Jesus Christ, our Lord, who with the Father and the Holy Spirit lives in glory for endless ages. Amen.